MASTER OF MANHATTAN

The Life of Richard Croker

RICHARD CROKER
IN 1901

MASTER OF MANHATTAN
The Life of Richard Croker

BY

LOTHROP STODDARD

Author of "The Rising Tide of Color," "Re-Forging America"

LONGMANS, GREEN AND CO.

NEW YORK   TORONTO

MDCCCCXXXI

CONTENTS

v

LIST OF ILLUSTRATIONS

Master of Manhattan

PROLOGUE

THE COMING OF THE GREEN-EYED BOY

IT WAS a crisp autumn afternoon of the year 1846 when the packet *Henry Clay*, three weeks out from Queenstown, Ireland, entered the harbor of New York. As the trim craft slipped past the Narrows and sailed up the bay, her decks were black with an immigrant throng. Irish peasant-folk they were, fleeing from blight and famine.

Eager to be ashore after the long sea voyage, the immigrants had fetched their luggage from below and stood or sat in groups about their scant belongings, talking or gazing open-mouthed at the wide panorama of bay and land and sky. It was a peaceful scene. No towering skyscrapers awed the voyager from afar; no Statue of Liberty greeted the newcomer with uplifted torch; no babel of hooting tugs proclaimed the commercial gateway to the New World. Instead, the bay was flecked with sails, Staten Island was a quiet realm of farms and wooded hills, Brooklyn a small town, while a few villages clustered here and there along the Jersey shore. Only the lower tip of Manhattan teemed with a bustling energy foreshadowing the mighty growth that was to be.

As the *Henry Clay* drew abreast of Governor's Island, the drone of the city came across the water to the immigrants' straining ears. Yet, from that angle, there could be no gaug-

ing of its size; since in those days New York was a city
of brick or wooden houses seldom more than three stories
high, with church spires rising, here and there, above a
jumble of pitched or gabled roofs. Furthermore, the broad
expanse of Battery Park, fringed by fine old trees toward
Bowling Green, masked Manhattan's southern tip, pleasantly
screening what lay behind.

Up toward the bow of the packet stood a family group:
man, wife, and clutter of goods and children. Not a distinguished group, yet obviously a bit above the run of those
around them. The father was a brawny man with that in-
definable something about him which often marks one whose
life is closely associated with horses. A glance at the packet's
steerage-list would have told you that he was one Eyre Coote
Croker, late veterinary and smith of the village of Blackrock, County Cork. A most un-Irish name, that; for Sir
Eyre Coote, his namesake, had been a famous British general, while the surname *Croker* had an equally English ring.
Yet the man came by it rightly enough, since he was descended from Cromwellian soldiers planted in southern Ireland two centuries before. His wife was likewise of migrant
stock. She was a Wellstead — a yeoman family of Scottish
origin, though settled in the County for a couple of generations. And the Lowland Scotch of her showed in her
prim yet pleasant face.

Eyre Coote Croker was the scion of a line which had come
down in the world. Originally, the Crokers had been independent landowners living in fair prosperity. But roystering forebears had scattered the ancestral acres and forced
the youth with a general's name to earn his bread as a
veterinary surgeon. Married young and with an abundant
brood, easy-going, open-handed Eyre Coote Croker had done

nothing to redeem the family fortunes. Even his black-smithing had barely sufficed to balance the domestic exchequer. So, when times grew hard and the dark shadow of famine lowered over Ireland, he had given up the struggle and joined the rush to America.

What thoughts crossed his mind that autumn day as he neared the New World, we do not know. Never fluent of speech, he has left scant record behind. But the scene must have heartened him, as it did all about him; for he spoke cheerily to wife and children, the youngest included — a boy some three years old, unusually sturdy for his age, with a mop of black hair and odd, grayish-green eyes. Lifting the little fellow to his broad shoulder, the father pointed, saying: "Look, Dick — New York. 'Tis New York." And the boy, following the pointed finger, gazed, uncomprehendingly yet steadily, across the narrowing strip of water at the sward of Battery Park and the autumn-tinted trees and the mass of red-brick buildings beyond.

Thus did Richard Croker first view Manhattan — that island-metropolis which, some forty years later, he would rule as an uncrowned king!

CHAPTER I

LITTLE OLD NEW YORK

NEW YORK in the forties, and for a generation thereafter, was an amazing place. For New York in those days was sky-rocketting from a town to a metropolis. And that was something wholly beyond American experience. When our Republic was founded, it had not even a good-sized city within its borders, and the census of 1790 showed only five places with more than 8000 inhabitants.[1]

This lack of cities did not worry our forefathers; on the contrary, they deemed it a blessing and hoped it might never be otherwise. Jefferson undoubtedly voiced the feeling of his day when he compared great cities to great sores. The Fathers of the Republic had no municipal problems and did not bother their heads about such things. The non-existent city was ignored. The future was left to take care of itself.

So matters stood for about a generation. Then, suddenly and without warning, embryo cities appeared in America. Faster and faster they grew, confronting an uncomprehending and indifferent public with problems whose gravity was long ignored. And in New York these problems took on a peculiarly intense and aggravated form. The growing-pains which racked Manhattan in its transformation from town to city and from city to metropolis are seldom appreciated. Yet this chaotic transition epoch was precisely the

4

period of Richard Croker's boyhood, youth, and prime. By it his character was moulded; from it he grasped his opportunities. Unless we comprehend this environmental background, his career and personality alike lose most of their true significance.

The outstanding fact is that, despite a veneer of sophistication, the New York of the eighteen-forties was a gigantic frontier community, with the spirit of a mining camp and no civic standards worth mentioning. Furthermore, New York had become so, suddenly, within the preceding fifteen or twenty years.

New York's metropolitan beginning dates from 1825 — the year of the opening of the Erie Canal. Before that, New York's commercial hinterland had been virtually the Hudson River valley, a fertile but restricted area hemmed in by mountainous uplands. Not until those geographical barriers were broken could Manhattan island capitalize its splendid harbor and become the commercial (and thereby the financial) pivot of America.

It was modern methods of transportation that brought this about. And the Erie Canal was the first phase of an economic expansion which the turnpike, the railroad, and the ocean-going steamship were to extend overland to the Pacific and overseas to the uttermost ends of the earth.

The swiftness of New York's transformation after 1825 is astounding. In a couple of decades, not merely the outward aspect but also the very spirit of the place was radically changed. Before 1825, despite a steady growth in prosperity and population, New York was essentially a " Knickerbocker " town. Its ruling genius remained that of its staid Dutch burghers, with their love of order, moderation, and decorum. Compactly seated on Manhattan's southern tip, the city extended very little above Canal Street. The most fashionable residences were still around the Battery, and up Broadway and Greenwich to Courtland. New York's civic life was on so modest a scale that the cargo of one modern ocean liner would presumably have stocked all its warehouses, the passengers on a single train into Grand Central or Pennsylvania Station would have overflowed all its hotels, while its annual municipal budget barely exceeded $1,000,000.

This last item is, however, less surprising when we discover that New York then had almost none of those public services today deemed indispensable even by small towns. Until 1844, New York had no regular police force, but merely a few watchmen wearing curious leather caps, who came on duty at dusk and patrolled the streets hourly until dawn. There was likewise no fire department, and every blaze might become a conflagration and burn down a whole section of the city — as happened several times. There was no health department, no sewage system, and practically no muncipal street-cleaning or garbage disposal — most of the latter being done by scavengers in the shape of hogs ranging the streets at their own sweet will. Until 1815, there was but one public school, and that maintained, not by taxation, but by subscription. Water was furnished by a private corporation through bored wooden logs laid underground from a reservoir in Chambers Street. In 1825 the city was agog, not only over the Erie Canal but also over a great municipal improvement — the introduction of gaslights in the main thoroughfares, to replace the wretched whale-oil lamps which smoked and sputtered and usually went out before morning.

Nothing better illustrates the spirit of this old New York

than its Sabbath and its isolation. The Knickerbocker Sabbath was an awesome thing. From early dawn all secular affairs were piously eschewed; no hot meals were served; no sound save the tolling of church bells broke the solemn stillness. Lest some chance vehicle, rattling over the cobblestones, disturb worshippers, the churches stretched chains across the streets during services held thrice in the day. Woe betide the Sabbath-breaker! He was ostracized by the community.

As for the limitations on trade and travel, they seem almost inconceivable to us of today. Local water transportation by sloop or crude paddle-wheel steamer was slow enough, but it was far swifter than travel by land. Think of one lumbering stage-coach per day for Albany and another for Boston, while passengers for Philadelphia would cross to Jersey City in the evening, sleep there at a tavern, and start by stage early the next morning, arriving in the Quaker City (mayhap!) in about twenty hours. No wonder Western trade languished until the opening of the Erie Canal.[2]

Such was Knickerbocker " Gotham "; narrow and provincial, yet more livable and with a broader outlook than perhaps any other American town of that period. Now, compare the situation after two decades. By the late forties, New York was a big city. In 1820, its population had been just over 100,000; the census of 1850 gave it a round half-million. So swiftly had it marched up Manhattan Island that the smart residential section ran from Bleecker to 14th Street, including both Broadway and lower Fifth Avenue. Beyond lay a wide fringe of settlement — fairly built-up to 23rd Street and trailing off into country villas and squatters' shanties almost to Yorkville and Harlem on the East and to Bloomingdale on the West Side; these villages, though within the corporate limits, being still deemed separate communities. The lower East Side was a noisome slum, centering about the district known as the Five Points. Downtown New York, as far as Fulton Street, had ceased to be residential and was frankly given over to business. New York was now a great port, and both water-fronts of lower Manhattan were belted with wharves and fringed with a forest of masts. In short, New York had become America's metropolis — recognized as such, both at home and abroad.

But this sudden rise to metropolitan greatness produced the inevitable result: it made New York a magnet for the ambitious, the unscrupulous, and the pleasure-seeking from far and wide. The myriads of poor immigrants who descended upon Manhattan like swarms of locusts are a commonplace. But what is not so well-known is the other immigration of native stock, which even more powerfully affected the situation. From every part of the Union they came, by the thousands and tens of thousands — canny " up-State " New Yorkers, shrewd New England Yankees, hard-headed Westerners, and fiery Southerners; an adventurous host, determined to win fame and fortune, and seldom finicky as to how these should be gained.

This two-fold invasion of Manhattan produced great economic results. The wholesale influx of brains, brawn, and abounding energy furnished just the combination needed to exploit New York's new opportunities. Wealth increased by leaps and bounds, and prosperity begot new prosperity.

Yet there was another side to the story. All these fortune-hunters flocked to Manhattan much as their fellows were flocking to San Francisco at about the same time. For New York itself they cared little; of its traditions and culture they knew next to nothing and recked even less. It was a bonanza, a gold-rush, essentially like the other one across the continent. So, like "'Frisco," New York became a "boom town," with all the usual unsightly trimmings such as frenzied speculation, new-rich vulgarity, vice, crime, political corruption, and a general lowering of both civic and social ideals.

In the early forties, Charles Dickens visited New York, and in his *American Notes* he set down his impressions of Manhattan's amazing mixture of luxury and squalor with a pungent sarcasm which raised a howl from Gotham's "high society."

"Once more on Broadway! Here are the same ladies in bright colors, walking to and fro. We are going to cross here. Take care of the pigs. Two portly sows are trotting behind this carriage, and a select party of half-a-dozen gentleman hogs have just now turned the corner. . . They are the city scavengers, these pigs. Ugly brutes they are; having, for the most part, scanty brown backs, like the lids of old horse-hair trunks. At this hour, just as evening is closing in, you will see them roaming towards bed by scores, eating their way to the last." [3]

All contemporary accounts stress the prevalence of violence and disorder. In the early forties, the lack of a police force was keenly felt. The old night watch was not worth its salt. Crime was rampant, and in certain sections of the city respectable persons walking along the streets were insulted, robbed, and beaten in broad daylight by gangs of ruffians who infested those quarters. At night the streets were absolutely unsafe. The upshot was that a police force was organized, but it was so inefficient that, for a time, improvement was barely perceptible.

A decade later, conditions were about the same. When

Mayor Wood made an official survey in the mid-fifties he found the streets ill-paved, filthy, and jammed with unregulated traffic; crime, drunkenness, and prostitution rampant; and a graft-ridden municipality which did nothing to better the situation.[4]

This survey is well-known and is the one usually cited for the period. Its accuracy is confirmed by the remarks of an English observer. This man, an unusually intelligent and well-read artisan, emigrated to New York in 1855. He was a convinced republican and came hither in high hopes. Three years later he returned to England, utterly disillusioned, and wrote a book warning his fellow-countrymen against " that huge mantrap, the U. S. A." [5]

His disillusionment began the moment he landed, when he and some companions were lured to an immigrant boarding-house. " A fortnight in one of these horrible dens," he says, "was enough for us, and we were glad to cross the water to Brooklyn, where things have not got to such a pitch of dirt, discomfort and indecency." [6] New York was filthy and crime-ridden, and " the state of the streets such that there are holes deep enough to break the legs of horses." [7]

He contemptuously describes the New York police as " of all ages and sizes, including little withered old men, five feet nothing high, whose first impulse on seeing a street row is to pocket their ' star ' and bolt down the next alley. The bulk of these gentry spend their time when on duty in bar-rooms or at the doors of them, cigar in mouth and hands in pockets. Some wear uniforms, others do not." [8]

By this time New York had a semblance of fire protection in the shape of volunteer fire-companies. But they seem to have been a very mixed blessing, for our British informant terms them mere gangs of rowdies and asserts that every

TAMMANY HALL, 1830

fire was literally a riot. " As they drag their engine along
the streets they shout and scream, and whoop and yell, more
like Indians or demons than reasonable men going to per-
form a duty which requires coolness and judgment. When
they arrive at the fire, confusion worse confounded; engines
running into one another; a mob of men, women and children impeding operations, and their ever-present thievish
hangers-on busy in *removing* goods." [9]

Our intelligent workingman's crowning disillusionment,
however, was the state of New York politics, which conclusively demolished his republican principles and sent him
back to England metaphorically shouting: *God Save the
King!* He roundly damns both parties; there is not a pin's
difference between Whigs and Democrats regarding bribery,
corruption, and plug-ugly tactics. His description of the
Presidential election of 1856 reads like a carnival of violence
and barefaced fraud.[10]

But, it may be asked, was not public opinion aroused by
such conditions? Was there no party pledged to resolute
reform? No, practically speaking, there was not. Plaints
and protests, of course, there were aplenty; but no organized,
constructive movement of any significance.

Perhaps the only thing which could have kept New York's
evolution within ordered bounds would have been a long-
established upper class, seasoned to authority — a true aristocracy, whose intellectual and cultural attainments would
have commanded genuine respect. But the Revolution had
made this impossible. Colonial New York had been a Tory
stronghold,[11] and when Revolution triumphed, over 10,000
loyalist refugees sailed away with the British fleet; among
them the strongest and staunchest of the city's colonial
leaders.

The truncated remnant of the old upper class which remained never regained its former prestige; and this, not merely because it was faced with an aggressive democracy, but also because it no longer deserved either prestige or authority. Knickerbocker society, from the Revolution to the Civil War, was a dull, pretentious affair, snobbish rather than aristocratic. Its few really fine old families were hopelessly diluted by a lot of brummagem Knickerbockers, mostly the mediocre descendants of Dutch peasants whose farms, turned into house-lots, yielded fortunes due to luck instead of ability.

Incapable of true leadership, Knickerbocker society fenced itself off from New York's turbulent reality behind a Chinese wall of etiquette. Politically, the Knickerbockers were as impotent as the Royalists of Paris, who, from their grim old mansions in the Faubourg Saint-Germain, sigh for a king and sneer at the Republic. But, like the Paris Royalists, the New York Knickerbockers never admitted their impotence and maintained an air of lofty superiority, consistently opposing the popular side in politics, whatever it might be. This did them no good but the city considerable harm, since it injected into municipal politics an element of snobbery and class-hatred which hampered civic progress.

Another hindrance was New York's peculiar geographical situation. Forced to expand in one direction only, the city flowed northward up the long, narrow island of Manhattan, like a gigantic snake forever casting its skin. Scarcely had a particular neighborhood established itself than it disintegrated, was torn down, and was rebuilt as something else. This was a serious handicap alike to social stability and the growth of civic feeling.

Coming now to the small minority with real municipal

ideals, we find their efforts hampered by lack of knowledge and their thin ranks divided for want of a common program of action.   Incredible as it may seem to us of today, the would-be reformers of municipal ills in the forties and fifties simply did not know what to do.   We have already seen that cities were then wholly new to American experience. The city just didn't fit into the scheme of things so nicely arranged by the Fathers of the Republic.   Most men regarded municipal problems as an annoyance, turned with a sigh of relief to the more familiar field of national politics, and bade civics go to the devil — which they promptly did.

Thus the reckless, roystering, devil-take-the-hindmost spirit of Boom-Town gripped Manhattan, and metropolitan New York proceeded cynically (yet rather splendidly) on its way; whither, few knew, or cared.   Those were great days, if you had a shrewd head, a hard hand, and plenty of nerve. Little old New York was no place for weaklings.

CHAPTER II

SHANTY-TOWN

THE sun was near its setting, with a tang of frost in the autumn air, when the *Henry Clay* was warped into her berth and her human cargo put ashore. Down the gangplank swirled the immigrant stream, spreading out upon the wharf and mingling tumultuously with the crowd that waited on its coming. There was no inspection, no regulation; in the mid-forties, Castle Garden was still a concert-hall, while Ellis Island and quota laws were both far below time's horizon. It was the age of *laissez faire;* which, in plain English, means " do as you dam' please."

The dockside throng that awaited the packet's warping was a motley lot. Some were honest laboring-folk, come to meet relatives from the Old Country and take them in friendly charge. Others, however, were of a different kidney. Bold, brassy fellows they were; Irish, too, for the most part, but of a garish prosperity and self-assurance which set them quite above their hard-working fellow-countrymen. These were immigrant " runners " — a sinister craft that flourished exceedingly in those free-and-easy days.[1]

And well the runners knew their job. As the immigrants stood huddled on the dock, bewildered by the tumult and for the most part with no kin to greet them, the runners swooped down on them like hawks upon their prey. Needless to add,

the Croker family was soon spotted by one of the slickest
of the tribe.

Puffing false friendship with every draw on his big
cigar, a burly, red-faced man, sporting a stove-pipe hat and
a flowered waistcoat, strode up to Eyre Coote and bade him
jovial welcome. The dazed, slow-spoken veterinary-smith
was quite overwhelmed by the rapid-fire of the runner's
discourse.

"What County? . . Ye don't tell me. . . And from
Blackrock, too. . . Och, the luck of it; me happenin' here
today! . . Sure, a County-man's always a comrade, sez
I. . . Now, we'll be lavin' this shalloo for a dacint, quiet
place I know of; jist made fer yez an' the childher,
ma'am. . . And the cost iv it? Niver a penny ye'll pay *me*,
ma'am. Amment I yer frind? "

So forth from the bedlam on the wharf fared the Crokers
and their new-found " friend " who helped Eyre Coote with
the baggage and favored each child with a cheery word, not
forgetting little Dick, whom he called " a broth of a bhoy."
Under his efficient convoy they safely ran the gantlet of
rival runners, furtive Jewish money-changers, and miscellaneous ruffians hovering in the background. The big, red-
faced fellow had proved his mettle too often for others to cut
in on his game.

A short walk of a few blocks brought them to their des-
tination — a dilapidated brick building set in a block devoted
to similar purposes. The whole street, indeed, was a nest
of immigrant boarding-houses, of which there were then
nearly two thousand in New York City, belting both water-
fronts just back from the wharves.[2]

The aspect of the " quiet, dacint place " was far from in-
viting. The ground floor was a combination lounging-room

and " family grocery " stocked with dubious supplies such as maggoty hams and shoulders, strings of dried onions, salt fish, pipes and tobacco, and above all, barrels of whiskey. These goods the proprietor practically forced his guests to buy at exorbitant prices.

Uneasy at the prospect, Eyre Coote and his wife were half-minded to seek other lodgings. But where? Their jovial guide, having delivered his quarry, had promptly disappeared. To venture forth again into the dark streets infested with prowling thugs was impossible. Better endure their present lot, lest worse befall. So Eyre Coote and his brood soon found themselves crammed into a dingy chamber, there to pass an uneasy night from the abundant vermin in the frowsy pallets, the scampering of rats in the mildewed walls, and the quarrelling of drunken neighbors.

Morning, however, found the family unharmed. The place was just a typical immigrant boarding-house, run by a man, grasping, indeed, yet no bad representative of his kind. No robbery or violence was practised on the premises, as happened in many dens where luckless new-comers were stripped of all their goods and flung, penniless, into the streets.

Still, Eyre Coote and his wife agreed that this was no fit abode, even for a brief stay. The father must see his family safely bestowed while he sought a job and a home. Fortune favored, and a few days later the Crokers were installed in lodgings better answering the " quiet, dacint place " the immigrant runner had so glibly promised.

But the job was still lacking. What Eyre Coote wanted was a post as veterinary to some stable or concern with many horses. He had had enough of blacksmithing in the Old Country and was resolved to ply his surgeon's craft in the new land. That, however, was easier said than done. The city was well supplied with horse-doctors, which made it hard for an unknown stranger from overseas. Vainly did Eyre Coote seek a professional opening, both in New York and elsewhere. Meanwhile funds were getting low. What was to be done?

At this point the harassed man decided to try his luck in the queer no-man's-land which then extended from about 23rd Street northward to the settlements of Bloomingdale and Harlem. This outer fringe of the metropolis long remained one of the strangest anomalies in New York's evolution.

Manhattan Island is geologically a rock-mass — a lower counterpart of the Palisades. Despite the Harlem flats and some good farmland here and there, the rocky core outcropped sharply in steep hills and bold ledges, especially through the middle section of the island (the site of Central Park), trending thence northwesterly to the Hudson River right to the island's rugged northern tip, which is not wholly built-up even today.

Manhattan is now so tamed and pruned by the hand of man that it is scarcely possible for our generation to reconstruct in fancy the topographic past. Only some bits of Central Park and the eastern face of Morningside Heights give us a clue to the semi-wilderness of cliff and crag, bald ledge and dank hollow, which stubbornly confronted the city's onward growth. Too barren for agriculture and too broken for easy suburban development, Manhattan's " badlands " were despised and neglected until the buccaneering vision of Boss Tweed, abetted by some great land speculators, solved the problem by giving the city Central Park and Riverside Drive.

However, those municipal glories were undreamed-of
when poor Eyre Coote Croker, despairing of finding a professional niche in the city proper, resolved to move to the
highly improper districts beyond the city's settled fringe.
So he decided to try his luck in " Shanty-Town."

From time immemorial, the bad-lands of Manhattan had
harbored a strange, half-nomad population, known as
" squatters," from the fact that they dwelt precariously on
lands to which they had no title but on which they were suffered by indifferent owners to remain.   Even in Colonial days
these worthless tracts had been pre-empted by a scattering
of gin-soaked Indians, vagrant whites, and runaway negroes.
As time passed, this mongrel population was steadily aug-
mented by waifs and strays from the growing city to the
southward, and when the foreign tide set in, large numbers
of immigrants, driven by poverty and distaste for crowded
slums, sought refuge in this sordid sanctuary.   Most numerous were the Irish, who soon so outnumbered the other
squatters that the term *Shanty Irish* covered the whole motley tribe.

This curious population persisted for many years, until
finally evicted by the northward thrust of the city.   A New
York artist gives us these colorful word-sketches of squatter
life:

" If you stand in the hollow at the corner of 86th Street
and Eighth Avenue, you will see a long reach of garden with
a weathered old cottage in the middle, and if you do not
raise your eyes, it will seem that you are in Ireland.   When
the shadows fall, the land has a sear and brown look, and
the hollows remind one of Ireland more than ever.   But
later in the afternoon the crimson splendor in the west is
reflected upon the old shanties perched above the level, and

SHANTY-TOWN

their frail and weatherbeaten shingles glow with the transmitted warmth. . .

"The afternoon is waning, and the squatters are lighting their lamps in the shanties. A door is open, and we peep in. The furniture is scant, and much the worse for wear. A goat is curled up before the rusty little stove, and a mummy-like old woman is talking Gaelic between the puffs of her pipe to a barefooted girl who is kneading bread."[3]

Here it was that Eyre Coote Croker and his family took up their abode in a dilapidated dwelling in what is now the western portion of Central Park, on or near the old Bloomingdale Road. In these squalid surroundings the Crokers lived for about three years. Their little house seems to have been somewhat better than the average squatter's shanty, and we may be sure that the patient, thrifty mother did her best to maintain in her home circle the decent cleanliness to which she had been reared. The father picked up a living by an itinerant veterinary practice among the horses, cows, and pigs of truck-farmers and market-gardeners, eked out by odd jobs of various sorts. It was a poor life, yet better than stewing in the foul tenements of the Five Points or Cherry Hill.

For little Dick and the other Croker children such a life had its compensations. There were wide open spaces to range and play in, and plenty of fresh air — albeit somewhat scented by nearby piggeries and dumps. Also, food was usually ample: goat's milk, fresh vegetables, eggs, and pork; since, in lieu of cash, many of Eyre Coote's customers presumably paid in kind. It was a healthful, open-air existence — if you dodged typhoid fever and malaria.

Anyway, it did Dick no harm. He throve on it and grew sturdier every day. We can picture the life he led — romping with his brothers and sisters, tussling with rough little squatter brats, scaling gray rock ledges, and gleefully dodging the charges of irate billy goats. Perhaps few memories of those early days remained in his conscious mind. Yet those years in Shanty-Town undoubtedly played an important part in shaping his personality. For early childhood is nature's moulding-time.

Thus Richard spent his boyhood up to his seventh year, when a great event happened — his father got a steady job. By some lucky chance, Eyre Coote landed a post with an East Side stable on the edge of town, i. e., around 34th Street. It was nothing to boast of, that job. But it paid a fair wage, and it brought the Crokers out of the wilds of Squatterdom.

A few years later, Eyre Coote got a better job as assistant veterinary to the stables of a horse-car line, also on the East Side. This meant a further improvement in the family fortunes. At last the humble horse-doctor had found his professional niche. He liked his job, held it, and abode content.

Richard's boyhood was thus passed a bit above the poverty-line and in the same neighborhood, his family living first on 26th Street and later on 28th Street, near Third Avenue. With a steady-going father and a thrifty mother, the Croker children were brought up in a self-respecting home. Though their abode was on the edge of the notorious " Gas House District," it was not in the slums.

Richard was thus spared the squalor of the swarming tenements. Yet he dwelt in their very shadow, and they colored his youth as they did that of most lads of his class and time. Indeed, the close-herding of the masses into more or less squalid tenements was for generations the root-ill of New York life.

And the basic cause of this stubborn evil was neither greedy landlordism nor corrupt politics, but geography. New York began as a small town on the tip of a long, narrow island flanked by broad rivers. When New York suddenly expanded, the inevitable result was acute congestion. Rapid transit was as yet unknown. A single stage-line up Broadway, and a few primitive ferry-boats to Brooklyn and Jersey summed up metropolitan transportation.

This meant that the urban masses were literally heaped up around their jobs. How could a workingman afford five-cent fares to the embryo suburbs (even if he could afford the time) when a dollar a day was considered a good average wage? At the very least, it meant foregoing cherished pleasures such as a mammoth schooner of beer for a nickel or a big drink of fairish whiskey for a dime!

With population far outstripping new construction, the laboring masses were jammed into ever closer quarters. First, single dwellings and ex-Knickerbocker mansions were converted into makeshift tenements by being cut up into small rooms, with jerry-built annexes covering the former garden-plots in rear. Then came the real tenements — big rookeries subdivided into tiny suites, which often rose several stories high and occasionally occupied a whole city block. And still the congestion grew. The lower East Side was soon so densely packed that its population touched 290,000 per square mile — worse than the slums of China.[4]

As late as 1890, Jacob Riis, the well-known social worker, stated: " The tenements today *are* New York, harboring three-fourths of its population." [5] A decade or so later, the situation changed for the better, chiefly owing to the mar-

vellous development of suburban rapid transit. But that
was well into the present century. During the entire period
with which we are here dealing (the period of Richard
Croker's active life) the basis of metropolitan existence was
the congested tenement. As Riis well says, the tenement *was*
New York. Sociologically, *and politically*, it was the tenement which set the civic tone, rather than the wealthy
" brownstone-front " districts along Fifth Avenue.

From the rough, hard school of poverty and adversity
sprang the line of political chieftains who ruled the New
York of those days. For Boss Tweed was born and bred in
the old Fourth Ward, " Honest John " Kelly was cradled
in the slums, while Richard Croker spent his early childhood amid squatters' shanties and his youth in the tenement
shadow.

It was a tenement atmosphere little Dick Croker breathed
whenever he set foot beyond the narrow confines of his home.
And he was afoot most of the time; for Dick was no home-
body, but an upstanding, aggressive spirit, thirsting for action
and adventure. Though small for his age, Dick was so
sturdily built and such a natural-born fighter that he was
well able to take care of himself. Soon, the toughest boys
in the neighborhood learned to walk wide of one whose
fistic prowess was known for blocks around.

Understand, that was no small reputation; for New York
then swarmed with hordes of street-arabs, many of whom
were homeless waifs living much like the " wild children "
who roamed about Russian cities after the Great War. Incredible though it may sound, there were no public agencies
for their up-bringing. Prowling like alley-cats, they lived
as best they might; foredoomed to grow up thieves and
thugs, should they survive.

Those were the tough customers Dick and the other neighborhood boys were apt to run up against every time they went out to play. For, in those days, there were no public playgrounds, no boy-scouts, no organized recreation of any kind. The street, the back-alley, and the wickedly dangerous waterfront were the only juvenile breathing-spaces; and whichever a boy chose, he had to dodge the cops and fight his way among his own kind. It was no place for Little Lord Fauntleroys; but those boys who could stand the gaff grew up to be " men of their hands." And young Croker was one of the best.

Sandwiched in between play and fisticuffs, Dick got a little schooling. By this time, New York did have public schools, of a sort. Dick attended a primary school on the site of the famous Madison Square Garden. It was a one-room schoolhouse, where, instead of a blackboard, the teacher traced letters with a pointed stick in a box of white sand.

After a year or two of this primary " education," Dick went to a grammar school on East 27th Street. Here the schoolmaster was a sour-tempered New England Yankee named Olney, who belabored his pupils with a hickory ruler on the slightest provocation.[6]

So the years passed, and Richard evolved from child to boy, and from boy to adolescent youth. A rough, care-free life it was, with games, scraps, brushes with the cops, and vagabond roamings with a few chosen companions. Those explorations into strange territory usually led to the East River, with its fascinating maze of wharves, and shipping, and water into which to plunge whenever the spirit willed. On such occasions Richard might be away from home for days at a time, foraging for food like the veriest street-arab, or earning a few pennies by some slight service like fetching

a pail of beer from a waterfront saloon to sweating steve-
dores or thirsty boatmen.

And every year, Richard grew brawnier. His chest deep-
ened, his limbs muscled, his grey-green eyes grew bolder, his
battle-scarred fists held a punch amazingly beyond his age.
While yet a boy, he had almost a man's strength. Rough
lads, years his senior, acknowledged his supremacy; even
obeyed him gladly. Before he was well into his teens, Dick
Croker was a juvenile gang-leader.

CHAPTER III

DICK THE GANGSTER

IN ROUGH times men must hang together or hang separately. No man then dares stand alone. He must belong to some crowd, or get the worst of it. The rougher the times, the closer men stick. The same is true of boys. And all such spontaneous groupings are, in the last analysis, " gangs " of various kinds.

Now the New York of Richard Croker's youth was, socially, in the Dark Ages. So every boy of his class (barring a few hopeless cripples or mollycoddles) joined a gang and became a loyal gangster. There was nothing else a boy could do, even if he had wanted to.[1]

In those days almost every block had its juvenile gang, and if you didn't belong, you were fair game for any boy to pick on the instant you set foot outside your home. Once a member in good standing, you had the freedom of your block; but the very next block might be forbidden ground — the realm of a rival gang, on which you trespassed at your peril. So a boy seldom roamed about alone, but usually joined forces with one or more tried companions. It was all very complicated, you see: a little world of loyalties and feuds, forays and defensive battles, truces and alliances solemnly pledged by gang leaders and rigidly kept by their followers.

Though forever warring among themselves, the gangs had one common bond — hatred of the police. The cop was always the enemy, and a boy fleeing from a bluecoat was sure of sanctuary even among his bitterest foes.

This perpetual feud between police and tenement youth was natural and inevitable. Allowed no legal outlet for their play-impulses, boys were bound to get their fun unlawfully. Milk cans were stolen from doorsteps, and fruit or vegetables were snitched from grocers or pushcart venders, to grace gang-feasts. Staid old gentlemen had their top-hats knocked off by snowballs in winter-time. Pranks innumerable were played on householders who incurred juvenile displeasure. All this was harmless enough at the start, but it fostered a deep-seated contempt for law and order.

New York was thus a sort of Gangland, in which an infinite variety of gangs, of all ages, sizes, and conditions strove tumultuously against the police and one another. Those old-time associations should be carefully distinguished from the so-called " gangs " of today. Modern gangsters are professional criminals, organized for specific purposes in relatively small groups which the underworld terms " mobs." The old-time gangs were of quite a different calibre. They were more like barbarian clans, bound together by a strong sentiment of solidarity, enthusiastically loyal to their chiefs, and often so large that a famous gang might put a thousand men in battle-array.

Though some gangs were frankly criminal, others were not; and the basic motive seems to have been, not sordid crime but rather a brawling independence. A joyous fighting spirit was literally in the air. The Volunteer Fire Companies were practically gangs, and the " silk stocking " Companies rampaged as lustily as did those from the Bowery; while boys in middle-class districts, equipped like gladiators with wooden swords and wash-boiler-top shields, engaged in fierce affrays.[2]

With boys so bellicose, the turbulence of their elders may be imagined. Marshalled under such piquant emblems as *The Dead Rabbitts, The Bowery Boys, The Plug-Uglies,* and *The True-Blue Americans,* the exploits of these great fighting clans still ring down the years. Some gang feuds kept whole wards of the city in riotous tumult for days at a time.[3]

And what, you may ask, were the police doing while all this was going on? Well, the police were nibbling on the outskirts of the battle, arresting stragglers but not daring to plunge into the thick of the fray. What happened when they did is pithily narrated by an old-time New Yorker who tells how a squad of 100 policemen marched valiantly down Leonard Street from Broadway to quell a mob fight, " and in a few minutes came flying out again, hatless, coatless, and bloody. It was only the Bowery Boys ' doing up ' the Five Points Boys, and when the police appeared, both gangs threw them out of the Five Points and then turned again to their own difficulties." [4]

Bearing all this in mind, the amount of police protection accorded the average citizen can be readily guessed. Minding your own business did not help. In fact, a quiet demeanor often invited trouble. In other words, the only way for a man with neither money nor position to get on in the world was to pack a punch in both fists — with a length of leadpipe or a pistol in his pocket for special emergencies.

The ideal of every upstanding New York youngster outside the well-to-do classes was the Bowery Boy — the hard-bitten, picturesque fellow, ready for a fight at the drop of a hat, and able to take care of himself under almost any circumstances. And the Bowery Boy, remember, was neither a crook nor a loafer; he was usually a husky butcher or mechanic, who earned an honest living, fought fair, and scorned to molest women or aged men.

The Bowery, indeed, set the tone for the rough, breezy democracy of old New York. Says a writer of the period: " There is no respect for persons in the surging Bowery. It treads on your heels; turns molasses, milk or liquor over your clothes; tears your garments or whirls you into the gutter; yet never explains in the least or asks your pardon. If you want manners, you should not be there. You must submit to the customs of the quarter, or fight, if you are aggrieved." [5]

Such was the Bowery in the heyday of its glory, immortalized by the famous popular ditty relating, in many verses, the sad experiences of a tenderfoot, and ending always with the poignant refrain:

Oh, the Bowery! The Bowery!
They say such things, and they do such things
On the Bowery, the Bowery;
I'll never go there any more!

That, then, was the situation. But it was a situation which exactly suited young Dick Croker. For, before he was out of his teens, Richard was a formidable person. Abnormally strong for his age, he already gave promise of what he would be in his prime — a tremendously sturdy body, massive shoulders, deep chest, and powerful arms shaggy with black hair; the whole topped by a grim-jawed face and those penetrating, gray-green eyes which, on occasion, could flash like lambent flame. Thewed like a bull, and with almost a

BOWERY GLIMPSES IN ITS HEYDAY

gorilla's strength, here was a young man fit to batter his way far in a rough world — if his wits matched his frame.

Assuredly, Richard made the most of the physical gifts which nature had bestowed upon him. Loving exercise as much as he hated books, the lad showed early aptitude in various forms of sport — in swimming; in wrestling; and, above all, in the use of his hands. Attending a boxing gymnasium kept by a veteran pugilist, Richard soon became the star pupil, and one fine day knocked out his master.

Indeed, had Fate not decreed otherwise, Dick Croker might have won fame in the prize-ring, for he gained quite a reputation in sporting circles and had a string of victories to his credit against good local talent. These fights were informal affairs, like those held in a cellar near his home, and a certain whirlwind bout with one " Pat " Kelly, staged in a saloon.

His most famous battle, however, was wholly impromptu. Richard was attending a picnic at Jones' Wood when the party was invaded by a notorious bully named " Dickie " Lynch, known as a " mean " slugger and a generally bad actor. Though outclassed in both height and weight, Richard went for the intruder like a prize bulldog, and administered a terrific beating. This notable triumph so enhanced young Croker's reputation that thenceforth few men cared to stand up to him in hot blood. However, Croker was deemed a fair fighter, in days when a great deal " went " and the benign influence of Queensberry Rules was as yet unknown.[6]

Young Croker fought for fun, not profit. He had a job — that of machinist in the shops of the New York Central Railroad; and he was a good machinist, too. For many years, half-mythical legends lingered in the car-shops about

that strapping youngster and his phenomenal prowess.   It
was said that as a blacksmith he could wield a sledge in either
hand.   We are told how he built a locomotive, ran it out of
the shops, and turned it over to the company after testing its
speed on a trial trip.   There is a fine touch of romance in the
thought that, some twenty years later, the highest officials
of that great railroad would be politely conferring with the
man who, in his youth, had worked for them at a slender
weekly wage.

Work and boxing, however, by no means summed up
Richard's activities.   Like many other brisk young men in
various walks of life, he belonged to a Volunteer Fire Company, and he won the plaudits of his fellows by his ability as
stoker of Engine 28, much as Bill Tweed did when foreman
of " Big Six."   Last, but emphatically not least, Croker was
a gangster of some note.   And it was these two avocations
which led him into his political career.

Had Richard lived on the lower East Side, he would
probably have become either a Dead Rabbitt or a Bowery
Boy.   Since he dwelt further north, he joined the livest organization in his part of town — an enterprising outfit known
as the Fourth Avenue Tunnel Gang.   And once in, he
rapidly promoted himself by a rare combination of punch,
loyalty, shrewdness, and dogged perseverance.

The Fourth Avenue Tunnel Gang seems to have been
neither better nor worse than the average of its kind.   Its
members were rough young fellows, ready for a fight or a
frolic, and more or less mixed up with the seamy side of
ward politics.   In short, they typified their times.

And the times were boisterous.   Not only did bad social
conditions foster lawlessness; racial and religious differences
inflamed popular passions and envenomed local politics.

Young Croker breathed an atmosphere which grew more and more stormy until, in his twentieth year, he lived through a great explosion which nearly left the metropolis a heap of smouldering ruins. This catastrophe was the Draft Riots of 1863.

The Draft Riots were no chance happening. They were the logical climax of a situation which had long portended trouble and which produced far-reaching political consequences.

New York politics had always been bitter and unscrupulous. But immigration had complicated the situation, especially the great Irish influx of the forties.

When the Irish influx began, New York City was about evenly divided between Democrats and Whigs. At first, both parties looked askance at the Irish. Tammany Hall (already become the regular local Democratic organization) was for a while strongly " Native American " in its attitude. However, Tammany swung around, championed the immigrant, and corralled most of the Irish vote. The Whigs tried to straddle the issue. The result was that they pleased nobody, got very few Irish votes, and lost a large part of their own followers to a new organization, the Native American or " Know-Nothing " Party, which came out flat-footed against immigration in general and the Irish in particular.

The issue was now squarely joined, and public opinion grew more and more inflamed. Many Democrats joined the new party, especially native workingmen, disgruntled by the competition of immigrant labor. In return, however, the immigrants tended to become Democrats.

The effects of popular passion upon practical politics were only too evident. Fraud, violence, and corruption became intensified. All three parties maintained standing armies of repeaters and thugs to cast fraudulent ballots and intimidate peaceful citizens at the polls.

These bravoes also fought one another on every possible occasion. The Native American champion, Bill Poole, a heavyweight boxer familiarly known as " Bill the Butcher," staged a series of Homeric combats with the Democratic champion, a gigantic Irishman named Morrissey. At length Bill was shot up in a saloon by some of Morrissey's friends, and expired, gasping: " Good-bye, boys; I die a true American! " Bill Poole's last words became the battle-cry of his comrades in many a bloody mêlée.

The Civil War further complicated the situation. Local politics were in chaos; for the Native American Party had evaporated, the Whig Party had gone to pieces, the Democrats were badly shaken, and a new party, the Republican, had appeared on the scene. From the very beginning of the war, the turbulent metropolis was an uncertain quantity. And as the war dragged dismally on, New York's attitude became more doubtful. Democrats murmured that the war was a failure, Southern sympathizers whispered busily, while the great foreign population muttered in its tenements, cursing war-prices and the growing toll of blood.

So matters stood when, in the spring of 1863, Congress decreed the Draft. In New York City the passage of the Draft Law was greeted with a chorus of wrath. Many men swore that they would never submit to it and talked wildly of a new rebellion.

Then, just before the Draft was held, the South dealt its supreme blow. At the head of the finest army the Confederacy ever put into the field, General Lee struck due north and invaded Pennsylvania. The fate of the Union

THE SHOOTING OF BILL POOLE

DRAFT RIOTERS MARCHING DOWN SECOND AVENUE

hung in the balance. In the opening days of July, the scales tipped at Gettysburg.

But the thunder of the guns at Gettysburg had barely ceased when, in New York, the Draft wheels began spinning. And they had spun but a day when the city was aflame with insurrection. Out of the slums and tenements huge mobs sprang as if by magic. With even the home-guards in the field against Lee, New York was virtually defenseless. The police were overwhelmed, and for two days and nights most of the city passed under mob control. It was an orgy of plunder, arson, and lust.

Then a stream of veteran regiments fresh from the front turned the tide. The raving mobs were blasted by howitzer salvoes and mowed down by rolling volleys of musketry fire. Within a week, the insurrection was crushed. But — suppose Lee had won at Gettysburg!

The Draft Riots had taught the Federal Government at Washington that here was a danger-spot. So, until the end of the war, New York City was carefully watched, was garrisoned by Federal troops, and was more than once placed under what amounted to a veiled form of martial law.

From the Federal standpoint, all this was necessary and proper. Yet, most New Yorkers had their own ideas on the subject. For whether or not the war-measures of the Republican administration were justifiable, New Yorkers generally chafed under them, Democrats were deeply embittered, and partisan hatreds were correspondingly sharpened.[7] The final result was a great accession of Democratic strength, many ex-Whigs becoming rockribbed Democrats. The close of the war saw New York City a Democratic stronghold.

In fact, for the next generation, the Manhattan Democracy

was so strong that it could split two or three ways, and still carry the city against the Republicans on a straight party line-up. The local Republican organization was in many ways like the Republican " carpet-baggers " of the Southern States during the Reconstruction period. It depended almost wholly upon Albany and Washington, and had scant vitality of its own.

Of Richard Croker's doings during the Draft Riots nothing definite is known. The war apparently meant little to him. Though he was eighteen years old when it began and twenty-two when it ended, he never tried to enlist. That much is obvious; for if a recruiting sergeant had ever caught sight of his stalwart frame, Dick would never have gotten away!

No. Richard had his mind on other matters. He was getting into politics. And, needless to add, he was a good Democrat.

CHAPTER IV

DICK CROKER GETS INTO POLITICS

TOUGH towns breed tough politics. Any political party that intends to get somewhere under such circumstances must play the game. Otherwise, it will simply be counted out.

From the very start of our national life, politics were stormy — especially municipal politics. For, as already remarked, the city was quite beyond the ken of the Fathers of our Republic, and was long regarded as something unworthy of statesmanlike consideration. The story of municipal government in the United States, from its beginning right down to about 1890, is a sort of political Rake's Progress, getting steadily worse and with few hopeful signs for the future. No wonder that Lord Bryce, writing in the late eighties, declared pessimistically that city government in America was "a conspicuous failure."[1]

Looking backward, the reasons for this lamentable civic decline are self-evident. "The task of governing the early American town was simple enough. . . Their populations were homogeneous, their wants were few; and they were still in that happy childhood when every voter knew nearly every other voter, and when everybody knew his neighbor's business as well as his own, and perhaps better."[2] In other words, these were real *communities,* in the organic sense, with traditions, standards, and a civic consciousness that embraced all classes.

35

Then those compact little towns swelled prodigiously into big cities — and promptly lost their civic souls. For, as Bryce well says: " What is a modern American city? A huge space of ground covered with houses. . . More than half of the lower strata had lately come from their far-off Old World homes. . . They were not members of a Community, but an aggregation of human atoms, swept hither and thither like grains of desert sand." [3]

What wonder, then, that these mushroom cities should, almost without exception, have wallowed in an orgy of political corruption? What wonder that, with no effective safeguards, elections became ruthless partisan battles? What wonder that *all* parties were literally forced to vie with one another in fraud and violence? Finally, what wonder that New York, where conditions were most hectic, should have been the worst offender of them all?

As far back as the thirties, New York City politics had become notorious for turbulence and venality. By that time, the Tammany Democracy had mobilized the slum gangs for ruthless political service. But the Whigs did their best to keep up with the game; and, in default of enough local talent, they imported gangs of thugs and rowdies from Philadelphia and other Whig strongholds. So both sides competed merrily in every species of election fraud: they stuffed ballot-boxes, colonized " repeaters," forged ballots, and engineered election riots which sometimes needed the militia to put them down.

The most picturesque personality of that early epoch was Captain Isaiah Rynders. This hard-faced, heavy-handed old ruffian had begun life as a gambler and dirk-fighter on the Mississippi. Drifting to New York, like so many other adventurous spirits, he plunged zestfully into its rough-and-tumble politics, and was soon one of the ward-captains of the local Democracy. There was nothing that Rynders would not do; and his grim visage, scarred by bullets and bowie-knives, warned opponents of what they might expect at his hands.

If Rynders typified ward politics, the party leaders, though more urbane, were imbued with the same spirit of ruthless partisanship. The "spoils system" which so long dominated American politics was first clearly formulated in a speech by Senator Marcy of New York, in the year 1833. Defending the politics of his State against an attack by Henry Clay, Marcy declared roundly in open Senate: "It may be that the politicians of New York are not so fastidious as some gentlemen are. They boldly preach what they practise. When they are contending for victory, they avow their intention of enjoying the fruits of it. If they fail, they will not murmur. If they win, they expect to reap all the advantages. They see nothing wrong in the rule that *to the victors belong the spoils.*"

The Civil War intensified the unfortunate trend of the times. The war sharpened partisan hatreds and raised the doctrine of "party regularity" almost to a religious dogma. It also fostered an era of unbridled extravagance and corruption. One political party was as bad as another. If in New York City the local Democracy was debauched by the brazen effrontery and gigantic peculations of Boss Tweed, the Republicans at Washington were disgraced by colossal scandals like the Credit Mobilier and the Whiskey Ring.

The most sinister feature of the post-war epoch, however, was the close alliance between politics and "big business." The financial demoralization of the war-period — the job-

bery in army-contracts, the sudden growth of ill-gotten fortunes, and the gambling spirit aroused by an unstable paper
currency, had spawned a horde of unsavory millionaires.
And this crew of new-rich profiteers, reckless and unscrupulous to the last degree, were past-masters in the art of prosti-
tuting politics to their own ends.　In national, State, and
municipal politics, it was the same story.　Jim Fiske and Jay
Gould were but the prototypes of a sordid era in which franchise grabs, grafting contracts, and special privileges of all
kinds were the order of the day.

The debasing influence of the times is strikingly shown in
the career of the arch-villain of the piece — Boss Tweed.
Contrary to the general impression, Tweed did not scheme
from the first to get into politics.　His modern biographer [4]
brings this out very well.　He shows us young Bill Tweed
as a youth of good habits, fairly launched in business, and
happily married to a nice girl at an early age.　When this
self-respecting, popular young fellow is waited on by a
delegation and asked to run for office, he declines, saying
that he wants to stick strictly to business.[5]

Then the Presidential election of 1844 takes place.
" Tweed, after casting his vote, loitered around the polls.
He saw both sides offering money for votes, bidding against
one another.　He went home to his bride that night, mar-
velling at the brazen manner in which it had been done.　He
had heard and read of these things. . .　Then he recalled
his father-in-law's opinion of politics.　Was not politics a
corrupt game? . .　There was no magic in it.　It was just
plain theft.　The Whigs stole in the Whig strongholds, and
the Democrats in the Tammany strongholds.　Ballot boxes
were stuffed, incorrect tallies reported by crooked tally
clerks, and the thugs of Rynders and his ilk went from one

JOHN T. HOFFMAN

WILLIAM MARCY TWEED

polling-place to another, impersonating honest citizens. Both sides did it." [6]

A few years later, Tweed decided to enter politics. But in this brief period, his youthful ideals had been quite shattered. " More than that, he had fixed ideas as to his future line of conduct. Politics were corrupt. He would have to be corrupt to be successful. And he was determined to succeed. His political *credo,* as recited by him before the Aldermanic Committee that made a pretense at investigating the Tweed Ring frauds after his downfall, was thus transcribed by the official stenographer:

" ' The fact is, New York politics were always dishonest — long before my time. A politician in coming forward takes things as they are. This population is too hopelessly split up into races and factions to govern it under universal suffrage, except by the bribery of patronage, or corruption." [7]

Such, even in the hour of defeat and disgrace, was the deliberate judgment of the man whom young Dick Croker acknowledged as his political liege-lord from the time he entered politics until he was nearly thirty years of age; the man whose career Croker studied, just as Tweed did the career of the notorious Fernando Wood and others of his time. The bosses passed, but the game of politics went on, essentially unchanged. And how should beginners learn the rules, if not from the master-players?

Yet this conscious modelling upon the doings of the great was an afterthought, which came to Dick Croker only when he was fairly launched upon his political career. The first steps were slight and unpremeditated; perhaps even Croker himself could not have told you just when the earliest was taken. The truth is that Dick just *drifted* into politics — as naturally and inevitably as he had drifted into his boyhood

gang. Under the circumstances, it was the normal thing
for him to do.

Consider his situation: A strapping youngster, marked out
among his fellows both by fighting ability and capacity for
leadership, he could not fail to be soon noted by lynx-eyed
ward politicians whose business it was to weigh and appraise
every man and boy within their compact domain. First the
block-lieutenant, then the precinct captain, then the district
leader, knew that here was a pup who showed the marks of
a good dog. And of course those shrewd appraisers were
Democrats. For Dick lived on the edge of the old Gas
House District. And the Gas House District was a Tammany stronghold.

The leader of the district in those days was a redoubtable
personage long known in Tammany annals as Jimmy
O'Brien the Famous. For many years he ruled his district
with a master-hand; rewarding the faithful, chastising the
unruly, crushing the disloyal, and fostering latent talent
with an almost tender solicitude. For a good district leader
cherishes the rising generation. It is through such wise
foresight that Tammany endures.

A Tammany sage gives us the key to Richard Croker's
humble entrance into politics. In his remarkable book,[8] so
crammed with the lore of practical politics, George Washington Plunkitt (of Croker's own generation, and raised,
like him, among the squatters of Central Park) thus describes
the typical first steps in a Tammany career: "You can't
begin too early in politics if you want to succeed at the game.
I began several years before I could vote, and so did every
other successful leader in Tammany Hall. When I was
twelve years old I made myself useful around the district
headquarters and did work at the polls on election day.

Later on, I hustled about gettin' out voters who had jags on or who were too lazy to come by themselves. There's a hundred ways that boys can help, and they get an experience that's the first real step in statesmanship. Show me a boy that hustles for the organization on election day, and I'll show you a comin' statesman." [9]

Thus Tammany (even then almost a century old) took young Dick Croker in hand. With rough yet genial efficiency, it taught him its commandments. Some of these were new to him. Others he had already glimpsed in the gang; for the gang-code of old New York was a good apprenticeship for a Tammany " worker."

First and foremost, Tammany taught discipline. Tammany is a volunteer army, and strict obedience to orders is the basis of its power. As in Napoleon's armies, the rawest recruit carries a marshal's baton in his knapsack; the " career is open to talent." Yet straight and narrow is the path to advancement. Promotion comes only through a merit system, rigid as the law of the Medes and Persians, which even the big Boss never breaks. And the first article of the Tammany code is that he who would lead must first serve; he who would command must know how, promptly and implicitly, to obey.

Tammany taught loyalty. For Tammany, remember, is a fraternity — governed paternally. Hence, the big Boss, though the absolute head of the clan, must be loyal to his clansmen, who are his brothers; and they, in turn, must be loyal to him. As an old veteran of the Wigwam put it: " There's nothing sticks so tight as Tammany." [10]

To call Tammany a brotherhood may seem strange when we recall the fierce strivings for place and preferment which go on eternally within the organization, and which have sometimes so rocked the Hall with factional strife that its foes have gleefully predicted its speedy dissolution.

Yet this is a surface view. One of the secrets of Tammany's success has been that it is run on the stern principle of the survival of the fittest. From the big Boss down to the youngest precinct captain, every man in authority must not only win his place but must hold it by efficient service against a crowd of eager aspirants. In other words, he must everlastingly " deliver the goods." Results, not excuses; election majorities, not alibis, are what is wanted — and required. As soon as results are not forthcoming, the man responsible is deemed to have " fallen down on the job " — and some one grabs the job away from him in short order. That keeps the whole organization forever " on its toes " and gives it at all times the " fighting edge " needed for victory.

Tammany makes both a business and a fine art of politics. The men who rise in Tammany Hall work systematically and intelligently. They take their politics as seriously as other men take their business or profession. In short, Tammany has evolved a marvellous political technique, based, not on theory, but upon the practical experience of succeeding generations.

Tammany's unique feature is its unrivalled knowledge of what may be termed the " human equation." Of *politics*, in the narrow sense of the word, Tammany has no monopoly. Other machines have been as well built, as strictly disciplined, as shrewdly aware of the tricks and dodges of " practical politics." But in its profound grasp of everyday human nature, Tammany stands alone; and it is therefore not as a mere machine but as an essentially human institution that Tammany has no rival in the political field.

Tammany taught Dick Croker, the rough young gangster, "To be kind to those in trouble; to look after the sick in the tenements in his precinct; to see that the widows had food and fuel, that the men had jobs, and the orphan children clothes; to mourn with those that mourn and to rejoice with them that rejoice." [11]

This never-failing charity, dispensed with fraternal kindliness, has characterized Tammany from its early days. Two typical instances may suffice: "The winter following the panic of 1837 was marked by unemployment, poverty, and suffering in New York. A Whig administration in power did nothing for the unemployed. Tammany promptly organized relief committees in the various wards, which distributed food, fuel, and clothing. . . Boss Tweed ran true to form in this line. During the winter of 1870–71, when another historic panic had paralyzed the country, Tweed gave $1000 to each alderman to buy coal for the poor. He distributed $50,000 in his own ward. Of course, it was later proved that he had stolen the money he gave away in charity; but New York recalled other venal persons who did not feel moved to share ill-gotten gains with their poverty-stricken fellow-citizens." [12]

The strength of Tammany's hold on the masses was never more strikingly shown than by the popular attitude toward Boss Tweed. Although convicted of gigantic frauds, disgraced, and unsparingly condemned by the bulk of public opinion, Tweed kept the affection of his humble friends. The tenement wards remembered his lavish bounty and jovial good fellowship, and stood by him to the end. During his trial, a Tweed champion, speaking at a popular mass-meeting, brought down the house by shouting: "Tweed's heart has always been in the right place, and even if he is a thief, there's more blood in his little finger and more marrow in his big toe than the men who are abusing him have in their whole bodies! " [13]

Another thing to be remembered is that Tammany charity makes no distinction of race, creed, or even political allegiance. No man down on his luck who seeks aid at the district clubhouse is ever asked his politics. Tammany figures, on a liberal percentage basis, that, whatever party a man may belong to at the start, after he has been helped out once or twice he will be a good enough Democrat to lend Tammany his vote most of the time.

Such was the lore which Tammany imparted to Richard Croker, as to all others who have risen in its service; not at once, but bit by bit, the lessons were learned, mostly practical experience. Yet, once learned, they were never forgotten.

At the start we can picture young Dick Croker doing slight political jobs and getting small personal favors from minor henchmen in return. Of course he was far beneath the public notice of the great Jimmie O'Brien, his district leader. Dick Croker was then merely one of a dozen promising lads worth watching for future eventualities.

But as Dick battled his way toward headship in the Fourth Avenue Tunnel Gang, the situation altered. Dick was proving himself. Then came the impromptu battle with Dickie Lynch, the notorious bruiser, in Jones' Wood. That smashing victory over long odds not only clinched young Croker's fistic reputation; it also stirred the district leader to action. The promising pup *was* a great dog! There was much work for him to do. It was high time he was taken aboard.

With Jimmie the Famous, to decide was to act. Wherefore, the district was promptly given to understand that

Dick Croker had been taken under O'Brien's wing and was part of "the organization." Dick had made his formal debut on the political stage.

O'Brien's discerning eye had already spotted his new henchman's special field of usefulness. Dick Croker was to be a boss "repeater." In those days of lax registration laws, election repeating was one of the mainstays of "practical politics," and Jimmie the Famous had developed it to a fine art. Nowhere was there a better organized corps of repeaters than that of the Gas House District; not even Isaiah Rynders could do better downtown in the "Bloody Ould Sixth Ward." On election days Jimmy O'Brien's "regulars," after making the home district safe, voted all over the city.

Indeed, on crucial occasions, they might be hired for an "outside job" as far away as Philadelphia or Albany; and they never failed to do yeoman service. It surely was not one of those efficient workers who committed the gross social error, immortalized by Senator Plunkitt, of trying to vote the name of the Episcopal Bishop of Albany, William Croswell Doane. Amazed at the fellow's effrontery, the election clerk remonstrated: "G'wan! You ain't Bishop Doane." To which the repeater answered heatedly: "The hell I ain't, you —— —— ——! "

Young Croker was certainly well qualified for his task. Besides great personal strength, he brought with him a considerable following — brisk boys of the Fourth Avenue Tunnel Gang. Around this trusted nucleus it was easy to build up an effective organization.

That Dick soon mastered the tricks of the trade is shown by certain fragmentary yet enlightening evidence. It was in 1864 that Richard Croker, having reached man's estate, cast his first vote. The very next year he did even better; he voted no less than seventeen times for William H. Lyman, the Democratic candidate for Constable in Greenpoint.[14] And three years later, a New York newspaper, describing the various gangs of repeaters loaned for heavy duty in the Philadelphia elections, ended its tally with the words: " Last, but not least, 150 metropolitan bandits under the notorious Dick Croker, all well-armed and spoiling for a fight." [15] As usual with whatever he undertook, Dick was forging ahead and gaining a reputation.

Repeating was not precisely a peaceful trade. The other side always objected in principle, and frequently in practice. Such objections had to be met in equally practical fashion. This led to numerous incidents like the one in the elections of 1868, when Croker's gang assaulted Christopher Pullman, a Republican politician, on the corner of 32nd Street and Second Avenue. Pullman was badly beaten up by the Croker boys and received injuries from which he never recovered.[16] A couple of years later, the *New York Times* printed a news item concerning an election brawl between Croker and one James Moore, on the corner of 21st Street and Third Avenue, in which Mr. Moore got very much the worst of it.[17] Shortly afterwards the same paper referred to Richard Croker as " a rowdy and election bully of well-established fame." [18]

Nothing is more amusing than the way Croker's enemies in after years would hold up their hands in holy horror over these and similar incidents of his early political career; while, on the other hand, his friends would gloze them over or angrily deny them altogether.

Yet, surely, both sets of gentlemen displayed a sad lack of historical perspective — to say nothing of a sense of humor. Why seek either to magnify or to minimize the obvious fact that Richard Croker began as a ward heeler? Morally, he was neither better nor worse than the average of his kind. He was merely doing (extremely well) what they all did — or tried to do. Furthermore, he was obeying orders, as part of a highly disciplined machine. The responsibility was not his, but his superiors'. His business it was to hear and obey; nothing more.

Croker entered politics with his brawny fists. His course was clear. For what had he seen, what had he learned, to teach him that politics was anything more than sordid, brutal strife? We have noted his up-bringing from his earliest years. His surroundings had moulded him; made him what he was — a super-roughneck.

So Dick Croker the ward heeler was well pleased with himself. And (what was more to the point) his ward boss, Jimmie the Famous, was pleased as well. The new henchman had loyally " delivered the goods." Therefore he must be suitably rewarded. That was the unwritten law of the clan.

The usual wires were pulled, and Dick Croker presently found himself on the City payroll. His first municipal job was largely a sinecure — that of Attendant in one of the Municipal Courts, at a salary of $1200 per annum. His next job was more in his line; he was made engineer on one of the City's steamers.

Then, in 1868, when he was but 25 years old, Croker received a real mark of his suzerain's regard. Jimmie O'Brien having been promoted from the Board of Aldermen to the office of Sheriff of New York (a very fat plum!), Dick Croker was duly seated in his stead. An Alderman at twenty-five! Richard was getting on.

CHAPTER V

RICHARD CROKER's path to power was a long and rocky road. Full twenty years was his apprenticeship; years fraught with strife and checkered by reverses, one of which proved well-nigh fatal. That he beat down all barriers and bested all foes bespeaks his iron will and dogged endurance.

Young Croker first rose from the ranks in Tweed's heyday. Yet he rose, not under the Big Boss's immediate eye, but as the faithful henchman of Jimmie O'Brien, his district leader. Tammany is a feudal hierarchy, with clearly graduated obediences. Each district leader is a sort of baron, almost supreme within his own domain. To him, the local vassals owe primal fealty. Hence, when Boss and baron fall out, the district leader may fairly count upon the support of his trusty followers, even against the Boss himself. These domestic conflicts were frequent in earlier times, when Tammany was looser jointed than it is today.

It was in one such feudal warring that Richard was presently embroiled. Barely had Croker blossomed forth as Alderman, than Jimmie the Famous quarreled with Boss Tweed. The cause need not concern us — nor did it concern Richard overmuch. As Jimmie O'Brien's lieutenant, he followed his district leader into battle as naturally as the retainer of a feudal lord against his distant sovereign. So the Braves of the Gas House District formed an insurgent faction, which the newspapers played up as an "anti-Tammany movement." That, of course, was absurd. The Gas House District was a Tammany stronghold, and political divisions there were purely personal. It was just a family row, which would presently blow over.

Meanwhile, however, the row waxed exceeding hot. Jimmie O'Brien gained allies in other districts, and the Big Boss was stirred to wrathful action. Unable to shake the rebels in their home wards, Tweed invoked the aid of Albany. The Democrats then controlled the State, so Tweed had plain sailing. A pliant legislature voted a new charter for New York City, so designed that the rebel Aldermen were turned out of office, while Jimmie O'Brien lost his Sheriff's job. That was just a sample of the so-called "ripper bills" by which America's metropolis was apt to be civically upset at any moment through partisan schemes hatched at Albany, 150 miles away.

It is interesting to learn that Alderman Croker was among those present in the gallery of the Senate Chamber when the Big Boss cracked the whip and his legislative puppets jumped to obey. "He must have watched the fantastic scene thoughtfully, for he then learned a great deal concerning what to do and what not to do when it came his turn to rule New York." [1]

Within a year, the war was over. The Big Chief and his rebellious Sachems smoked the pipe of peace, and the insurgent Braves trooped back into the Wigwam. Naturally, Jimmy the Famous saw to it that his right-hand man was properly taken care of; so ex-Alderman Croker got a job in the Comptroller's office at a good salary, with plenty of spare time for his district duties.

Croker needed that spare time, because a deputy district

leader had countless duties. He had to be on the job twenty-four hours a day, if O'Brien's political fences were to be kept in good repair. Every complaint must be promptly heard, every appeal of needy constituents quickly satisfied.

Besides his routine chores, Richard had special election duties, as when he sat in some corner saloon, distributing ballots,[2] listening to reports of precinct captains, marshalling gangs of repeaters, and himself leading them forth to the fray in emergencies. It was a strenuous life, but it was his chosen calling and he throve mightily thereon.

By 1871, Croker was apparently well on his upward way. Then came the first rumblings of the political earthquake which hurled Tweed from power. So shattering was the upheaval that a year later, Tammany lay defeated and discredited. Never was the organization nearer complete dissolution. The solid front of the New York Democracy was broken into factions, not to be re-welded for many years.

It is a mistake to think (as often asserted) that Tammany recovered its grip on the city soon after the Tweed debacle. New York remained Democratic, because the Democratic majority was so large that it could split internally and still retain party control. But there were several distinct factions, the largest being one known as the County Democracy, with Tammany ranking second, Irving Hall third, and some flea-bite " Democracies " combining around election-time to gouge an office or two out of the bigger organizations.[3] The local Republican Party was then too small and morally too contemptible to be in the running.

New York politics thus degenerated into a welter of factional strife, wherein the best led and most compactly disciplined organization would ultimately win. Fortunately for Tammany, it already possessed the tradition of " regu-

" HONEST JOHN " KELLY

larity," and it now produced a leader who was to steer it successfully through the lean years that lay ahead.

Tammany's new leader was a man named Kelly, who delighted in the prefix " Honest John." [4] Kelly's right to the title may appear somewhat dubious to modern eyes, but he seems to have merited it by the standards of his day. Besides a moral reputation vastly above Tweed's, " Honest John " possessed other qualities essential to his strenuous chieftainship. Raised in the hard school of the slums, Kelly had battled his way to the front. When he came to power in 1872, he was in the prime of robust manhood. Kelly was physically a larger edition of Richard Croker. Six feet tall, his two hundred pounds of bone and muscle gave promise of tremendous fighting power — a promise not belied by his grim mouth and stubborn jaw.

Kelly pinned his faith on iron discipline. A dictator by nature, he demanded blind obedience, and when he had once made up his mind he could be moved by neither arguments nor threats. Opposition was to him an unpardonable sin, never to be forgotten.

Such was the man, in all his strength — and limitations. For " Honest John " lacked Croker's flexibility and cooler vision. Also, Kelly was susceptible to flattery. The result was that he raised up a host of needless enemies, while harboring many false friends; and these together were responsible for the political failures which embittered his later years and finally brought him, broken-hearted, to an untimely grave.

Meanwhile, Croker, as a member of Tammany, had shared its misfortunes in the crucial days which marked the downfall of the Tweed Ring. His old leader, Jimmie O'Brien, deserted the apparently sinking Tammany ship,

and like many other political war-horses, switched allegiance
to one of the new Democratic factions which now arose.
What was Croker to do? Should he follow Jimmie the
Famous into the new camp? Or should he stick to the ship
and follow the rising star of Tammany's new chief, "Honest
John"?

Perhaps it was the prompting of discipline, perhaps instinctive liking for a personality so kindred to his own; any-
how, Croker remained loyal to Tammany and became
Kelly's man. Kelly, on his side, approved of Croker from
the first, and Richard's fealty was soon rewarded. Through
Kelly's influence, his henchman was appointed City Mar-
shall and the next year Croker was elected Coroner — an
important office with fees worth $15,000 a year.

However, there was trouble ahead. By this time, Kelly
and O'Brien were enemies, and the nature of both men made
it inevitable that this enmity should become a bitter personal
feud. In the elections of 1872, O'Brien ran for Mayor in a
three-cornered fight, the other contestants being the Tammany candidate and the nominee of still another Democratic
faction. This man won; but the Tammany candidate came
in a close second, whereas O'Brien finished a bad third.

That further envenomed the Kelly-O'Brien feud. As the
elections of 1874 drew nigh, the two rivals girded their loins
for a decisive trial of strength. And in that grim struggle,
Richard Croker was destined to encounter the gravest peril
of his entire career. He was to come within the shadow of
the gallows.

CHAPTER VI

IN THE SHADOW OF THE GALLOWS

ELECTION morn dawned gray and sullen; a November day of the year 1874. Everybody in the district knew that trouble was brewing. The local campaign had been a whirlwind of billingsgate and brickbats — verbal and otherwise. Jimmy O'Brien was running for Congress. The Tammany candidate was Abram S. Hewitt, a millionaire merchant with a penchant for politics, ready to " open a barrel " to further his hobby. Hewitt was thus an ideal candidate for the occasion. With plenteous funds, Boss Kelly might hope to beat Jimmie the Famous even in his home ward. On the other hand, O'Brien had his back to the wall. Defeated there, his power would be so shaken that he might thenceforth be politically down and out. All of which meant a fight to a finish, in which almost anything "went."

Jimmy's ex-lieutenant, Richard Croker, was in the front rank of the Tammany attack. And his strong arm was needed, for Jimmy was fighting hard and rough. Long before noon, gangs of embattled O'Brienites were patrolling the district, stuffing ballot-boxes and beating up Tammany voters. Owney Geoghahan, a notorious bruiser, spread terror with his pile-driving fists; and a gang of West Side repeaters, hired for the occasion, was aiding the O'Brienite forces.

The Tammany men were not taking all this lying down. Their patrols were also in the field; and it was one of these, headed by Croker, which presently came upon a knot of the West Siders at the corner of 34th Street and Second Avenue.

Striding up to the intruders, Croker asked their leader, a strapping fellow named Billy Borst, what he and his friends were doing over on the East Side. Before Borst could answer, who should come around the corner but Jimmy O'Brien himself.

Instantly the air grew tense. With a venomous side-glance at Croker, O'Brien addressed his hired henchman, asking pointedly, " Billy, what is that damned loafer saying to you? "

" I am no damned loafer," growled Croker, advancing a pace.

" You are a damned loafer, and a God damned loafer, and a repeater! " shouted O'Brien. Both sides instinctively bunched together behind their respective champions.

" You're a damned thief," rejoined Croker; to which O'Brien answered: " You damned cur, I picked you out of the gutter, and now you're supporting a rich man like Hewitt against me for Congress."

Thud! Thud! The fight was on. O'Brien swung heavily to Croker's head, and Croker landed a stiff one to the jaw, which cut O'Brien's mouth. " Come on, boys! " yelled George Hickey, a Crokerite. " Let's give it to the sons of bitches! "

Snarling and cursing, both sides leapt into the fray. For a few seconds there was a milling blur of flailing arms and fists. Then — crack! crack! Two pistol shots, followed by a scream of mortal agony.

Sullenly the fighters drew apart as the police came on the

scene. Hitherto, the guardians of the peace had kept discreetly in the background; but gun-play at close quarters was too much of a good thing.

They found John McKenna, an O'Brienite, prone on the sidewalk, shot in the head and obviously dying. Limp and white, the stricken man was carried to a nearby drug-store. The police sergeant, who knew McKenna personally, bent over him. "John," he said, "it's my place to know. Tell me how it happened."

McKenna groaned, and gasped: "For God's sake give me a drink of water!"

Again the sergeant asked: "John, who shot you?"

And the dying man muttered thickly, "Dick Croker —"[1]

Richard was in a very tight place. For, regardless of his guilt or innocence, there was high politics involved. Jimmy the Famous had managed to hold his home ward. Hence, he was still a power in the land. And every ounce of his pull would be thrown against his ex-henchman, whom he hated as a renegade. Indeed, if Croker were innocent, his conviction by "railroading" methods would redound doubly to O'Brien's prestige; it would inform all and sundry that double-crossing Jimmie the Famous emphatically did not pay! Buttressed by McKenna's dying words, the case against Croker was strong. And Dick the ex-gangster's reputation was none of the best.

Croker's main hope was in his Boss. For here, again, innocent or guilty, political prestige was at stake. Kelly was bound to exert himself for a loyal follower who had come to grief in party service. The only drawback was that Kelly stood before the public as the apostle of a better Tammany and cherished his title of "Honest John." Still, within limits, Croker might rest assured that Kelly would do his best.

The Boss gave no sign of side-stepping his obligations. When Croker was sent to the Tombs prison to await his trial for murder, both Kelly and Hewitt visited him, and when Croker assured them of his innocence, they publicly backed him and engaged eminent counsel in his defense.

From the first, Croker had emphatically denied his guilt. At the time of his arrest he roundly stated: " I never carried a pistol in my life, and never will as long as I can use my hands." When his case came to trial some months later, " the evidence was conflicting and thin. Some eye-witnesses testified that they saw Croker fire the shot; others testified that Croker did not have a gun and never carried a gun. The jury remained out for seventeen hours and then re-turned to announce that they stood equally divided, six for conviction and six for acquittal, and that they could not agree.

" Croker was thereupon released, and he was never tried again. It was generally believed in later years that he did not fire the shot that killed McKenna, but that it was fired by his friend, George Hickey. General Wingate, who was of Croker's counsel, said after Croker's death that the man who fired the shot was standing next to Croker during the trial and intended to declare himself the murderer if the verdict was one of guilty. Croker, according to his lawyer, refused to permit proof to be submitted that his friend had fired the fatal shot." [2] Furthermore, Judge Barrett, who presided at the trial, stated many years later that, from what he had since learned, he was convinced that Croker was in-nocent of the crime.

Croker had thus won clear of the shadow of the gallows.

Yet its aftermath had to be lived down. He was out of a job, and none was in sight. Kelly was well disposed towards him, but for the moment he could do little. It was one thing to get his henchman out of jail; it was quite another publicly to favor a man very much under a cloud. Remember: Croker had not been acquitted; he had merely been released through the disagreement of a " hung " jury. His trial had been widely featured in the newspapers, and his enemies had done their best to blacken his name. So notorious a person simply could not be put on the city payroll.

Unfortunately for Croker, he had no savings to fall back upon. Free-handed with his friends, and already devoted to the race-track, money had slipped through his fingers and he found himself almost broke. A New York journalist who knew Croker well gives us a striking glimpse of the straits to which the future Boss of Tammany was reduced during the next few years.

" I never see Richard Croker in these days of wealth and renown," he writes,[3] " but I recall his disagreeable experiences after being released from prison. He was shunned by men of his own class, and found little assistance in his attempts to remove the stigma of prison from his name. He was in almost abject poverty. John Kelly gave him the opportunity to redeem himself. I do not believe the circumstances have ever been related in print.

" Croker appealed to Kelly to use his influence with the Mayor to appoint him to a job of minor importance. Kelly and the Mayor were not on good terms; but Kelly, who was friendly to Croker, sent for a mutual friend and urged him to assist his protégé. That friend has since told me of his first meeting with Croker.

" Kelly called Croker from an adjoining room. Croker,

in a suit of clothes almost threadbare from constant wear, and twirling a well-worn soft brown slouch hat in his hand, came in and stood looking stolidly at Kelly.

" 'Now, Richard,' said Kelly, 'I want you to tell this gentleman what you are after. He will help you.'

" In a few jerky words, Croker said that he had applied to several officials for a position. He knew there was a vacancy in one of the departments. 'But they won't give it to me,' he said, 'and I don't know what to do. I've got my district behind me, and I go to City Hall every day and hang about and try to see the Mayor. He won't see me. When I speak to him in the halls, he don't notice me. I guess it's because of that case against me.'

" 'What case? ' asked the Mayor's friend.

" 'For killing McKenna,' replied Croker. 'They think I did it. I didn't, though. I want work. I've just got to have it.'

" Croker remained standing during the entire interview, twirling his slouch hat and looking at the floor, until Kelly dismissed him, after saying to the Mayor's friend: 'Now, I know that Richard is a worthy boy (Croker was then over 32 years old). I know he means well and is a good party worker. I wish you would help him.'

" Ten minutes later, when the Mayor's friend came down from Kelly's office in the building at the corner of Park Place and Broadway, he found Croker leaning against a lamp-post. Night was coming on, and it had begun to snow. Croker wore no overcoat. He looked disconsolately at the crowds shifting and separating through City Hall Park; his hands in his pockets, and his face wearing an expression of utter dejection. He admitted, when interrogated, that he did not have the money to pay his fare uptown to deliver to the Mayor the letter which had been given him. In this hour of sore need, the Mayor's friend assisted him; and it is a tribute to Croker's sense of gratitude that he has since returned the loan with interest ten thousandfold." [4]

So Croker was once more on the payroll. It was a poor job — a terrible come-down for one who had held a Coronership worth $15,000 a year. But Croker took it thankfully, and dug harder than ever into politics. Never was there a more faithful and tireless party "worker." And this indomitable persistence was bound to reap its reward in the long run.

However, for the time being, progress was discouragingly slow. Plodding away at his job and his district chores, " his sole diversion was the race-track, which he followed as persistently as he did politics. It was only a short time after his appearance in Kelly's office as a suppliant for a $3 a day job that he confided to a friend at Saratoga that he had lost his last dollar on a race, and didn't know how he was going to get back to New York. He complained at that time that ' That crowd in New York won't let me in. I can't make any money.' " [5]

These lean years of set-back and obscurity played their part in forging the iron of Croker's soul. His arrest and imprisonment for a crime he probably did not commit tempered his character and hardened his self-control. In the easy days of his first prosperity, Croker still retained much of the rough swagger of his gangster days. When he again began climbing fortune's path, he had become shrewdly silent; saying little, observing much, cautiously testing each step of the way.

It was Boss Kelly who gave Richard what ultimately proved to be his golden opportunity. As already remarked,

Kelly had liked Richard from the first.   Watching him carefully, Kelly noted Croker's silent industry and devoted party
zeal.   Might not Croker make an ideal right-hand man? —
the confidential assistant at headquarters whom Kelly needed
and had long been looking for?   It was worth trying.

So, one fine day, Croker found himself in the Boss's private office.   And, once there, he stayed.   More and more,
he made himself indispensable to his chief; more and more,
Kelly leaned upon his model subordinate.

Richard was climbing again.

CHAPTER VII

CROKER GATHERS UP THE REINS

In the score of years which elapsed between Richard Croker's humble entry into politics and his arrival at the headship of Tammany Hall, the man underwent an extraordinary transformation. In 1864, the 22-year-old henchman of Jimmie the Famous was a mere ward heeler, doing the dirty work of his hard-handed, unscrupulous political superior. A brawling gangster and election bully, young Croker was distinguished from dozens of his fellows only by tremendous physical strength, unflinching courage, and a certain innate capacity for command displayed since boyhood days.

In 1885, the leader who seized the reins of power from John Kelly's dying hands had not only mastered Tammany but had also mastered himself. The truculent gang-chief, graduate of street brawls and eager for a fight at the drop of a hat, had become a man of silence and self-control. Though retaining all his courage and dominating energy, Croker had learned to govern by moral force, instead of by the fist. He had discovered the power that is in a word or look, rather than brutal shoutings and rough-and-tumble exploits on the pavement. His dogged will had subordinated his lower and more repulsive instincts, and had steadily developed his higher qualities.

In fact, the former uncouth rough had become a really presentable figure. He had learned most of the social conventions, spoke fairly correct English, and dressed inconspicuously and in good taste. His usual manner was quiet, reserved, and dignified. Most significant, his inborn genius for leadership, evolved by practice and fortified by success, so suffused his personality that even the casual observer realized that here was a master of men. This striking evolution can be accounted for primarily, no doubt, to innate force of character; to good latent qualities beneath the rough exterior. Yet even these hidden traits would hardly have flowered so conspicuously unless fostered by favoring conditions. Full-grown men do not thus alter the tenor of their ways without the aid of new and compelling circumstances. And as we scan Richard Croker's early manhood, we see but one major factor which could have wrought the change — the selective discipline of Tammany Hall.

To be John Kelly's right-hand man was to sit at the feet of a master in the school of practical politics. And Richard proved an apt pupil. Silent, efficient, never openly opposing, somehow getting results, Croker became indispensable to the grizzled autocrat who had fewer friends and more foes with every passing year.

Banking on Richard's ability and loyalty, Kelly opened his confidence. Bit by bit, the old Boss gave his henchman the benefit of his ripe experience, until Croker knew every trick in the game. It was from Kelly that he absorbed his profound knowledge of organization detail; from Kelly, also, he caught the pose of eloquent listener which he used so effectively in later life. Croker studied Kelly like a textbook, committed him to memory — and bettered the instruction in the end.

To outward seeming, Croker's life was an eventless one. Quit of the brawling turmoil of ward politics and moving in the shadow of his exalted patron, Richard was out of the limelight. That, however, was as it should have been. Richard had had too much publicity of the wrong kind. Luckily, the public has a conveniently short memory. And there were several matters which Richard wanted forgotten.

Though Boss Kelly's confidential man was unknown to the average citizen, he was well-known to insiders at Tammany Hall. They saw which way the wind was blowing, and as the Boss devolved upon his trusted deputy an ever-larger measure of responsibility, they accorded him a corresponding measure of deferential respect. More and more, Croker became the man to " see "; the man to consult; the man to take orders from. It was a process of evolution, slow but sure. Shrewd observers realized that Croker was " in line " to succeed Kelly. For, as a Tammany notable once put it: " The headship of Tammany Hall is not an appointment, but a growth."

So time unobtrusively went by. Richard had apparently foresworn his hectic youth. A married man with a growing family, he lived quietly, and no scandal tarnished his name. Beneath the surface, of course, he was deep in politics. And New York politics were then tangled beyond description. As already remarked, the upheaval against Tweed had shattered the local Democracy into jarring fragments, and Tammany was merely one of several factions which wrangled endlessly for power and patronage.

In this long struggle the chief protagonists were Tammany Hall and the County Democracy. Both had their strong and weak points. The County Democracy boasted a somewhat larger following, and was led by men of wealth and social distinction, such as Abram S. Hewitt, the millionaire merchant for whom Croker had so strenuously battled; William C. Whitney, the Wall Street magnate; and that leader of the " silk-stocking " Democracy, William R. Grace. On the other hand, the County Democracy could not match Tammany in discipline and aggressive driving-power. Kelly was a martinet who drilled his followers till they performed at the polls like regiments of grenadiers. As someone has aptly said: " Kelly found Tammany a horde; he left it a political army." Compact, flexible, trained down hard and fine, Kelly's Tammany was a perfect machine, capable of great performance at the touch of a master-hand.

But Kelly *just* lacked the master-touch. He could prepare magnificently, but he often bungled in action. Rigid, obstinate, vengeful, and intolerant of the slightest opposition, " Honest John " was foredoomed to blunder whenever he got outside his special field. That field was New York City politics, and here Kelly functioned well. Unfortunately, Kelly ventured into State and national politics; and then he led his devoted battalions to pitiable disasters which spelled defeat abroad and discomfiture at home.

Kelly's first big mistake was his feud with Samuel J. Tilden, the Democratic State leader. Tilden was a man of wealth and ability. He had gained great popularity through his reform activities against the Tweed Ring, became Governor, and in 1876 almost won the Presidency. Such a man was one to walk wide of. Yet Kelly fell foul of him over matters of patronage. The quarrel came to a dramatic climax in the State campaign of 1879. Determined to block Tilden's candidate for Governor, Kelly ordered the Tammany delegates to " bolt " the Democratic State Convention, hold a rump convention of their own, and nominate Kelly himself. So iron was Tammany discipline that the delegates obeyed without a murmur. On election day, Kelly polled nearly 100,000 votes; and with the Democracy thus split, the Republican candidate nosed in by a small plurality.

Kelly had thus won his immediate point. But his " victory " struck at the very heart of Tammany's prestige. If Tammany stood for one thing, it was party regularity. From its earliest days the Hall had denounced " bolters " and " kickers " as the worst of traitors. Yet here was the Boss of Tammany Hall committing the very crime its traditions so strongly condemned!

" Honest John " might hold his own followers stiffly in line, but he could not control the wave of wrathful indignation which rolled over the rest of the Democracy. Reprisals came swiftly. The Democratic Mayor of New York refused Tammany its expected share of patronage, avowedly as punishment for its disloyal attitude. Worst of all, in the State Convention of 1881, the Tammany delegation was ruled out, and the County Democracy was declared the " regular " organization.

Here, indeed, was a body-blow to the Tammany Tiger! Had it come a few years earlier, it might have been fatal. But now, so splendid was discipline that the organization merely closed ranks and marched on; somewhat lean and hungry, yet unbroken.

These misfortunes should have taught " Honest John " a lesson. Apparently they did not; for within three years he had locked horns with another great Democrat — Grover Cleveland.

By this time a new spirit had begun to stir America's political life. The old shibboleths of hidebound party loyalty and ruthless spoils-mongering were losing somewhat of their charm. A body of independent voters, known as " Mugwumps," had appeared. Also, influential citizens of both

parties condemned the spoils system and preached " civil
service reform." And Grover Cleveland was avowedly
sympathetic to both these developments.

To Boss Kelly, all this was anathema. He stood four-
square on the dogma of party discipline and the extremest
application of Marcy's dictum: " To the victors belong the
spoils! "

Between two such contrasted natures, both equally determined, friction was inevitable. Kelly certainly did nothing
to avoid a major clash. At Albany, the Tammany Senators
and Assemblymen stubbornly opposed Governor Cleveland's
reform measures, and when the Governor protested to Kelly
against these obstructive tactics he met with a rebuff. The
fight was on!

It came to a head at the Democratic National Convention
of 1884. Grover Cleveland was the favorite. But John
Kelly was so blinded by rage that he could not see the trend
in the National Democracy. So once more the Tammany
battalions were sent into a losing battle. Doggedly they
fought on the Convention floor. Tammany's star orator,
Thomas F. Grady, delivered a bitter philippic against Cleveland, virulently assailing not only his public career but his
private character as well. This, however, proved a boom-
erang. Grady was hissed; and the Convention broke into
thunderous applause when General Bragg of Wisconsin rose
and uttered his famous retort: " We love him [Cleveland]
for the enemies he has made! " In the eyes of the nation
Tammany stood discredited — and a bit ridiculous.

Even Kelly's stubborn spirit winced under the blow. Yet
he set his teeth and went grimly forward. Grover Cleveland had been nominated. So be it. But he would be defeated. Kelly openly made that boast. Tammany would

FROM THE COLLECTION OF MR. EDWIN P. KILROE, COPYRIGHTED

HIS GRACE, THE DUKE OF TAMMANY

RICHARD CROKER, COMMANDER-IN-CHIEF OF THE ANCIENT AND
DISHONORABLE COMPANY OF WARD HEELERS

not bolt this time; it would go through the motions, as per schedule. But the real work would be put into the local Mayoralty campaign, where a Tammany candidate was running against William R. Grace, of the County Democracy. For against Grace, also, Kelly bore a personal grudge.

The campaign was duly fought; November came — and Cleveland and Grace both won!

"Honest John" Kelly cracked and toppled like a sturdy oak before the axeman's stroke. Physically and spiritually broken, he was literally a nervous wreck. True, he was still nominal leader of Tammany Hall, and the news of his breakdown was carefully kept from the general public. But the insiders knew; and they also realized who was now in effective control. It was Richard Croker.

Every afternoon, Kelly's lieutenant would visit the broken Boss at his home on West 69th Street, and would confer with the grizzled veteran as he sat in his big arm-chair. Then Croker would go forth to execute Kelly's orders — as he, Croker, saw fit. There was no open usurpation; the conventionalities were carefully observed. But the reins of power had slipped from the old Boss's nerveless fingers, and stronger hands must promptly gather them up. It was the inexorable law of the tribe.

Alfred Henry Lewis, in his political novel, *The Boss*,[1] wherein Croker (somewhat disguised) is the hero and Kelly appears as "Big John Kennedy," has a striking bit of dialogue between the pair in Big John's last days. The conversation is of course imaginary; yet it is so instinct with the cynical realism of that grim era that it is substantially true.

Aware that he is done for, Big John gives his lieutenant the following sage advice:

" You've got things nailed, an' I'm glad it's so. Now let me give you a few points; they may help you to hold down your place as Boss.

" When it comes to handin' out th' offices an' th' contracts, don't play fav'rites. Hand every man what's comin' to him by th' rules of th' game. It'll give you more power to have men say you'll do what's square, than that you'll stick by your friends. Good men — dead-game men, don't want favors; they want justice.

" Never give a man the wrong office; size every man up, an' measure him for his place th' same as a tailor does for a suit of clothes. If you give a big man a little office, you make an enemy; if you give a little man a big office, you make trouble.

" Flatter th' Mugwumps. O' course, their belfry is full of bats; but about half th' time they have to be your pals, d'ye see, in order to be Mugwumps. An' you needn't be afraid of havin' 'em around; they'll never ketch onto anything. A Mugwump, as some wise guy said, is like a man ridin' backward in a carriage; he never sees a thing until it's by.

" Say ' No ' nineteen times before you say ' Yes ' once. People respect th' man who says ' No,' an' his ' Yes ' is worth more when he passes it out. When you say ' No,' you play your own game; when you say ' Yes,' you're playin' some other duck's game.

" Don't be fooled by a cheer or by a crowd. Cheers are nothin' but a breeze; an' as for a crowd, no matter who you are, there would always be a bigger turnout to see you hanged than to shake your mit.

" Always go with th' current; that's th' first rule of leadership. It's easier; an' there's more water down stream than up.

" Think first, last, and all th' time of yourself. You may not be of account to others; but to yourself yer th' whole box o' tricks. Don't give a man more than he gives you. Folks who don't stick to that steer land either in bankruptcy or Bloomin'dale.

" An' remember: while you're Boss, you'll be forced into many things ag'inst your judgment. The head of Tammany is like th' head of a snake, and gets shoved forward by the tail. Also, like th' head of a snake, th' Boss is th' target for every rock that is thrown.

" Have as many lieutenants as you can; twenty are safer than two. Two might fake up a deal with each other to throw you down; twenty might start, but before they got to you they'd fight among themselves.

" Always pay your political debts; but pay with a jolly as far as it'll go. If you find one who won't take a jolly, throw a scare into him and pay him with that. If he's a strong, dangerous mug with whom a jolly or a bluff don't work, get next to him as fast as you can. If you strike an obstinate party, it's th' old rule for drivin' pigs. If you want 'em to go forward, pull 'em back by th' tails.

" The whole science of leadership lies in what I've told you; an' if you can clinch onto it, you'll stick at th' top till you go away, like I do now, to die." [2]

Thus spake Big John Kennedy in the story. And thus thought " Honest John " Kelly in his last days.

When the grim old Boss died, he left his confidential man in position to seat himself firmly on the vacant throne.

CHAPTER VIII

CROKER TAKES STOCK

WHEN Richard Croker grasped at the reins of power shortly before Kelly's death, he found he had a real job on his hands. Defeated and discredited alike in National, State, and City politics, Tammany had no friends and next to no patronage. The County Democracy ruled Manhattan; and Mayor-elect Grace would see to it that the Tiger was kept off the payroll. Tammany's only visible assets were iron discipline and a fairly good reputation; for " Honest John " had kept down graft, and even Tammany's enemies had to admit that it was considerably improved since Tweed's day.

The Tammany Tiger was thus very much alive. But he was pretty hungry, and unless he soon got substantial nourishment he might starve and die. It was up to the new leader to get busy and get results. Otherwise, not even Kelly's veterans would keep step much longer.

Croker's first moves were cautiously circumspect. No flourish of oratorical trumpets blared in the new régime. At the old leader's death, Croker took the apparently inconspicuous post of Chairman of the Finance Committee of Tammany Hall. That post, however, was the key to the situation. The Finance Committee of Tammany was a peculiar institution. It was a Committee that rarely met — and that kept no books. All organization moneys passed through the Chairman's hands. Accountable to no one, he could expend Tammany's revenues as he saw fit and controlled absolutely its vital sinews of war.

There was no slackening of the reins, no let-up in discipline. But the method was different. Kelly had been an autocrat who liked to make men feel it. Croker was after results, and realized that the iron hand should oft be hid in the velvet glove. Affecting an air of almost genial simplicity, Croker treated his district leaders as friendly equals, took pains to confer with them, and let every man have his say.

Behind the scenes, action was really decided on by Croker and a few chosen colleagues. Here, again, Croker was taking no chances. He made no attempt, at this stage of the game, to play a lone hand. So he allied himself with a small knot of leaders; notably, Hugh J. Grant, Bourke Cockran, and Thomas F. Gilroy.

Each of these men had some special quality needed for an effective combination. Grant was young, rich, well-educated, with a pleasing personality. He lacked the forceful intelligence of his colleagues, but Croker did not want Grant for his brains; he wanted him for his " availability." Completely dominated by Croker's stronger personality, Grant made an ideal Tammany candidate for high office whenever the time was ripe.

Bourke Cockran, already known as " the silver-tongued orator," could stir a crowd and draft a platform like no one else. He was enormously popular with the masses, and was a great publicity manager. As for Gilroy, he was an organization veteran, with hosts of " contacts " and with the trick of getting things smoothly and quietly done.

Such were the " Big Four " who guided Tammany for the next few years. Later on, there were to be disputes and quarrels between them. But for the moment, the quartet sang sweet and low as a band of brothers. With Tammany out of power, there were no rich spoils to fight over.

Their first step was to repair some of Kelly's blunders. They started with the State situation. So long as Grover Cleveland was in active control of the State Democracy, little could be done. But when the President-elect moved on to Washington in the spring of 1885, conditions changed. Cleveland, as Governor, had championed civil service reform, and had relied both upon the progressive wing of his party and the independent voters known as Mugwumps. However, Cleveland had thereby offended most of the old party war-horses, and as soon as he left Albany a swift reaction ensued. David B. Hill, Cleveland's successor in the Governor's chair, was an old-line politician who hated Cleveland's new-fangled notions as heartily as John Kelly had done. Furthermore, Hill was rapidly building a personal machine which was to dominate the " up-State " Democracy for many years.

Holding as they both did to the old Jacksonian ideal of partisan politics, Hill and Croker had much in common, and a mutual friend now brought them together. This obliging intermediary was Edward Murphy, a prominent up-State Democrat. The son of a wealthy brewer of Troy (New York), Murphy controlled the local Democratic organization there and had recently become one of Hill's chief supporters. Murphy also knew Croker and had laid the basis for the close friendship which was thenceforth to subsist between them.

Heartened by the prospect of Hill's support, Croker prepared to deliver his first blow in home politics. The year 1885 was an " off-year," but there were the County offices to be voted for, and these would serve as an excellent trial of strength against Tammany's chief rival, the County Democracy. It would be a hard fight, for the rival faction held the County offices, as it did about everything else. Yet Croker knew that his leadership was on trial, and that defeat would mean not only a body-blow to Tammany but his own political finish as well.

Swiftly and surely, Croker planned his initial campaign. The big political prize to be fought for was the office of Sheriff, a post with fees worth $50,000 a year. Hugh J. Grant should run for Sheriff; his personal popularity would go far to elect him, and would boost the rest of the Tammany ticket into the bargain. As for the Tammany platform, it was a red-hot assault on the County Democracy, straight from Bourke Cockran's sizzling pen. And the County Democracy, in its recent tenure of office, had certainly laid itself open to attack.

The campaign was a whirlwind. The opening salvo was a series of sensational articles in the *New York World*, charging the County Democracy with gross corruption, especially in the matter of street railway franchises given away by boodling Aldermen, many of whom were County Democrats. Hugh Grant had been on the Board of Aldermen and knew the "inside story" — though he had kept himself clean. The articles in the *World* made a great sensation and led to the famous "boodle trials" of the ensuing year.

Next, Governor Hill came to town and openly supported Tammany. It was at this time that he made his famous speech beginning: "I am a Democrat!" His address extolled the principle of party regularity, assailed civil service reform, and ridiculed the Mugwumps in savage fashion.

Then Bourke Cockran outdid himself in oratory designed

to play upon racial and religious feeling. Hugh J. Grant
was a prominent Irish Catholic. Accordingly, " Cockran
appealed to the Irish vote to support Grant, who was a credit
to his race. Cockran had the Irish from one end of Manhattan Island to the other ablaze with racial pride and enthusiasm. Some of them, after listening to Cockran's flights
of oratory, believed that Grant's election would ensure Home
Rule for Ireland." [1]

The result was all that Croker could have hoped for.
Grant won in a walk, and practically the whole Tammany
ticket pulled through. The proud County Democracy had
been sadly jolted; Tammany Hall went wild with joy, and
Croker's position was assured.

Croker was further aided by the general course of events.
The trial of the " boodle Aldermen," which began in the
spring of 1886, was the biggest scandal since the Tweed
Ring. For months, New York was in a fever of excitement
as disclosure after disclosure revealed wholesale bribery and
corruption. Although some Tammany men were involved,
it was proved that both Kelly and Croker had condemned
their conduct, and Hugh Grant's clean record redounded
strongly to Tammany's credit. So Tammany gained notably in public favor, while the County Democracy was dealt
a blow from which it never recovered.

Croker thus emerged with flying colors from his first
strenuous ordeal. Tammany's standing was vastly improved.
It had acquired powerful up-State friends; it had defeated
and partially discredited its most dangerous rival, and it
once more had a good slice of patronage. No wonder that
Croker easily maintained discipline and rapidly strengthened his grip on the organization. Here was a leader after
Tammany's own heart, and the Braves obeyed him gladly.

RICHARD CROKER
IN THE EARLY NINETIES

When Richard Croker became the titular Boss of Tammany Hall, he was in his forty-third year, and at the very height of his physical and mental powers. His burly frame, with its herculean shoulders, bespoke untapped reserves of health and vitality; his black beard, though close-cropped, was of such plenteous growth as partially to conceal his grim mouth and jaw; his gray-green eyes, half-screened by shaggy brows, were alight with commanding authority. Indeed, Croker was the very archetype of the American Boss; the dynamic leader, rising from the social depths to the political heights by the sheer force that was in him.

Yet, with all Croker's picturesqueness of personality, and despite his undoubted touch of genius, we must not view him as a strange, solitary apparition on the political scene. Croker was an outstanding and striking member of a class: the class of *Bosses*, who flourished abundantly throughout America in his day and generation. There was hardly a city of any size, from New York to San Francisco, and from Minneapolis to New Orleans, which did not generate a Boss of the authentic breed.[2]

Alfred Henry Lewis, who knew Croker well, has this to say of the great Boss: " At Tammany Hall he is perpetually surrounded by a throng of henchmen. And in their midst is Croker; smooth, silent, bland. Yet there is not one about him whose measure he has not taken. In short, it's a game — the game of politics. And Croker defeats these folk; and turns them, and twists them, and takes them in, and moves them about, and in all things does with them what one, expert, might do with children at a game of cards." [3]

Croker had no theories. He was practical and factful. He indulged in no day-dreams. " Doing things," he once said, when asked how he accounted for his success. "While most men sit around club windows, or at dinner, discussing political plans, I go among my people to find out what they are saying and doing. I don't waste any time in theories. I want reports that give me facts and figures. I don't make plans, to be forgotten overnight. I never went to bed on a theory in my life. As a matter of fact, I never went to bed at all if there was a plan to carry out, until I had learned whether it would suit or not. The best plans are those that result from a system. We don't have any theories at Tammany Hall." [4]

Organization and discipline were the guiding stars in Croker's career. This he avowed many times. "Every successful enterprise," said he, "must have organization; without it, all things fall to pieces. Be it a store, or an army, or a church, or a political party, it must have organization and a head. If I'm a 'boss,' then a merchant, a bishop, or a general is a 'boss'; and the President is the big 'boss' of all." [5]

In his novel, *The Boss*, Lewis makes his hero (who is, of course, Richard Croker) say, very truly: "Tammany was never more sharply organized. I worked over the business like an artist over an etching. Discipline was brought to a pitch never known before. My district leaders were the pick of the covey; and every one, for force and talents of executive kind, fit to lead a brigade into battle. Under these were the captains of election precincts; and a rank below the latter came the block captains — one for each city block. Thus were made up those wheels within wheels which, taken together, completed the machine. They fitted one with the other: block captains with precinct captains, the latter with district leaders, and these last with myself; and all like the wheels and springs and ratchets and regulators of a clock; one sure, too, when wound and oiled and started, to strike the hours and announce the time of day in local politics with a nicety that owned no precedent." [6]

Of this elaborate machine Richard Croker was the master. Yet, in practice, his dictatorship had its limits; and this, not from lack of dominating will-power, but because he instinctively knew when to " go with the game." So close was Croker's finger upon Tammany's pulse that he sensed just when he was about to run counter to a tide of sentiment in the organization which might prove too strong for him. The instant he felt this, he changed his course.

Croker was habitually close-mouthed and rarely spoke his mind. Perhaps the most revealing utterances he ever made were in a series of conversations with the famous English editor, William T. Stead, when they were fellow-passengers on a voyage from Liverpool to New York.

" ' Politics,' declared Croker, ' are impossible without the spoils. It is all very well to argue that it ought not to be so. But we have to deal with men as they are, and with things as they are. . .

" ' Look the facts in the face. There are in our country and in New York a small number of citizens who might reasonably be expected to respond to the appeal of patriotic and civic motives. They are what you would call the cultured class; the people who have wealth, education, leisure. . . From them, no doubt, you might expect to meet with such response to your appeals as would enable you to run your State upon high principles and dispense with spoils.

" ' But if you were to expect any such thing, you would be very much disappointed. What is the one fact which all you English first notice in our country? Why, it is that the very crowd of which we are speaking, the minority of cultured leisured citizens, will not touch political work — no, not with their little fingers. All your high principles will not induce a Mugwump to take more than a fitful interest in an occasional election. Why, then, when Mugwump principles won't make even Mugwumps work, do you expect the same lofty motives to be sufficient to interest the masses in politics?

" ' And so,' I said, ' you need to bribe them with spoils? '

" ' And so,' Mr. Croker replied, ' we need to bribe them with spoils. Call it so, if you like. . . When you have our crowd, you have got to do it in one way, the only way that appeals to them. I admit it is not the best way. But think of what New York is and what the people of New York are. One-half, more than one-half, are of foreign birth. We have thousands upon thousands of men who are alien born, who have no ties connecting them with the city or the State. They do not speak our language, they do not know our laws, they are the raw material with which we have to build up the State. How are we to do it with Mugwump methods? I tell you, it cannot be done. . . There is not a Mugwump in the city who would shake hands with them. Except to their employer, they have no value until they get a vote.'

" ' And then they are of value to Tammany? ' I said, laughing.

" ' Yes,' said Mr. Croker imperturbably, ' and then they are of value to Tammany. And Tammany looks after them for the sake of their vote. . . If we go down into the gutter, it is because there are men in the gutter; and you have to go down where they are if you are to do anything with them.' " [7]

To think of Croker solely as the great Boss; the grim,

silent leader, always on the job and forever plotting political campaigns, is to neglect the other Croker — the red-blooded devotee of sport, with his close friendships, and warm loyalties, and chuckling sense of humor. The Boss's stern silence was to some extent a pose, picked up under Kelly, found useful, and cultivated until it became second nature. The Croker who mingled familiarly with the crowds at race-tracks and football-matches, who laughed and joked with his cronies, who was accessible to the lowliest of his followers, was the human Croker, when off-duty and having his fun.

One of Croker's friends gives us some amusing glimpses of his lighter side. " Croker," he writes, " got much of his fun by playing horse with the politicians round him. . . Croker's ability to discover the weak spot in any one amounted almost to genius. Any one he considered a ' character,' and who was smart enough to let Croker have fun with him, was sure of success at Tammany Hall.

" It was also a fad of Croker's to pick out the under-dogs of life and push them to the front. If any one developed the big head, Croker was through with them. A leader was sure of making a hit with the Boss by hunting up some boyhood friend of Croker's who was in need of help, particularly if the person had ever done Croker even a slight favor. Such a person would either be given an office or be put in a position to make money. I remember one old fellow who had been a machinist in the New York Central Railroad shops. Croker had been his helper when a boy. He had grown poor. Croker heard of this and put him in the contracting business. The man became rich. His son is one of the rich men in New York today.

" ' Gratitude is the finest word I know,' said Croker. ' I

would much prefer a man to steal from me than to display ingratitude. All there is in life is loyalty to one's family and friends.' This was at once Croker's strength and weakness. By a supposed friend he was easily imposed on. Those who had a great personal affection for him were in the vast majority, and to them Croker's word was law." [8] Such was Croker the man.

CHAPTER IX

TAMMANY HALL DEFENDS FIFTH AVENUE

BENEATH the stable crust of American politics an underground trend now and then comes to the surface. America was founded in revolution. That revolution was quickly stabilized. Yet a radical minority existed which hoped to carry the revolutionary process much further, and its doctrines have never been forgotten.

Under favoring circumstances, a radical ferment generates, usually taking the form of mushroom "third parties." Whenever this has happened, the two regular parties have tended to adjourn their differences and down the radical upstarts — who threatened them both.[1]

New York City has had its share of these radical ferments. New York's bad housing conditions and glaring inequalities between poverty and wealth made social unrest inevitable. Furthermore, radical agitation in the metropolis involves peculiarly dangerous possibilities, owing to the presence of desperate elements ready for trouble on the slightest provocation.

In the metropolis, as elsewhere, the two-party system has acted as an efficient stabilizer. It has kept within bounds social unrest and class hatreds which might otherwise have gotten out of hand. This is certainly true of Tammany Hall, the traditional Democratic organization.

Tammany has always posed as the champion of "the masses." It has consistently denounced aristocracy, ridiculed " silk-stockings," and proclaimed the rule of " the plain people " in a way to delight the plebeian heart. On the other hand, Tammany's successive " regular " opponents (Federalists, Whigs, and Republicans) have catered to the upper and middle classes, and have capitalized the social and religious attitudes which regarded Tammany as wicked and vulgar.[2] Thus both sides have banged the bass drum of prejudice — and have kept their respective followers in line.

Occasionally, however, politics have become abnormal. Now and then a new crowd has appeared on the political scene; a crowd which refused to play the regular game and proposed sweeping changes in the rules. These disturbers denounced both the old parties and promised the people all sorts of alluring things which could be gotten only by tampering with the established social order and the vested rights of private property. In short, their program was radical and socialistic in character.

When this happened, both the old parties promptly took alarm. That the Whig, and later the Republican, organization should have done so is self-evident. They were bound by the fears of their upper and middle class supporters.

What is not so plain is that Tammany was threatened in even more fundamental fashion. Yet this was the case. Tammany depends for its very existence upon the voting masses. It is the masses who are most affected by radical propaganda. Therefore, for every Whig or Republican vote which might switch to the new party, Tammany would lose at least five. Furthermore, Tammany was estopped by its very nature from keeping its backsliders from marching over to the radical camp; because Tammany, while Democratic, is not radical. In fact, Tammany Hall is essentially a conservative institution. Rooted in tradition and based upon hierarchic discipline, Tammany instinctively shrinks from sweeping changes.

Herein, Tammany typifies all our " regular" political organizations. " Though the reformers fumed and raved, the hated political bosses were in truth (as that cool observer, James Bryce, quietly remarked) buffers between the rich and the poor; buffers who taxed the one to keep the other in good humor. The political levies and sometimes the flagrant corruption to which party managers resorted were chiefly for the purpose of acquiring the funds necessary to ' take care of the boys '; that is, to amuse them with balls, outings, and picnics, to supply them with clothing and funds in hard times, and to lend them money on occasion. Naturally there were brokers' charges on the collections, but these were small as compared with the cost of riots and revolutions." [3]

Tammany has shown itself to be an unusually effective safety-valve against a radical explosion. A well-known writer puts the matter aptly when he says: " The 90,000 men who have surrendered their citizenship to Tammany might do far worse with it. In all their ignorance, and greed, and mendacity they might use that citizenship. If the time ever comes when they do use it unrestrained by the intervening agency of Croker, or his heirs or assigns, heaven protect wealth and social order in New York City! Take away the steel hoops of Tammany from the social dynamite, and let it go kicking around under the feet of any cheap agitator, and then look out for fireworks. . .

" With all the mould of feudalism which Tammany preserves, the Tammany-made citizen is more trustworthy than the citizen the red anarchists would make. . . For Tammany preaches contentment. It tolerates no Jeremiahs." [4]

It was an upsurge of radical agitation that Croker had to face at the beginning of his chieftainship. There had been others before his time,[5] but none so well-led or so determined. The whole country was affected by a current of unrest. In New York the radical trend crystallized into a powerful " Labor Party " headed by the redoubtable Henry George, whose book, *Progress and Poverty*, had been an international sensation.

Henry George's special panacea for society's ills was the " Single Tax "; but he had assembled beneath his banner a varied following, ranging from mildly dissatisfied workingmen to radicals of the reddest shades. Hard times and labor disputes started the ball rolling; the persuasive oratory and magnetic personality of Henry George did the rest. The movement grew by leaps and bounds. Radical enthusiasm ran through the tenement districts like a swift contagion. By the summer of 1886, the old parties realized that they were menaced by a popular tidal wave which might engulf them both.

Forthwith the party leaders conferred together against the common peril. How far was united action possible? For the scattered clans of the Democracy to adjourn their factional quarrels was relatively easy. Accordingly Tammany and the County Democracy agreed to present a united front in the autumn campaign.

The coalition champion was none other than Abram S. Hewitt. From every point of view, Hewitt was the ideal candidate for the occasion. Though a member of the County Democracy, Hewitt had no special feud with Tammany and was well liked by Croker, who did not forget the old merchant's efforts on his behalf when he stood on trial for his life. Furthermore, Hewitt, the millionaire merchant, with his good business reputation and his financial contacts, could rally the moneyed interests as the " savior of society " against the threat of " mob-rule."

That was the key-note. And it worked. Bankers and business men, regardless of party, opened wide their purses; and Richard Croker, the coalition campaign manager, soon had a record-breaking camapign fund.

He needed it! For his confidential reports told him unmistakably that, in default of heroic measures, Hewitt was beaten and the Laborites would take the town.

Now, how about the Republicans? In this supreme emergency, could they not be swung into line under Hewitt's banner? The Republican leaders were, for the most part, willing enough; but they found it impossible to " deliver " the bulk of their followers. Party regularity was too strict in those days for such an ultra-realistic manoeuvre. Rather than vote Democratic, thousands of Republicans would undoubtably plump for Henry George. So a Republican ticket had to be provided for these hidebound partisans, headed by a Mayoralty candidate in the person of Theodore Roosevelt, a strenuous young man just getting into the political game.

Croker's campaign strategy that autumn was a masterpiece of " practical politics." His spellbinders rang all the changes on the " red peril " and frightened timid middle-class voters almost into fits with dire predictions of the revolutionary wrath to come.

Croker knew, however, that he could not compete with Henry George in oratory. So other methods were used — less spectacular, but highly efficacious. " The boys " were flush with greenbacks as they never had been before. Down in the tenement districts, each block and precinct captain conned his voting-list as piously as a churchman tells his beads, and put on the last ounce of pressure to hold wavering followers in line. And (unless the weight of evidence be false) a host of repeaters was mobilized, not only from local sources but also from Philadelphia and the Jersey towns.

Election day came; the votes were counted — and Abram S. Hewitt topped the poll by more than 20,000. The Tammany dyke had held! The radical wave had broken in a welter of foam and spray.

Laborites might cry " Fraud! " and indignantly protest that they had been grossly counted out. That did them no good. Their hour had passed. The old parties could feel reasonably sure that, though Henry George might run again in the next election two years hence, the radical wave would then have so far spent itself that it would be a minor factor. As a matter of fact, Croker was never called upon to confront a similar crisis again.

This momentous victory completed Tammany's comeback, and of course clinched Croker's hold on the chieftainship. For who within the organization could successfully challenge his authority? Had he not restored Tammany to party primacy and fed it deep on patronage? Was not the new Mayor pledged to give the Tiger its full share of the spoils?

And the Boss did not forget himself. Promptly after inauguration day, Mayor Hewitt appointed Richard Croker to the post of Fire Commissioner of New York at a fat salary.

As Big John Kennedy remarked: " A good cook always licks his fingers."

CHAPTER X

FOR many years the plight of the local Democracy had been a grief to campaign managers and a scandal to the faithful. Split into snarling factions gnawing on the same bone of patronage, these family rows were as sordid as they were interminable.

Though Republican weakness kept New York City safely Democratic, the local situation reacted badly on Democratic State and National politics. Despite their best efforts, outsiders were often involved, and then the disgruntled faction would take its chance at the polls. Boss Kelly's personal feuds cost the State Democracy a Governorship, and Kelly hurt Tilden's Presidential chances in 1876, while his opposition to Cleveland was notorious. Much the same was true of the other Democratic factions, who sometimes made traitorous " deals " with the Republicans for their own selfish ends. Indeed, Democratic " soreheads " would often desert, bag-and-baggage, to the common enemy. When we come to view the local Republican organization we shall find that many of its best party " workers " were ex-Democrats — even ex-Tammany men.

Richard Croker had, from the first, determined to reforge the local Democracy, shattered since Tweed's day. Henry George's radical eruption had compelled him to suspend his attack upon his chief rival. In fact, the Laborites

87

were still so vociferous that Tammany and the County Democracy prolonged their truce through 1887, putting up a joint ticket for the County offices. The elections showed that the Labor Party was definitely on the wane. Its vote fell off one-half from that of the Mayoralty contest the previous year, and the coalition ticket won easily. Exultant at the end of the radical peril, and further cheered by a victory up-State, Democratic enthusiasm ran riot. The *Herald* reported: " Last night the city was in a roar of excitement over the great Democratic victory. All the incidents of the feverish day were swallowed up in the one tremendous fact that the triumphant Democracy had scattered its enemies. The streets were ablaze with bonfires, and around the flaming heaps thousands of boys danced and whooped. The hotels fronting on Madison Square were packed with squirming, delirious multitudes." [1]

Behind the scenes, Tammany and the County Democracy were girding on their armor for a fight to a finish. Their immediate tactics, however, were a joint hunting-expedition against their minor rivals. A number of little factions still survived, such as a rump of the old " Irving Hall Democracy," and these guerilla bands were a chronic source of trouble. Both Tammany and the County Democracy determined to conscript the bushwhackers into their respective forces. It was a race to see which should get the most recruits, and honors seem to have been fairly even. But the immediate objective was attained. The guerilla organizations were practically exterminated, and the two regular armies, strengthened in numbers, made ready for clean-cut battle.

That battle was due in the next Mayoralty election. Long before the actual campaign, however, Croker had thrown out a far-flung net of skillful preparation. The year 1888 was a Presidential year. Grover Cleveland would undoubtedly be renominated for another term in the White House, while Governor Hill wanted to succeed himself. Croker planned uproarious support for both, thereby advertising Tammany's " regularity " on a national scale and winning at least their neutrality in his own local war.

Tammany certainly needed some good advertising, for its reputation with the nation was very bad indeed. The whole country still thought of Tammany in terms of the Tweed Ring. Furthermore, Kelly's blunders had so compromised Tammany with the National Democracy that at the last three National Conventions its delegates had been openly booed and hissed.

A piquant description of the Tiger's notoriety during that period is given us by a well-known political writer, who says: " I first knew Tammany Hall when I was a little schoolboy in Saint Louis. The Democratic National Convention of 1876, which nominated Tilden for President, was held there. I was attending a boarding school on Chanteau Avenue, and the boys were told that it was not safe to be out after dark when Tammany arrived in town. The two dear old ladies who conducted the school gave their pupils to understand that Tammany was located in a part of New York City known as the Five Points, where all the inhabitants were thugs and murderers. Some of the older lads, who surreptitiously read dime novels, told the younger boys that Tammany would probably shoot up and rob the town. One Saint Louis paper, a Tilden organ, actually advised the merchants to bolt their doors and put up the shutters when Tammany arrived. A couple of my more adventurous companions and myself slipped out after we were supposed to be in bed. We started for one of the big hotels, but had not gone far when we saw two flashily-dressed men in high white hats and adorned with Tammany badges. Their cigars stood in their mouths at an angle of 45 degrees. We boys ran across the street. We felt it our duty to warn our neighbors that Tammany had invaded Chanteau Avenue." [2]

Such was the evil heritage, alike in nation and party, with which Croker had to reckon. He may not have sweetened the Tiger's reputation much with the average citizen, but among the politicians he certainly got results. In a widely-heralded press interview, Croker announced: "Tammany Hall this year is going to demonstrate by its united, hearty, and loyal support of the National ticket that it is entitled to be called the exponent of true Democracy; and the results will prove that, as well as being the oldest, it is the strongest and most faithful Democratic organization in the country. We will sink or swim with the National ticket this time, for the day has gone by when any doubt can be raised as to Tammany's loyalty."

Croker also gave orders that Tammany should make a grand showing at Saint Louis, where the Democratic National Convention was to be held. Every Tammanyite who had the price was ordered to attend in full regalia. The resulting turn-out was a show worth coming far to see. Tammany, with Croker at its head and a dozen bands, marched into Saint Louis — and was received with open arms. What a change from its reception twelve years before! Tammany and Croker were roundly cheered, in and out of the Convention Hall. It was a great triumph for them both.

The reward was soon apparent. The County Democracy prided itself upon being a "Cleveland" organization, and had endorsed the President's ideal of civil service reform;

whereas Tammany was frankly for the spoils system and could not, in its heart of hearts, be wildly enthusiastic over Grover Cleveland. The County Democracy had therefore hoped for the President's support, or at least his approval. Throughout the ensuing municipal campaign, Cleveland and his entire administration maintained a strict neutrality.

At the Democratic State Convention, likewise, Croker won an important political skirmish. Governor Hill was resolved to succeed himself. But " Cleveland Democrats " had no love for this avowed " spoilsman," and talked of nominating that prominent member of the County Democracy, ex-Mayor William R. Grace. This gave Croker the chance to come out strongly for Hill. The Governor promptly recipro- cated by pulling wires in the Convention whereby the num- ber of Tammany delegates was increased and the strength of the County Democracy was proportionately cut down. Here again, what a change since Kelly's day, when the Tam- many delegates had been thrown out of the State Convention and the County Democracy declared the " regular " organi- zation! The priceless asset of party regularity was once more in Tammany's grasp. And it alone meant thousands of otherwise doubtful votes.

Meanwhile, the course of events in Manhattan itself was in Tammany's favor. The County Democracy would run Mayor Hewitt again; no doubt about that. He was their man, and they were pledged up to the hilt. But during his term, the Mayor had committed several political blunders which rendered him somewhat of a liability. Old and irasci- ble, Hewitt lacked tact; as, for instance, when he had deeply offended the Irish by refusing to review a Saint Patrick's Day parade. Furthermore, Hewitt prided himself on his independence, and bristled at anything that savored of dictation. This had led to a breach with Croker over matters of patronage. The old debt of friendship dating from the McKenna trial was cancelled.

Croker felt well satisfied with the outlook. A bit of clever baiting roused Hewitt's wrath and led him to give out a heated interview about the Tammany Boss; to which Croker replied sarcastically: " I understand that Mayor Hewitt has alluded to me as a 'spoilsman.' If I am a 'spoilsman,' as he says, I never neglect to secure employment for a deserving needy man, instead of having him turned away from the door by an English lackey." ³

The line of attack was plain. In the coming campaign, Hewitt would be denounced by Tammany's spellbinders as a millionaire, an aristocrat, an Anglomaniac, and a camouflaged A.P.A. That, indeed, was the key-note a fortnight later, when Bourke Cockran made the Wigwam rock with oratory, while the Boss, silent and watchful as usual, sat on the platform and smiled grimly behind his beard as " the boys " went wild.⁴ On that same occasion the Tammany standard-bearer was duly led forth — Croker's prize candidate, Hugh J. Grant.

The campaign was one of the liveliest in years. A Mayoralty contest filled with emotional appeals and bitter personalities, coinciding with a close-fought Presidential contest, kept Manhattan in the throes of political fever. On election eve, near-riots broke out, quelled only by prompt police charges and vigorous clubbings with heavy nightsticks.

With so strenuous an election eve, the scenes on election night can be imagined. The polls had barely closed when it became clear that Hewitt had been snowed under and that Grant had won a sweeping victory. Indeed, so badly had the old Mayor been beaten that he actually ran behind the Republican candidate, while Grant's plurality was nearly 40,000. The County Democracy had been routed, horse, foot, and artillery; and Tammany owned the town!

Down on 14th Street, the scene baffled description. As the press reported it: " At one time last night nearly 6000 men filled Tammany Hall and almost made the walls bulge. Never had there been such enthusiasm shown in the old Wigwam. There were no seats on the floor. Men were packed together as close as — well, they were as close together as postage stamps on an envelope. It was a mystery how that wedged mass of humanity could breathe, let alone move. The 69th Regiment Band was on hand early and discoursed inspiring music. Later in the evening there were Irish airs and war-dances."

Over at Mayor-elect Grant's headquarters in the Union Square Hotel, the Boss stood amid a surging crowd of frenzied admirers and issued this significant statement: " It is a momentous victory. Next year, Tammany Hall will hold its centenary anniversary. It will then be, as it always has been, the only real Democratic organization in the city. When Mr. Grant assumes the reins of government, he will be a reform Mayor in action; not in words or garrulous letters."

Meanwhile, the Presidential contest hung in the balance. So close were the returns that victory wavered continually, and not until long after midnight was it known that Cleveland had been defeated and that Benjamin Harrison, the Republican candidate, had won the race. So nothing dimmed the enthusiasm of triumphant Tammany or of the predominantly Democratic city crowds.

" Under the stars the city waited to see which party had

won. And what a city it was! A city that thrilled and throbbed from river to river; its streets aflame with thousands of bonfires, and great black multitudes roaring and surging about with no thought of sleep — now in convulsions of delight, and now in agonies of despair. . .

" It was a close fight, and everyone knew it. All they could do was to wait and strain their eyes and shout till their throats were hoarse. None could possibly know the result early in the evening; none, unless they were the party managers — and they sat pale and nerveless in their inner dens, sending forth alternate bulletins of hope and dread.

" In Madison Square, 30,000 people stood in front of the *Herald* bulletin, and the sound of their voices was like the beating of wild waves through a cavern. Along the edges of this vast multitude were the blazing corridors of the hotels, in which half-crazed men with flushed faces and bloodshot eyes waved handfuls of money, and with blasphemous boastings sought out their opponents. Crowds of drunken men swirled into the tumultuous scene from every corner of the city. Dainty ladies, who had ventured from their homes, shrank back from the wild, savage uproar of the city's unwashed hosts. White-haired, feeble men crept out and got into snug positions where they could watch the varying returns and tell the roystering young men around them that it was a more glorious night than even the old times ever saw.

" Down in front of the newspaper offices a prairie of faces seemed to be spread out from grim Saint Paul's to the Brooklyn Bridge. When the cars passed through them, the crowds parted like water and flowed together again in the wake, hurrahing and swaying with passion.

" From Democratic headquarters at the Hoffman House

A TAMMANY SOUVENIR

came a steady roar of 'Four! Four! Four years more!',
and ladies could be seen leaning out of the windows of the
Fifth Avenue Hotel beating time with bandannas and shouting Democratic war-cries at the top of their voices. Through
the quieter streets rushed hundreds of newsboys, filling the
air with wild, mad cries." [5]

Dawn brought National Democratic defeat. Yet Tammany men had lost little thereby. The White House was
not in their bailiwick, and Grover Cleveland was not of their
kind. Everything that really mattered had been won. Tammany now owned Manhattan; it had routed its rivals; it enjoyed the favor of its up-State ally, firmly seated in the
Governor's chair. Who could reasonably ask for more?

By contrast, the camp of the County Democracy was filled
with gloom, though the leaders whistled to keep up their
courage. As one of them, William M. Ivins, remarked:
" I think the organization will plug along as usual. There
must be a watch-dog on Tammany, you know. If the
County Democracy were to dry up and blow away tomorrow,
there would be another anti-Tammany organization in this
city within twenty-four hours."

That, however, was cold comfort to those who faced the
dreary prospect of losing their jobs on New Year's Day
when Mayor Grant would take over City Hall. One hope
alone remained — to climb swiftly on the Tammany bandwagon. So the ranks of the County Democracy began to
thin.

Thenceforth the County Democracy rapidly declined.
Though it allied itself openly with the Republicans in the
elections next year, Tammany beat this Fusion ticket and
won nearly all the remaining offices.

In 1890, the County Democracy's waning hopes were re-

vived by two important events: Richard Croker sailed for
Europe in bad health; and the Republican State machine ap-
pointed a Legislative Committee of inquiry into New York
City politics known as the Fassett Investigation.[6]

Heartened by these developments, the County Democracy
and the Republicans again launched a Fusion ticket; and a
real non-partisan Reform organization, the People's Municipal League (created by the Fassett disclosures) fell into
line. Yet Tammany triumphed over the coalition, and
Mayor Grant was re-elected by a reduced plurality of about
20,000. The County Democracy was now a mere shadow
of its former self and had become little more than a satellite
of the local Republican machine. Vainly did it call itself
" The Cleveland Democracy." It might acclaim Grover
Cleveland, but that gentleman was not minded to recipro-
cate. He was again a Presidential candidate, and would certainly not jeopardize his chances in pivotal New York by
lending ear to a discredited faction. Moreover, Richard
Croker was on hand with convincing proofs of Tammany
loyalty. At the Chicago Convention of 1892, the Boss appeared at the head of the snappiest body of uniformed men
that Tammany had ever turned out on parade.

That autumn, the Democracy won all along the line.
Cleveland was given another term in the White House, while
Tammany elected another Mayor — the astute Thomas F.
Gilroy.

Those were great days for Croker and for Tammany.
The organization was at its best. It was social as well as
political. In each of the thirty districts the Tammany organization owned a substantial club-house. Meetings were held
once or twice a week, and were well attended. Croker insisted that the small shopkeepers in the different districts be

given prominence and that every courtesy be shown them. They were made to feel that they were an important part of Tammany. This policy pleased them, and gave Tammany strength and respectability.

Everyone connected with Tammany seemed prosperous. The street railways were then spending vast sums in changing from horse to cable cars, and there were plenty of contracts to go round.

Croker, once more in good health, kept the wheels of the big machine turning from his sanctum at the Wigwam. The Boss's office was on the first floor, at the right of the entrance to Tammany Hall. It was a rather large room, furnished with plain, straight-backed chairs. The only decorations were a life-sized figure of an Indian chief clutching a tomahawk, a huge American eagle, and some portraits of Tammany Sachems upon the walls. In one corner stood a big iron safe.

The back of the room was equipped with folding-doors which, when shut, closed off a dark little cubby-hole where Croker's desk was placed. There, he could discuss, in absolute privacy, confidential matters.

In these characteristic quarters the Boss was to be found almost every day, and during campaigns until far into the evening. Thither the district leaders came to consult with the Boss and with one another; so that Croker's office became a general rendezvous for Tammany notables. They were sure to learn the latest news about politics; and it was also well to pay tacit homage to the Boss by being frequently under his eye.

Croker had now attained one of his goals: reunion of the New York City Democracy under the aegis of Tammany Hall. True, a few disgruntled cliques survived; but these guerilla bands, while sometimes annoying, could do no real harm.

The only foes worth considering were the Republican machine and the non-partisan Reform movement, which, though destined to become formidable, was as yet in its infancy. The outstanding fact in New York politics at that moment was that the once shattered Manhattan Democracy had been so well mended that the cracks barely showed.

CHAPTER XI

THE " EASY BOSS " COMES TO TOWN

By 1890, Richard Croker was Master of Manhattan. Within its boundaries no man or set of men remained who could effectively dispute his sway. Yet in that very year, the political stroke known as the Fassett Investigation disclosed the presence of a formidable external foe with whom the Tammany chieftain would have seriously to reckon. That foe was the head of the up-State Republican machine, Thomas Collier Platt.

When the Queenstown packet landed its immigrant cargo — three-year-old Richard Croker included — a pale, delicate-looking boy of thirteen, familiarly called " Tom " Platt, was going to school in the little town of Owego, Tioga County, Central New York.

Scarcely more than a village, Owego was a typical country town of the period: isolated, self-contained, and conditioned by the sincere yet narrow Puritanism of most rural communities. Tom's father, a local lawyer and a rigid Presbyterian, wanted his son to be a minister. In this, the elder Platt failed; but he did bring Tom up as a model youth — quiet, well-mannered, fond of study, regular at church and in personal habits.

Platt senior also determined his son's political faith. Young Platt grew to manhood in the stirring years before the Civil War. In those days Republicanism was sweeping

rural New York like a religious revival; and in Owego, the
elder Platt was one of the new Party's charter members.
Tom first voted in the Presidential election of 1856, and
naturally cast his ballot for John C. Frémont, the Republican
candidate. " The excitement of those days made a deep
impression upon his mind and furnished the root of that
unquestioning loyalty to the Republican Party which he displayed in later life." [1]

Herein, Platt typified his times. The Civil War split
the population of the Empire State along sharp lines of
sectional feeling. We have already seen how it turned New
York City into a rock-ribbed Democratic stronghold. But,
above the Bronx, the same process converted up-State New
York to equally rock-ribbed Republicanism. Thenceforth,
State and metropolis confronted one another in a political
war the bitterness of which was notorious even in times when
party regularity was the watchword throughout the Union.

This extreme partisanship was based upon much the same
differences which had envenomed metropolitan politics in
the forties, but which were now projected on a wider scale.
On one side stood the Manhattan Democracy, dominated by
(and largely composed of) Irish Catholics, with their Old-
World outlook and their spirit of clan and sept. On the
other side stood the bulk of the native-American Protestants,
with their staunch Puritan ideals and their upstanding
pioneer individualism. Now add to all this the innate antagonism between city and country; between urban and rural
manners, habits, and attitude towards life, and we can visualize the depth of the resulting political cleavage.

Under such conditions, political machines flourish and
bosses rule. Men thus deeply divided instinctively join one
or other of the political armies, cheerfully endure the strictest

party discipline, and obey orders so implicitly that their leaders can move them about like pawns on a chess-board. Furthermore, the ranks are automatically recruited from the rising generation, since sons tend to follow the political faith of their fathers as a matter of course.

It was, therefore, as a devoted partisan that young Tom Platt entered the Republican army as a private and began his long upward climb toward supreme power and authority. And it is interesting to note that, while the social and cultural conditions of his apprenticeship differed utterly from Richard Croker's, the political objectives were essentially the same.

In the first place, the political careers of both men began as an instinctive process rather than as the result of conscious determination. Platt himself tells us that he " drifted into politics — just drifted." [2] That was precisely what young Dick Croker did; only he drifted in by way of the gang and the corner saloon, whereas Tom Platt did so *via* — the drug-store! " In Owego, as in many other small towns of New York, saloons were frowned upon in the fifties, and the drug-store or general store was the centre where the 'elder statesmen' congregated to discuss politics and the questions of the day." [3]

Young Platt found himself strategically placed, because he started life as a drug-store clerk. Be sure that he used his ears and made useful acquaintances. Also, stimulated by the discussions he heard, he seems to have spent his leisure time reading and studying political literature, especially the speeches of famous Republicans like Thurlow Weed.

So greatly did Platt relish his calling that he presently established a drug-store of his own, which became the civic centre of his community. For many years thereafter most of the political work of the County was done in the little office in the rear of this store.

Slowly but surely, Platt became a power in County and State politics. He had his reverses, to be sure, but his net progress was unmistakable. Platt's cleverness in dispensing patronage was widely acknowledged; his appointees were to be found scattered everywhere in the State and Federal service.[4]

It was at approximately the same moment (about 1890) that Platt and Croker stood forth as the recognized Bosses of their respective organizations.

And it is then that the basic similarity of their Boss-ships becomes most apparent. Both men avoided high-sounding titles and ruled modestly as committee chairmen; Croker's Finance Committee of Tammany Hall being paralleled by Platt's Republican State Committee — the apex of a committee hierarchy which extended down to the smallest rural communities, yet which functioned organically as a smooth-working machine of the highest efficiency. Both used patronage and campaign funds as their sinews of power. Both exalted the same ideals of organization, discipline, and uncompromising partisanship. Both sincerely believed that party victory was an end which justified almost any means.

Platt and Croker alike owed their success in large measure to their intense concentration upon politics. If anything, Platt carried his political preoccupation to greater extremes. Croker had a love for horses and open-air sport as avocations. Platt had no hobby, and Roosevelt said truly that he could not find in Platt " any tastes at all except for politics, and on rare occasions for a very dry theology wholly divorced from moral implications." [5]

Platt's religion, however, did not interfere with his poli-

tics. In New York City, Platt attended Dr. Parkhurst's
church until, one Sunday, the militant Doctor nearly startled
his distinguished parishioner out of his pew by announcing
that one Platt was worse than five Crokers. Platt changed
his church at once.

Both in New York and in Washington, Platt lived at
hotels and rarely went out in society. Utterly absorbed in
his passion for politics, Platt could concentrate willingly
upon petty detail which Croker found boresome.

Yet, despite their similarities, how amazingly different
were the two men! Contrast the burly Tammany chieftain
with the slim, fragile leader of the Republican machine.
Croker looked like a prize-fighter; Platt like a shy recluse.
Croker was *The Boss* incarnate; Platt, with his parchment-
like skin and delicate figure, was perfectly camouflaged.
"Strangers who first saw him often exclaimed: ' That Tom
Platt? He must be smarter than he looks! ' . . The Senator did not make a very prepossessing appearance as he
hunched over his seat in the Chamber. He looked more like
a New England college professor or a retired clergyman
than he did like a seasoned political warrior. Quigg, his
faithful lieutenant, said that Platt was so little magnetic
that he performed listlessly even the act of shaking hands." [6]

These physical and temperamental contrasts give the key
to their differences in political technique. Croker, while
shrewd and resourceful, preferred direct action and posi-
tively enjoyed a knock-down fight; Platt revelled in sly
manoeuvres, and always preached " harmony." Croker insisted on full details; Platt demanded only results. The
methods employed did not interest him. That was why
Platt was called the " Easy Boss."

In action, Platt was a model of smooth decorum. Always

tactful and conciliatory, he habitually spoke in a low, soft tone, rarely raising his voice. Platt could never have mastered the rough democracy of Tammany Hall, while Croker's sledge-hammer methods would not have been tolerated by the touchy farmers and ultra-respectable middle-class folk who were the backbone of Republican power. Both men were thus eminently fitted for their respective jobs.

Such were the champions of their respective parties who, in 1890, clashed for the first time. Thenceforth, for a full decade, the manoeuvres of these two great Bosses give the clue to their epoch. Like master-players, Platt and Croker sat facing one another across the political chess-board, giving alternate check and counter-check.

Platt's entry into New York City politics was the first serious Republican intervention since the Civil War. For a whole generation, the local Republican organization had been left pretty much to its own devices. The reasons are not far to seek. So small and discredited was the metropolitan *G.O.P.* that only powerful outside assistance would yield worth-while results.

The up-State Republicans were unable to give such aid. During most of this period their State organization was split into rival factions, popularly known as " Stalwarts " and " Half-Breeds." The split started as a mere squabble over patronage, but it degenerated into a bitter feud which dragged on interminably and rendered united action impossible.

Indeed, the entire up-State political situation was about as complicated as the one in New York City. Both parties were patchworks of jarring local organizations. Only in the eighties did a process of consolidation set in which pres-

ently resulted in two efficient State machines: one dominated
by Platt, the other by David B. Hill.

The Republican machine was much the more powerful,
resting as it did upon the mass of the rural population and
the more prosperous townsfolk. The strength of the up-
State Democracy lay in the industrial towns and cities; for
here, as in the metropolis, the poorer classes, especially the
immigrants, tended to be Democrats. The up-State Democracy thus appeared as a series of isolated strongholds, set
against a solid Republican background. And this, in turn,
enabled the Republicans to control the Legislature even
under Democratic Governors; because the legislative seats,
apportioned according to territory as well as population,
favored the rural districts somewhat out of their numerical
proportion.

Because of this, even in "Democratic years," Platt was
able to strike shrewd blows from Albany against Croker and
Tammany, despite furious protests from the Gubernatorial
Chair. Platt's well-drilled legislative majority could be
depended on to obey orders and stolidly re-pass his measures over a Democratic Governor's veto.

It was in the late eighties that Platt, sure of his well-
oiled machine and his docile Legislature, was ready for aggressive action. In this expansive mood there came to him
emissaries from his political brethren to the southward, asking aid and promising much in return. So alluring were
their tales that Platt decided to investigate. Let us try to
visualize the conditions which met Platt's shrewd gaze as he
reconnoitred the metropolis.

Manhattan Republicanism had been from the first a sickly
growth. Through the seventies and eighties it was in a
hopeless minority, rarely polling more than twenty-five per

cent of the vote. Furthermore, the local Republican organization was parasitic in a twofold sense: it depended on
the Albany machine for its share of State and Federal patronage, and upon the Manhattan Democracy for local favors.

This last may seem a degrading occupation, yet it was
a recognized form of "practical politics." In that epoch,
professional politicians were always open to a " trade ";
and we will often find Platt and Croker, like Chinese generals, sandwiching a "deal" between two battles. So the
local organizations always maintained certain "gentleman's
agreements." For instance, there was a tacit understanding
that Republican election officials should be " taken care of "
by City jobs, even in the staunchest Democratic wards where
the Republican organization was a mere shell — the Republicans repaying the favor by minor State or Federal appointments at their disposal.

So far as mere politics went, there was little difference
between the Republican and Democratic machines. Theodore Roosevelt bears striking testimony to this when he
gossips about the political conditions of his youth.

"Almost immediately after leaving Harvard in 1880,"
he writes, " I began to take an interest in politics. . . It was
thus that I became a member of the 21st District Republican
Association of the City of New York. The men I knew
best were the men in the clubs of social pretension and the
men of cultivated taste and easy life. Although the Twenty-
first was known as one of the ' silk-stocking' districts of
town, when I began to make inquiries as to the whereabouts
of the local Republican organization and the means of join-
ing it, my friends laughed at me and told me that politics
were ' low '; that the organizations were not controlled by
' gentlemen '; that I would find them run by saloon-keepers,

horse-car conductors, and the like; moreover, they assured me that the men I met would be rough and brutal and unpleasant to deal with.

" I answered that if this were true it merely meant that the people I knew did not belong to the governing class, and that the other people did — and that I intended to be one of the governing class." [7]

When Roosevelt goes on to describe his District Association we find it much like a Tammany District club-house — minus most the latter's social and charitable features. He describes it as "a large, barn-like room over a saloon. Its furniture was of the canonical kind: dingy benches, spittoons, a dais at one end with a table and chair and a stout pitcher for iced water, and on the walls pictures of General Grant and of Levi P. Morton, to whose generosity we owed the room. We had regular meetings once or twice a month, and between times the place was treated, at least on certain nights, as a kind of club. . .

" I soon got on good terms with the ordinary ' heelers ' and even with some of the minor leaders. The big leader was ' Jake ' Hess, who treated me with rather distant affability." [8]

Young Roosevelt found his new friends very useful; for when he first ran for the Assembly he failed dismally to "get next to the voters." So he left this business to his friends the ward heelers — who did a good job.

Roosevelt makes the interesting statement that two of the minor leaders in his district were Irishmen — converts from Tammany Hall, who had been badly treated by some Tammany leader and had, in revenge, transferred themselves and their gangs to the Republican party. This was by no means exceptional; the two Irish leaders and their retinues whom Roosevelt mentions could probably have been duplicated in other districts in town.

Such was the situation of the Republican Party in New York City when Platt surveyed his proposed field of action. However, Platt's investigations unearthed one cheering fact: the Manhattan $G.O.P.$ was certainly growing in numbers. A decade before, it had polled a beggarly 20% or 25% of the total vote cast in the city. By 1890, it was polling an average of 35%.

The basic reason for this increase seems to be that the population of Manhattan had been changing in a pro-Republican sense. From the forties into the seventies, the chief contingent of immigrant settlers in the metropolis was Irish, who were ready-made Democrats almost to a man. But about 1880, the Germans outstripped the Irish; and rather more than half of the Teutons became Republicans. Also, there was the large contingent of Scandinavians, who showed strong Republican tendencies. Lastly, the vanguard of the great Jewish influx had arrived; and the Jews, then as always, were decidedly independent in their party affiliations. The upshot was that the tremendous Democratic lead in the metropolis was being slowly but surely cut down.

True, the Manhattan $G.O.P.$ had a very long way to go before it could hope to become a majority. Yet the more sanguine party leaders were coming to believe that if enough time, effort, and cash were put into the task, New York City might be converted.

Whether the wily Platt really expected anything so delightful is uncertain. What he apparently did hope for was so pronounced a gain in Republican strength as would force Tammany to hand over a large share of the local patronage. And that, in itself, was a prize worth striving after; for the

richness of Tammany's preserves must have made the little
up-Stater's mouth fairly water.

Platt calculated that he already held a high trump card:
legislative control. That control was theoretically limitless;
for the metropolis, like every other city or town, was legally
a mere creature of the State. From the State it had received
its corporate existence; and what the State had given, it
could take away. So far as the letter of the law went, the
Legislature could alter New York's charter at any moment,
or even abolish it altogether, putting the metropolis under
direct State control by a Board, Commission, or otherwise.[9]
The chief hindrance to such drastic action was the "Home
Rule" sentiment in New York City, which would presumably be so aroused by the loss of self-government that
Republicans and Democrats would join in a political uprising that might wreck the Republican Party.

Platt was too wise seriously to meditate any such extreme
measure. It was just a useful bugaboo, to be discreetly
trotted out on suitable occasions. But if Platt could so master
the local Republican organization that it became as subservient to him as his up-State organization; if, in other
words, he could weld the whole *G.O.P.* of the Empire State
into one big Platt machine, his bargaining power would be
vastly strengthened, and Tammany, in return for favors at
Albany, would have to surrender an ever-larger slice of
the metropolitan spoils.

A working model of the transfer method already existed.
This was the "bi-partisan" idea, which had been applied
to the Metropolitan Police Board for many years. It might
be extended to other departments as well.

Having reconnoitred the hostile *terrain* and found it to
his liking, Platt proceeded busily with his scheme of getting

the metropolis under his control. Platt's "invasion" of New York City was a characteristic performance; it was about as spectacular as the entry of a mouse into a cheese.

But the results were soon discernible to the professional eye. The local Republican organization felt in its every part the pressure of the "Easy Boss's" delicate yet efficient hand. Platt lieutenants soon commanded everywhere, and Platt himself established metropolitan headquarters at the Fifth Avenue Hotel, where he conferred with his staff-officers and tactfully issued his orders.

Platt's "council-chamber" is worth noting. At the end of the broad hotel corridor were two large sofas. Here, the "Easy Boss" held his conclaves. It was all so decorous that the conferences were jocularly dubbed "Platt's Sunday School Class." Yet the outcome of these conferences was so certain to be just what Platt wanted that the spot itself was called "The Amen Corner." Contrast the Amen Corner with Croker's quarters down at the Wigwam! There we get a graphic glimpse of the abysmal difference between the rival Bosses and their ways.

While Platt's Sunday School Class was holding its ultra-respectable sessions, "The Boys" were doing their un-respectable organization work — and no questions asked by the "Easy Boss," so long as they got results.

The machine must run without a hitch. And the best way to avert trouble was to get caucuses [10] of the "right" kind. Platt was a skilled manipulator, and had done considerable caucus "packing" up-State; but in the metropolis, this fine art reached full bloom. In 1896, an investigation of alleged election frauds reported that "the Republican enrollment in New York City was from 15% to 45% bogus." And Dr. Parkhurst remarked: "There is a brazen insolence and a colossal dare-deviltry about these enrollment frauds that is thrilling." [11]

It was in the autumn of 1889 that Platt felt himself strong enough to begin putting the screws on the Tiger. Accordingly, Platt quietly but insistently let Mayor Grant know that certain city appointments to deserving Republicans would be gratefully acknowledged. Grant, of course, promptly referred the matter to his Boss. The rival chieftains were face to face!

Boss Croker, however, did not at once throw down the gauntlet by a direct refusal. Whether he wished to find out what Platt had up his sleeve, or whether the ill-health from which he then suffered indisposed him to instant battle, certain it is that Croker temporized and put Platt off with vague assurances.

Yet before long it became evident that Croker had no intentions of "coming through." That decided Platt. So Croker would not "trade," eh? Well, he would have to be shown that Platt was in a position to make his wishes respected. A few low-voiced orders to Albany, and the Legislature appointed a Committee, headed by State Senator J. Sloat Fassett, one of Platt's trusted lieutenants, to examine into certain alleged abuses committed by the Tammany municipal administration in general, and by Mayor Hugh J. Grant in particular.

Thus began the first of the series of legislative investigations into Tammany's misdeeds which were to have such momentous consequences. It was also the first round in the great duel between Platt and Croker, destined to last more than ten years — until both Bosses were undermined by the rising tide of political change and rudely buffeted by the angry waves of reform.

CHAPTER XII

FIRST BLOOD FOR PLATT!

IN JANUARY 1890, the State Senate appointed its committee of inquiry, colloquially known as the Fassett Investigation. Platt's blow was well timed: it came early in a Mayoralty election year, and it caught the Tammany Boss when he was physically below par.

For some time, Richard Croker had not been a well man. During the past six years he had been working at top speed. He had wrought political marvels; but the continuous strain had taken its toll. Those interminable hours in his stuffy office at the Wigwam were not good for one who had trained down hard as a welterweight boxer, and who had from childhood been accustomed to open air and plenty of vigorous exercise.

Croker rarely touched liquor; but he was a hearty eater and a heavy smoker, consuming many strong cigars per day. Several years of sedentary life, together with intense nervous activity, had begun to entail unpleasant consequences. Croker was much over-weight; his bulging muscles were larded with fat; he had developed stomach trouble. The wind-up of the campaign the previous autumn had left him so exhausted that he had taken a two-months' vacation in the South; but it had produced no lasting benefit.

Croker was thus in poor shape to undergo a gruelling ordeal on the witness-stand — where Platt plainly intended to put him. He knew that Platt's committee would get him there. Croker had played the game of politics to the limit; and he had enemies who would not hesitate to stress the worst side of certain episodes that would not read well on the front pages of the newspapers. In short: Croker felt that he was due for a hectic time, whatever the ultimate political reaction might be.

This harassing prospect probably decided him to do what his doctors had long been urging — take a long rest under medical care. And since he knew that he would soon be politically under fire, he resolved to gain full liberty of action by two decisive moves: quitting official life, and going beyond the reach of subpœnas by travel abroad.

That was drastic action. It meant throwing up the post of City Chamberlain, with its $25,000 a year salary. It also would give his enemies the chance to claim that he was running away. Yet, early in February, he took the plunge, publicly announced both decisions, and appointed Thomas F. Gilroy to run things at the Wigwam.

This announcement came like a thunderbolt. Next day, the press reported: " Richard Croker's resignation caused great excitement in political circles. Croker will sail for Europe soon. He is a very sick man. Various names are publicly given by his physicians for his disease, the most common being dyspepsia. Mr. Croker says that frequently a pain seizes him in his left side about the region of the heart as if he were compressed by hoops of steel, and a faintness and dizziness attack him. Last Saturday he fainted away in his office.

" Speaking of his condition, Mr. Croker recently said: ' I am almost discouraged. I don't know what is the matter with me, but I am far from being a well man.' "[1]

The following morning, a front-page news story read: " Is Richard Croker going to resign the leadership of Tammany Hall? That he desires to do so was privately stated last evening by one of his trusted friends."[2]

Amid this jumble of fact and rumor, the Boss took his departure, heading straight for Wiesbaden, Germany, to undergo a thorough " cure."

Meanwhile, the Fassett Investigation was getting under way, and presently had Mayor Grant on the stand to explain alleged irregularities while he was Sheriff of New York, some years before. Grant's reputation had hitherto been so clean that these charges made a great sensation. The metropolitan press at once despatched special correspondents posthaste to Wiesbaden; and one of them, after interviewing the exiled Boss, reported:

" It is strange to see the Tammany chief idling the hours away, strolling about the *Kursaal*. One thinks of Mr. Croker as ' whooping it up for Tammany ' rather than sipping warm water at the *Trinkhalle*.

" But Richard Croker is here, all the same, diligently searching after his lost health. ' I am not here for fun,' said Mr. Croker to me today. ' A man does not quit New York as I did, throwing down a $25,000 a year office, unless he has to do it *P. D. Q.*, too, if he doesn't want to lose his health forever. The fact is, I was breaking down so rapidly that I had to drop everything in a hurry. The doctors here tell me that my trouble is pleuritic, not one of the heart, and that before long they will have it under control; but after my treatment here they insist that I must go to the mountains for three or four months, if the cure is to be permanent. If I do as they say, they promise to make me a well man and send me home in September. I shall be glad indeed to be back again. New York is good enough for me. I wish I was there now.' "

The interviewer having broached the subject of the charges against Grant, with the query whether Tammany would be hurt by this scandal at the next election, Croker answered quickly: " In no way, unless Tammany harbors and protects men after they have been *proven* guilty. If Tammany does that, it may as well put up the shutters, with a neat little card outside like this: ' Death in the family. Gone to meet the County Democracy! ' " [3]

So far, so good. Then came the big bombshell. Patrick H. McCann, Mrs. Croker's brother-in-law, went on the stand and proceeded to tell things about the Boss and the Mayor which needed a lot of explaining.

McCann began by asserting that, some six years before, Croker had shown him a satchel containing $180,000 in bills, which had been contributed by some big Tammany men to bribe members of the Board of Aldermen to confirm Grant's appointment as Commissioner of Public Works; albeit, the money had eventually been returned to the donors when Mayor Edson declined to appoint Grant to the office.

Furthermore, McCann testified that, a little later on, when Grant had been made Sheriff through Croker's influence, he presented Croker's six-year-old daughter, Flossie, with some strangely munificent gifts in the shape of envelopes, each containing $5000 in currency — the total amount of the series being estimated as somewhere between $10,000 and $25,000.

The sensation caused by McCann's testimony may be imagined! Croker promptly cabled: " McCann's charge is false. Would not believe him under oath and is a blackmailer." When burly " Pat " McCann was shown the cablegram, his big-jowled face grew crimson with wrath, and he growled to the reporters that he was ready to fight his brother-in-law any sort of way.

The fact is that McCann's testimony was the climax of a very pretty family row. McCann and Croker had once been good friends, and while Croker was still John Kelly's lieutenant he had prevailed upon his Boss to get McCann the lease of a municipal-owned restaurant in Central Park. Later, however, the pair quarrelled; and McCann asserted that Croker (now Boss) told the Park Commissioners not to renew McCann's lease — which was, in fact, given to another. Deprived of a very good thing, McCann had ever since been waiting to get even.

The obvious bad blood between Croker and his brother-in-law tempered the public's reaction to McCann's charges; especially the charge of attempted Aldermanic bribery — the more serious of the two. To the *Herald's* foreign correspondent, Croker said in an interview at Wiesbaden:

" Imagine me going around town showing McCann a bag full of money and telling him it was boodle. Rubbish! I'm not such a fool as to go hunting Aldermen with a brass band like that."

The Boss was still in bad physical shape, for the interviewer stated: " Croker is a pretty sick man; does not look nearly as well as when I saw him a month ago. He has had a severe hæmorrhage and seems to have lost a great deal of the strength which he then appeared to be gaining. Today he was in bed, and seeing how I was fatiguing him, I cut short the interview." [4]

It should be noted that, while Croker indignantly denied McCann's charge of attempted Aldermanic bribery, he was discreetly silent about his friend Grant's gifts to little Flos-

sie. There, McCann had evidently hit home; for Mayor
Grant admitted on the witness-stand that he had made two
such gifts, of $5000 each, naïvely explaining that he had
made them because he was Flossie's godfather and wanted
to do something handsome for the child. But Grant was
also forced to admit that he had never made any similar
presents, before or since; and later on, Croker had to confess
that he did not put the money in a trust fund, but apparently
used it for his own purposes.

Grant's " generosity " was, therefore, obviously a thinly
disguised payment of a political debt, and the episode had an
unsavory tang to it, even in those free-and-easy days.

On the other hand, McCann's lurid tale about the satchel
full of " boodle " was never corroborated by other testimony; and in face of flat denials by both Grant and Croker,
the general verdict at the time was: " Not proven."

One thing was certain: Croker was in a tight fix. Senator
Fassett's keen-edged drill had clearly " struck oil." The
Republicans were exultant; the public was whetting its ap-
petite for fresh disclosures; the reformers were in full cry
after Tammany; the Braves were showing signs of dismay.
Yet here Croker was, more than 3000 miles away from New
York City, flat on his back, and under doctor's orders to stay
there till he was better!

With his hand thus forced, Croker determined to compromise between health and politics. He would suspend his
" cure "; return to face his accusers as soon as he could
travel; and, that job once done and his political fences
mended, go back to Europe for the final stages toward physical recovery.

So, at the end of May, Croker cabled that he would be
home within a fortnight. It was high time. The air was

full of the wildest rumors, and a sinister whisper was going round that the Boss was dying. All this loose talk was squelched when Croker landed on schedule and, after a brief rest, appeared before the Fassett Investigation.

The dramatic scene which ensued is vividly described in a press account of the time:

" The court-room was packed like Tammany Hall on election night, and it was a Tammany crowd. It was a meeting of the Braves, who made no secret of their sympathies, but applauded and whoop-laed like gallery gods at every point which looked favorable to their side.

" McCann was there, of course. Joseph Choate, Republican, yet retained by the accused, sat beside Mrs. Croker and listened with sardonic face to the raps that fell now and then on Tammany, but sent many a hot shot flying into the ranks of the legal enemy, Ivins. Beside him sat Bourke Cockran, belligerent and mouthy, as the legal representative of Mayor Grant.

" It needed no physician to tell that Richard Croker was sick. His eye, his face, his voice, all told the story. The color in his usually swarthy face shaded up from the black beard, from the copper of his recently-acquired sea-tan to an ashy gray. The eyes were dull and sodden. The spiritless voice was half inaudible. Yet he sat patiently on the rack through five hours of weary questioning and gave no sign of pain.

" His answers were non-committal on all points save the things denied in the testimony of McCann, yet seemingly frank so far as he told anything. . . When Mr. Croker's name was called, he rose without a change of color or token of embarrassment. His wife, however, flushed painfully, and her fan fluttered for a moment. . . The way Mr.

Croker jumped on brother-in-law McCann's testimony was like the pounding of a pile-driver, and McCann's face got blue all the way up to the crown of his bald head." [5]

When it was over, nobody " had the goods on " Croker, in the legal sense.   No criminal act could be proved.   So the Boss was in no danger of sharing Tweed's fate.

From the ranks of Tammany arose a great sigh of relief, mingled with murmurs of sympathy and protestations of loyalty.   When Croker made his first appearance at the Wigwam a few nights later, he received a tremendous ovation.   The Braves yelled and stamped for minutes on end. The Boss was obviously much moved.[6]

Soon after this gratifying ovation, the Boss sailed away for his promised sojourn in the Swiss mountains.   With the dreaded ordeal past, and an easy mind for his political future, Croker could concentrate on his immediate quest — the full recovery of his health.

CHAPTER XIII

" HONEST GRAFT "

IN THE thick of one of his fiercest battles, Richard Croker snapped out an angry retort which instantly took its place in the history of politics, and which will probably be remembered long after all his other sayings have been forgotten.

This chance remark was uttered when the Tammany Boss was being grilled on the witness-stand during the Mazet Investigation of 1899; the third and last of those searching inquiries into New York City politics engineered by Platt. Frank Moss, head counsel for the Mazet Committee, had been pressing Croker regarding his hidden sources of income. At length, at the height of a sharp cross-examination, Mr. Moss asked with veiled sarcasm: " Then you are working for your own pocket, are you not? " To which the Boss instantly snapped back: " All the time — the same as you! " [1]

The grim directness of that retort; its naïve frankness and obvious truth electrified not merely New York but the entire nation. From Coast to Coast, Croker's words were caught up and pondered. For, as a lightning-flash illumines a dark landscape, so the Tammany Boss's laconic phrase lit up a whole code of conduct hitherto obscure. Well-meaning men everywhere were forced to face a political philosophy which, before this, they had tended to ignore. And the kernel of that philosophy can be stated in two words: *Honest Graft.*

The phrase is not Croker's. It was coined by another Tammany celebrity; by that genial sage of the Wigwam, George Washington Plunkitt. In his famous book (become a political classic) the Tammany philosopher thus states his case with his usual mordant humor:

"Everybody is talkin' these days about Tammany growin' rich on graft, but nobody thinks of drawin' the distinction between honest graft and dishonest graft. There's all the difference in the world between the two. Yes, many of our men have grown rich on politics. I have myself. I've made a big fortune out of the game, and I'm gettin' richer every day. But I've not gone in for dishonest graft (blackmailin' saloon-keepers, disorderly people, et cetera).

"There's an honest graft, and I'm an example of how it works. I might sum up the whole thing by sayin': 'I seen my opportunities and I took 'em.'

"Just let me explain by examples. My party's in power in the city, see, and it's goin' to undertake a lot of public improvements. Well, I'm tipped off, say, that they're goin' to lay out a new park at a certain place.

"I see my opportunity and I take it. I buy up all the land in the neighborhood. Then the board of this or that makes its plan public, and there's a rush to get my land, which nobody cared partic'lar for before. Ain't it perfectly honest to charge a good price and make a profit on my investment and foresight? Of course it is. Well, that's honest graft. It's just like lookin' ahead in Wall Street or in the coffee or cotton market. It's honest graft, and I'm lookin' for it every day in the year." [2]

There, in brief, we have the political ethics of a man who, according to his lights, seems to have been well-meaning and sincere. In those days, the test of conduct was, not what

was right, but what could get by the law. Sharp practices
were usually condoned as smart and clever. So long as a
man kept clear of the courts, his reputation was reasonably
secure.

A contemporary put the matter aptly when he stated:
" Between ' Thou shalt not steal ' and ' Honesty is the best
policy ' lies the history of unindicted men." [3]   And Theodore
Roosevelt sums up the ethics of the epoch in his statement
that: " The creed of mere materialism was rampant in both
American politics and American business, and many, many
strong men, in accordance with the prevailing commercial
and political morality, did things for which they deserve
blame and condemnation." [4]

This explains the sinister intimacy between politics and
" big business " which was so sensationally exposed by the
" muck-raking " journalists of the succeeding decade. Yet,
given the circumstances, that intimacy was virtually inevitable. Big corporations were willing to pay untold millions
for public service franchises and other special privileges;
while politicians had it in their power to harass those same
corporations almost out of existence by blackmailing " strike "
bills and municipal ordinances, unless properly " taken
care of."

A favorite slogan of Croker's political foes was the sardonic query: *Where Did He Get It?* Without trying to
discover where Croker got all of " It," we may at least
evaluate the main sources of a fortune which, from small
beginnings, rapidly swelled to a size estimated at several
millions of dollars upon his final retirement from politics
in the year 1902.

We have already noted Croker's early ups-and-downs: his
first prosperity, culminating in his Coronership with its

$15,000 a year perquisites; and his sudden descent to abject poverty, following the McKenna episode in 1874. Until Kelly's retirement a decade later, Croker was in moderate circumstances, living in a simple home in Harlem.

From the moment of his accession to power, Croker began to make real money; as witness Hugh J. Grant's payment of at least $10,000 in return for his appointment as Sheriff — doubtless only one among many cash settlements of political debts. The whole field of patronage must have been a veritable gold mine.

Then there was Croker's Chairmanship of the Finance Committee of Tammany Hall; a Committee which almost never met, and which kept no books. With the vast revenue of the organization passing, unchecked, through his hands, it was doubtless expected that a certain portion would stick to his fingers.

Croker always denied that he ever touched what Plunkitt calls "dishonest graft." The tribute from illicit liquor-selling, gambling, vice, and other tainted sources, may have been primarily the perquisites of lesser grades in the organization; and presumably not much of it reached head-quarters — at least, in its original form. But the damning fact remains that, whether much or little "dishonest graft" went into Croker's pocket, a lot of it went into the pockets of other Tammany men. The Lexow and Mazet Investigations proved to the hilt that in those days Tammany was reaping "dishonest graft" of the vilest kinds.

One major source of revenue was contracting. Here, however, the graft was very "honest." No more Tweed scandals! But — let a well-informed contemporary tell us how the trick was done:

"Generally, all is open and aboveboard. The contractor

agrees to do a certain amount of work for which he is to be
paid a fixed sum. The work is done and the money is paid.
Investigated, and everything is straight. The work has
been performed according to contract and no more money
has been paid for it than the stipulated price. Strictly honest
business, you see! Who can complain?

" But now suppose you put in a bid for one of these contracts. Do you get the job? Not much. At least, not until
you enter into a business arrangement with some city official
who is sent to you for that purpose, and you agree to put up
a fixed share of the receipts (*not* the profits) for the benefit
of somebody behind the scenes. Of course, if you did not
have to pay this tribute, you could do the work at less price
and the city would be the gainer. But it cannot be shown
that anybody has stolen any money out of the city treasury.
Who has stolen anything? The records are all straight." [5]

Another highly lucrative source of revenue was Croker's
real-estate connection. Soon after he became Boss of Tammany Hall, he entered into a partnership with one Peter
F. Meyer, and the firm of Meyer and Croker at once became
the most prosperous auctioneering concern in New York
City, having practically a monopoly of judicial sales of real
estate. The reasons for this, and for Croker's large profits
therefrom, came out in the Mazet Investigation of 1899.
Incidentally, it was at this point in the proceedings that
Croker made the avowal about his " own pocket " which
caused such a sensation.

The official record reads:

Mr. Moss: Let us see if my deductions are correct. The
judges elected by Tammany Hall appoint referees, who, in
line with their party obligations, appoint auctioneers —

Mr. Croker: That referee is appointed by the judge, and he appoints whatever auctioneer he pleases.

Mr. Moss: But if that referee is a good Tammany man, he should appoint an auctioneer who is in line with the party, should he not, as part of the patronage?

Mr. Croker: It all depends on the kind of a Tammany man he is.

Mr. Moss: If he appoints your firm (Meyer & Croker) he does a good party act, does he not?

Mr. Croker: Yes, sir.

Mr. Moss: Now, I ask you why he does a good party act when he appoints your firm?

Mr. Croker: Well, all things being equal, he has a right to do it. He is a Democrat himself, and he ought to appoint Democrats.

Mr. Moss: And he ought to do that thing which puts into your pocket money, because you are a Democrat, too?

Mr. Croker: Yes, sir.

Mr. Moss: So we have it, then, that you, participating in the selection of judges before election, participate in the emolument that comes away down at the end of their judicial proceeding; namely, judicial sales?

Mr. Croker: Yes, sir.

Mr. Moss: And it goes into your pocket?

Mr. Croker: I get — that is, a part of my profit. . .

Mr. Moss: Then you are working for your own pocket, are you not?

Mr. Croker: All the time; the same as you.

Mr. Moss: It is not, then, a matter of wide statesmanship and patriotism altogether, but it is wide statesmanship, patriotism, and personal gain mixed up, is it not?

Mr. Croker: It is " To the Party belongs the Spoils." I tell you that now right out, so that you can make it all right here. We win, and expect everyone to stand by us.[6]

A LITTLE later in the proceedings, Croker gave the committee this interesting information:

Mr. Croker: We will show you the books. There is Peter Meyer's there, and I want to say to you now that my half in that business has amounted to anywhere from $25,000 to $30,000 for the last seven years, right along.[7]

So MUCH for the Boss's profits through real estate. But he had other perquisites, even more lucrative. Almost every corporation which expected to do much business with the City found it convenient to make Richard Croker the holder of a sizeable block of its stock; and the aggregate value of these holdings, over a long period of years, must have been enormous.

The Mazet Committee tried hard to get Croker to talk on this subject, but he stubbornly refused, declaring that all such matters were his " private business," with which the public had no legitimate concern.

It is amusing to note how Croker made a shrewd counter-thrust at his accusers by drawing an interesting parallel between his corporation activities and those of his enemy, Platt. When asked to reveal his business enterprises, he protested: " All this talk is very well, but why don't you go and examine the man that created you, and sent you here? Go and investigate the office of Tracy, Boardman & Platt. There is more corruption in that office than any other office in this town. Go and investigate the man you get your retainer from, Mr. Moss; the man that made you possible. Platt is the man I mean."

Leaving the pot to call the kettle black, let us now turn to a further source of Croker's wealth, the cumulative importance of which is often overlooked. We refer to the Boss's relations with Wall Street.

The moving spirit in this matter seems to have been his friend Edward Murphy, of Troy. Murphy, who was born rich and who knew the financial ropes, pointed out to Croker his golden opportunities to make a fortune through judicious speculation.

The times were ripe; for New York City was then entering on an intensive stage in its development, and the great public service corporations were expanding, consolidating, and acquiring new franchises of enormous potential value. To cite only one instance: at this time, William C. Whitney and his associates were getting their grip upon the metropolitan street railways.

" In suggesting to Croker that he should seize the opportunity to improve his financial condition, Senator Murphy's words ran something like this: 'Richard, you have a hundred times more power than Whitney. All Whitney has put into this traction proposition is $450, and that was to pay the fees for filing the papers.'

" If Senator Murphy had told Croker he could jump to the moon, Croker could not have been more astonished. Soon after this, Croker showed unmistakable signs of prosperity. . . He got well acquainted with leaders of Wall Street, such as C. P. Huntington and James R. Keene." [8]

The tale of one notable financial " killing " will suffice to show how Croker enriched himself through his Wall Street associations. In 1892, a franchise was granted for the construction of a street railway through the outlying sections of the Bronx. This region was still so undeveloped that the new line was jocularly nicknamed: *The Huckleberry Rail-*

road. Yet its shrewd promoters realized its ultimate possibilities, and within a few years its stock (originally selling
very low) was extremely valuable. We do not know the
exact size of Croker's holdings, but in 1899 it was reliably
estimated to have run close to 1000 shares, for which he had
paid little or nothing.

And, over and above all specific transactions, was the fact
that Croker could always be sure of investing his money according to " inside information " and with the very best
financial advice. His Wall Street associates simply could not
let him lose; he was altogether too valuable to them.

Being a big winner, the Boss likewise showed himself a
good spender. Shortly after Mayor Grant's re-election in
1890, Croker disposed of his modest house in Harlem and
moved to a fine residence at number 5 East 79th Street.
This was in one of the smartest sections of town, just off
Fifth Avenue.

The price of the Boss's new home was understood to have
been $80,000; and the total cost, including the elaborate
furnishings, to have been nearly $200,000. The entire ex-
istence of the Croker household was on a munificent scale,
with a retinue of servants and a private Pullman car.

These domestic expenditures certainly suggest marked
prosperity. Yet even they were not so significant as Croker's
outlays on his life-long hobby — race-horses. In his lean
years we have seen Dick Croker betting his last dollar at
Saratoga. Now the great Boss spared no expense in gratifying his passion for " the sport of kings."

As early as 1891, Croker had purchased a stock-farm at
Richfield Springs, together with a string of thoroughbreds,
including *Dobbins,* a horse whose price was $20,000. Early
in 1893, Croker bought, for $250,000, a half-interest in

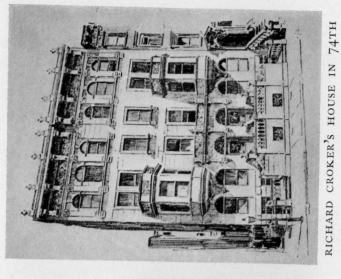

RICHARD CROKER'S HOUSE IN 74TH
STREET

[THE HOUSE ON THE LEFT]

RICHARD CROKER'S STOCK-FARM

AT RICHFIELD SPRINGS, N. Y.

Belle Meade Farm, one of the best-known stud-farms in the United States, and spent an extra $100,000 adding to his string, which now included *Longstreet,* a celebrated race-horse of his day. So successfully did Croker race that season that he became almost as much talked about on the turf as he was in politics.

All this time, be it remembered, Croker held no salaried office, and had no regular business. When he resigned his $25,000 a year Chamberlain's job early in 1890, he was through with official life and never again got on the municipal pay-roll.

As Big John Kennedy remarked: " 'Tis a great game, is politics; and can be made to pay like a bank! "

CHAPTER XIV

THE " GAY NINETIES " GET VERY GAY

The Gay Nineties is an apt phrase. It vividly depicts an epoch. Down the lengthening vista of the vanished years wafts its spicy flavor, evoking a certain naughty curiosity.

The Gay Nineties were the climax of previous decades; the rollicking close of America's pioneering age. The cream of a virgin continent was being skimmed; boundless natural resources were being wastefully coined into dollars; and the fortunate possessors spent lavishly and garishly. " Easy come and easy go! " was the slogan. From Nevada mining-camps to State of Maine lumber-towns, the spirit was essentially the same.

Yet where could a man have so gorgeous a fling as in " Little Old New York "? So the metropolis became the . nation's capital of pleasure. Here, new-rich millionaires from Pittsburgh and 'Frisco, from Michigan and the Texas Panhandle, foregathered to preen themselves as " big spenders." Thither flocked ambitious " country sports," " tired " business men, and miscellaneous joy-seekers: all after a " good time." And the average New Yorker was himself not precisely austere.

The demand for life's lighter pleasures was thus almost insatiable. And that demand, the metropolis did its best to supply. The spirit of the times was not censorious; Volstead and Mann Acts were then unthinkable. And what restraining laws did exist could be suitably evaded.

New York's world-wide reputation for gayety dates from the close of the Civil War. The let-down which always follows a great war, together with speculative finance and currency inflation, spelled " easy money " — and easy morals.

The results in New York were soon evident. Theatres, restaurants, dance-halls, gambling-joints, and disorderly houses sprang up like mushrooms on every hand. The " Red Light District " (formerly confined almost entirely to the Five Points and the Bowery) spread rapidly north and west. Some of the " resorts " were mansions, splendidly furnished and conducted with much style and ceremony. " On certain days of the month no gentleman was admitted unless he wore evening dress and carried a bouquet of flowers." [1]

Thus New York entered the " Flash Age "; so called because of the diamond studs (the bigger, the better) which every man who aspired to be " toney " wore on his ample shirt-front. It was a time of ostentation, blatant and unashamed. As one new-rich magnate, when criticized for vulgar display, blandly retorted: " Them as has 'em, wears 'em! "

The literary style of the " Flash Age " was as flamboyant as its manners. This is amusingly shown by the following description of metropolitan high society:

" All New York is in the midst of gaiety and dissipation. Splendid carriages, with liveried coachmen and sleek horses, dash up and down the avenues, depositing their perfumed inmates before brilliantly-lighted, high-stooped, brownstone fronts, whence the sound of merry voices and voluptuous music comes wooingly out, through frequently opened doors, into the chilly night. . .

" Dancing and feasting, flirting and gossip bind the hours with fragrant chaplets, and the duties and purposes of life sink into soft oblivion. The night reels, like a drunken Bacchant, away; and the stars grow pale as the revelers depart, with bounding blood and dazed senses, to the embroidered chambers that hold sweet sleep in silken chains." [2]

New York's fashionable thoroughfares reflected the spirit of the times. Broadway glittered with marble. Fifth Avenue, as far as 59th Street, was an almost unbroken expanse of brown-stone palaces, stretching oppressively, block after block and mile upon mile.

Even then, New York had its " Greenwich Village "; though in those days the " Bohemian " quarter centred around Bleecker Street, which had been the citadel of society's elect only a generation before.

In the " Flash Age," Bleecker Street was the abode of artists, actresses, kept women, and other unconventional persons; and the studios of the artistic colony were famous for their wild parties.

The centre of sporting life was, at the moment, around Union Square. But it was soon destined to drift northward; first to Madison Square, and thence up Broadway and Sixth Avenue.

This was the district known as *The Tenderloin*. The nickname arose out of a chance remark uttered by Police Captain Alexander S. Williams. After long service in quiet residential districts, where opportunities for police graft were scarce, the doughty Captain was promoted to the precinct covering the notorious vice and gambling area. Shortly thereafter, a friend saw Captain Williams breezing down Broadway, and, noting his jaunty air, asked him the reason. " Well," smiled Williams, " I've been transferred. I've

"SATAN'S CIRCUS" — SIXTH AVENUE AT 3 A.M.

had nothin' but chuck steak for a long time, and now I'm goin' to get a little of the tenderloin! "

The Flash Age, which had begun with the Civil War, ended suddenly and painfully in the great financial panic of 1873. Thereafter, New York was quieter for a few years; albeit, the cause was not so much better morals as less cash.

Indeed, even during its financial hang-over, the metropolis apparently did itself fairly well. Certainly, the seeker after pleasure would have found no dearth of entertainment if he took an evening stroll up Sixth Avenue, from 23rd to 40th Streets; for this was now the sporting centre — aptly termed *Satan's Circus.*

The ruin wrought by the panic of '73 was soon effaced by the flowing tide of national prosperity. All through the eighties, metropolitan life went forward with ever-accelerating tempo. To portray New York in the eighties would be virtually to repeat our description of the Flash Age. New York of the eighties was a little less vulgar, a little less strident; but it was basically the same in spirit, and there was even more money to spend.

So we emerge into the *Gay Nineties:* the climax of high living and low thinking; of liquor and women; of graft and gambling; of peerless " sports " and colossal " spenders " like " Lucky " Baldwin and " Betcha-a-million " Gates.

Perhaps the most astounding " exhibit " of this extravagant, pleasure-loving epoch was the Saratoga Club, Richard Canfield's gambling-joint *de luxe,* at number 5 East 44th Street. There, the master-gambler, whom his recent biographer calls *The Host to the Nineties,* received his select millionaire clientele. No man who could not sign his check for at least five figures was apt to get inside the massive bronze doors of this Palace of Chance, where fortunes were nightly lost and won, and whence John W. Gates, the arch-plunger, walked forth in the wee small hours, richer at a single sitting by a cool $100,000.

Canfield's resort was familiarly known as " next to Del's," from its situation close to Delmonico's, the smartest restaurant of the town. The Saratoga Club was then considered a marvel of interior decorating. The very office had matched panels of white mahogany inlaid with mother-of-pearl, and the entire mansion was filled with rare antiques and *objets d'art.*

" True to tradition, Canfield served a magnificent supper at eleven o'clock. There were tables for those who cared to sit down; for the rest, servants brought the food to the gaming tables. Delicious cold cuts, salads, and desserts were prepared on the premises. If a patron wanted something special, it was brought from Delmonico's, with no charge to the player except the tip of a white or a red chip for the servant. Costly cigars were dispensed free. . . The wine-cellar contained the finest vintages, as well as the more plebeian drinks." [3]

Canfield's was the most magnificent of hundreds of gambling-joints then operating in the city, all of them running in flat defiance of the law. Furthermore, the multitude of policy-shops, brothels, assignation-houses, and other forms of vice, together with illegal liquor-selling, constituted an immense volume of illegal activity.

These countless illegalities were condemned, not merely by moralists in New York City but also by the bulk of up-State public opinion, which was getting more and more censorious of metropolitan ways.

We thus witness an ever-growing antagonism between two

sharply contrasted attitudes toward life, which was to have momentous political consequences. The free-and-easy, pleasure-loving metropolitan majority was presently to be coerced by a resident minority backed by powerful up-State allies. The city majority promptly rebelled against this coercion and endeavored to evade or defy restrictive legislation.

The upshot was an emotional clash which became the paramount issue in local politics; an issue to which voters tended to subordinate all other matters.

In short, it was a small-scale rehearsal of the great "Wet and Dry" drama which agitates the nation today.

The first battle between the antagonistic forces came in the mid-nineties. It was precipitated by the vice disclosures of the Fassett and Lexow Investigations. Those investigations had been started by Platt for partisan purposes. But their revelations so dramatized conditions that both the moral and the political reformers were roused to unprecedented activity and joined forces in a common onslaught against the evils they respectively abhorred.

The champion of the moralists was the Reverend Charles H. Parkhurst, Pastor of the Madison Square Presbyterian Church, and probably the most eloquent preacher of his day. His sermons attracted widespread attention and had profound influence. A born orator, inspired by quenchless zeal, and tireless in action, Dr. Parkhurst was the ideal leader of a moral crusade.

Dr. Parkhurst fired the opening gun of the campaign against vice by his famous sermon preached on Sunday, February 14, 1892, whereof the text was: *Ye are the salt of the earth*. It was a blistering arraignment of vice conditions in the metropolis, and an equally scathing arraignment of the

Tammany administration which tolerated those conditions and profited by them. This sermon made a great sensation. Next day, New York was in a furor.

The Doctor was indefatigable. Aided by influential supporters, he and his agents investigated the ills he had so hotly denounced. As soon as he had gathered enough new data, Dr. Parkhurst would preach another sermon, describing realistically to his crowded congregation the horrors he had seen; and next morning the newspapers would broadcast it as a front-page story. It was amazingly effective propaganda.

Dr. Parkhurst's guide through New York's "underworld" was a certain Charles W. Gardner. This man was not only a competent detective but also possessed a lively sense of humor. Gardner wrote an account of his vice tour with the minister which was published in pamphlet form under the intriguing title: *The Doctor and the Devil: or Midnight Adventures of Doctor Parkhurst.*[4] This little volume, written in a racy style, is as amusing as it is informative.

Gardner had promised Dr. Parkhurst to " show him the town " for six dollars a day and expenses. On the appointed evening, the detective took the Doctor and a young assistant named Erving to his room on West 18th Street, and made them up. Gardner had quite a job disguising Dr. Parkhurst's ultra-clerical personality, but at length he had everything to his liking, and the trio sallied forth to " see life." That night they saw plenty — and on subsequent nights, as well.

The tour was not free from trials on both sides. Dr. Parkhurst's first ordeal came when, to avoid suspicion in a very tough joint, he had to take a stiff drink of Cherry Hill whiskey. "He acted," relates Gardner, "as if he had swallowed a whole political parade — torchlights and all."

On the other hand, the detective had his troubles. Not only was he worried lest his tenderfoot clients betray themselves; he was certainly made to earn his money. For, as Gardner complains: "the Doctor was a very hard man to satisfy. 'Show me something worse!' was his constant cry. He really went at his slumming as if his heart was in the tour."

Perhaps the most startling event in this memorable excursion was the notorious "leap-frog" episode. The detective arranged a "dance of nature" in a low-grade brothel run by one Hattie Adams. Five naked girls danced the can-can to the strains of a tin-pan piano played by a broken-down musician known as *The Professor*.

Says Gardner: "As I could not dance, and the Doctor, of course, would not if he could, young Erving was forced to do the dancing for us visitors. . . Then came the celebrated 'leap-frog' episode, in which I was the frog and the others jumped over me.

"The Doctor sat in a corner with an unmoved face through it all, watching us and slowly sipping a glass of beer. Hattie Adams was quite anxious to find out who Dr. Parkhurst was. I told her he was 'from the West,' and was 'a gay boy.' Then Hattie tried to pull Dr. Parkhurst's whiskers, but the Doctor straightened up with such an air of dignity that she did not attempt any further familiarities."

Dr. Parkhurst was not the only vice investigator. Another earnest seeker after the naked truth was Joel S. Harris, a special agent for the Mazet Committee; and his story, as told on the witness-stand, gives us in vivid fashion the flavor of the "Red-Light District" during this period:

"On the 6th day of July I was walking through 26th Street, between Sixth and Seventh Avenues. It was late at night. As I was passing number 116 West 26th Street, on the stoop there were three or four colored girls; and one of them solicited me.

"In fact, all three did, but one got up and grabbed hold of me while I was against the railing, and said: 'Come up stairs.'

"I said: 'No, I don't care about going.'

"She says: 'Come on! Come on!' and she put her arms around me, and at the same time she went in my pocket and took a dollar which I had there, with some other money — make-believe money, counterfeit, stage-money.

"This girl took the money out of my pocket (it was in my vest pocket) and ran up stairs, saying: 'Well, there's nothing in you. Good-bye, Honey.'

"So I felt and saw that I was robbed, and I went to look after an officer. I found an officer on the corner of 25th Street and Sixth Avenue. I said: 'Officer, I have got the rinky-dink.'

"He knew what I meant, all right. He said: 'Where? Down at that wench-house?'

"I said: 'I guess that is right. Will you come around?' and he says: 'I can't. It's not on my beat,' or something like that.

"I says: 'John, blow your whistle,' and he did, and three or four policemen came running up and asked what was the matter. I told them I had been robbed. . . So we got to the house. I began knocking on the doors and trying them, and an officer says: 'Here, don't do that. You'll have your brains blown out.' . .

"Then a door opened and a big fellow came out. He

says: ' Are you the guy that lost something? ' I said: ' I lost some money.' He said: ' Was it a dollar bill with a lot of stage-money? ' I said: ' That's me.' He says: ' I'll get it for you,' and walked inside.

"When he goes in for the money, the officer says to me: ' You are a cheap son-of-a-bitch making that holler over a dollar. I wouldn't have budged.' He said: ' You're so light you'd float, to make that holler over a dollar.' . . They were all kidding me, and calling me all kinds of names and everything else. . .

" Then the man came back and handed out the money and showed it to the officers, and went to show by that how cheap I was. He said: ' I wouldn't have had it happen for ten dollars.' He said: ' Here, a nice-dressed fellow like you making all this fuss over a dollar! ' " [5]

Mr. Harris' experience was not unique. Any well-dressed man who walked through " The District " was almost sure to be urgently solicited. A highly piquant instance of this happened to " Big Bill " Devery when he was still a Precinct Captain.

Strolling along one evening, off duty and in civilian attire, Devery was loudly hailed by some disreputable females from the windows of a low resort which he was passing.

Whether it was his morals or his taste in women that he deemed impugned, certain it is that " Big Bill " was very angry. Bright and early next morning, the proprietor of the offending bagnio was summoned to the station-house.

And the luckless proprietor testified before the Lexow Committee that as soon as he entered the Captain's presence " and he saw me, he says: ' You son-of-a-bitch, that's you, is it? ' ' Well,' he says, ' if them women cows of yours call me again, I'll take you by the neck and throw you out of the house! ' "

The sequel to this painful interview was that, a few days later, Devery's wardman called on the proprietor and ordered him to pay ten dollars per month more "protection money" for the gross insult to his Captain.[6]

Such was "York" of the Gay Nineties: wide-open and unashamed. Its pagan life might run the whole gamut from the superbly gorgeous to the drably sordid. Yet, in that composite picture, Canfield's gambling-palace "next to Del's," Hattie Adams' frowsy joint, and the 26th Street "wench-house," all had their place.

CHAPTER XV

THE REFORMERS SWEEP THE TOWN

THE EARLY nineties witnessed the rise of a deep-seated, constructive movement for municipal reform. Unfortunately, this new leaven stirred to action a motley host of zealots who, with their manifold programs, did much to discredit in the public mind the very cause they had so eagerly espoused. It was they who brought the word *Reformer* into such popular odium that level-headed persons seeking civic betterment soon came to avoid the term and purposely re-labelled themselves.

This distinction between Reform and " Reformers " must be carefully kept in mind if we are to understand the inwardness of " non-partisan " politics in New York City.

By the late eighties, thinking men had begun to realize that our municipal life was in a bad way. Accordingly, many of the country's best minds grappled with the problem. During the next few years a number of authoritative works on municipal government appeared,[1] and the stream of thought and discussion swelled rapidly, both in volume and in effect.

This movement for civic betterment was intimately connected with the reforming trend in national and State politics which had begun a decade earlier, and which had already produced results such as the Federal Civil Service Reform Act of 1883. It was only natural that the field of municipal

affairs should have been neglected for the more obvious problems of State and nation.

Yet many of those problems were common to all phases
of our political life. This was eminently true of civil service
reform (the " Merit System "), as opposed to the partisan
" Spoils System." It was equally true of reform in election
and party machinery, such as the secret (" Australian ") ballot, direct primaries, and public scrutiny of campaign funds.

Straight-thinking reformers realized from the first the
magnitude of their task and the obstacles they would encounter. They therefore tended to proceed realistically, according to scientific methods. Facts were gathered; assembled data were analyzed, and theories were frankly revised
if these did not work out in practice. It is to the patient
labor and clear vision of these long-headed, common-sense
builders (*re-formers*, in the literal sense) that the political
progress of the last few decades is primarily due. For, with
all its imperfections, the political life of today; national,
State, and especially municipal, is vastly cleaner and better
than it was a generation ago.

Our political progress is the fruit of strenuous effort. The
pioneers of the reform movement had a double task: they
had to awaken an indifferent or complacent public to the
magnitude of deep-rooted evils; and they had to educate the
public to a knowledge of practical remedies.

Orthodox politicians of every stripe were their enemies
from the start. Instantly scenting danger to themselves, the
old-line " regulars " of both political armies declared war to
the knife against these innovators, and covered them with
tirades of mingled abuse and ridicule. Just as the Mugwumps were damned as traitors to " regularity," so advo-
cates of the Merit System and the Australian Ballot were

persistently villified. Hard-shelled spoilsmen jeeringly dubbed the Merit System: "*Snivel* Service Reform."

Richard Croker was naturally a staunch believer in the traditional slogan: " To the victors belong the spoils! " And he never hesitated to say so frankly. His opinion of the Merit System was vigorously expressed during one of his verbal tilts with Mr. Moss during the Mazet Investigation:

Mr. Moss: That is the theory of the city government right through; that the organization in control should have all the offices in every department?

Mr. Croker: Yes, sir.

Mr. Moss: Judicial, executive, administrative and everything?

Mr. Croker: Yes, sir; that is what I believe the people voted our ticket for.

Mr. Moss: And that is why you have the emblem of the tiger, who has a large mouth, which is constantly open?

Mr. Croker: Yes, sir. That was so when we put you off the Police Board. You saw that in print, didn't you? [2]

LATER on in the proceedings, Croker stated: " I think the city would be better off without civil service. . . I think it is an obstruction to city government." [3]

In all these utterances there is a scornful note not wholly accounted for by the facts as thus far stated. The reason being that these " practical " politicians were thinking of their opponents in terms, not of the new movement's level-headed thinkers, but of the emotional zealots who did most of the talking and made nearly all the noise.

The psychology of this sort of " reformer " is in many ways intensely irritating, not only to politicians but to the average run of mankind. There is a cocksureness, a self-righteousness, a lack of human sympathy and understanding about him which tends to arouse mingled anger and contempt. In short: the " reformer " himself has probably been the greatest single handicap to reform.

Popular distrust was intensified by the fact that many upper-class reformers obviously distrusted the people, their attitude toward government being substantially that of Alexander Hamilton and his Federalist supporters. That attitude might have worked when our country was virtually an aristocratic republic; but applied to conditions of universal suffrage and " government by the people," its mere suspicion in the popular consciousness spelled something akin to political suicide.

The typical " reformer's " lamentable ignorance of human nature is strikingly revealed by his desire to coerce the public, by legislative acts or municipal ordinances, to matters which run counter to popular usage and therefore rouse the public to angry defiance. That, in turn, nullifies the special legislation, besides bringing all law into discredit.

" Nothing is easier to make than an unworkable law; and nothing is harder than to execute it. The art of government is largely the art of adapting laws to the foibles of mankind. It is the art of managing large bodies of cantankerous, obstinate, fickle, apathetic, and emotional men and women. Frame the laws as skilfully as you may — and you have taken only the first step. Applying the laws, interpreting them, enforcing them, and developing a popular respect for them — these are also steps that count. And all of them require the cooperation of men drawn from the ranks of the people." [4]

The " reformer's " gross lack of human understanding is

primarily due to the fact that he is usually obsessed by some fixed idea which he devoutly believes will regenerate mankind and solve society's problems, if only his idea be fully and resolutely applied. It may be any one of a dozen political nostrums advocated by rival reformist sects; yet in each case the psychology is the same.

This emotional obsession blinds the reformist zealot to the realities of the situation. Whence his deplorable tendency toward intolerance. " The mental process which the average reformer uses is simple enough. He begins by taking it for granted that he is right. Then it must follow, as the night the day, that if you differ from him you are wrong. And if you are wrong there can be no compromise with you, for truth cannot enter into any compromise with error. The reformer, when he runs true to type, is not open to argument concerning the validity of his convictions. He will not barter away his ' principles.' He will not arbitrate an issue of righteousness. As well ask him to dicker on the Golden Rule and the Ten Commandments." [5]

The moral reformers in the New York of the nineties were mostly of this uncompromising type. And Dr. Parkhurst, their spokesman, certainly knew how to fire their emotional zeal. When the Doctor began preaching against the wickedness of New York City, the Protestant, church-going middle class fell into line behind him like a crusading host.

Dr. Parkhurst was a good fighter. His first attack was a volley of hot shot fired straight at his foes. In his famous sermon of February, 1892, the Doctor proclaimed: " There is not a form under which the devil disguises himself that so perplexes us in our efforts, or so bewilders us in the devising of our schemes, as the polluted harpies who, under the pretense of governing this city, are feeding day and night on its quivering vitals. They are a lying, perjured, rum-soaked, libidinous lot. . . Every effort that is made to improve character in this city, every effort to make men respectable, honest, temperate, and sexually clean is a direct blow between the eyes of the Mayor and his whole gang of drunken and lecherous subordinates."

That certainly was plain speaking. And among the crowded congregation which listened in fascinated silence sat Boss Platt — still a member of the Madison Square Presbyterian Church, since the fiery Doctor had not yet denounced him from the pulpit as worse than five Crokers. " One can imagine Platt, rather shrivelled and somewhat dry, sitting up in his pew and exulting at the statements which the servant of the Lord was making in favor of the Republican Party. Dr. Parkhurst's intentions were of the best, but Mr. Platt could calculate, as he carefully held his silk hat between his knees, the number of votes that sermon would produce." [6]

Platt, however, was marking time. Shrewd political analysts like himself were already secretly aware that 1892 was a " Democratic year "; and the November elections were to prove a Democratic " landslide " which put Grover Cleveland in the White House, elected Democrats as Governor of New York State and Mayor of the metropolis, and even temporarily wrested the State Legislature from Republican control.

But Platt knew how to wait. He would bide his time. And meanwhile, Dr. Parkhurst thundered tirelessly on.

The very next year saw a turn of the tide; 1893 witnessed a world-wide financial panic, and the worst business depression since that of twenty years before. Unemployment and destitution rose to alarming proportions. The whole nation was filled with discontent. And, as usual, the party in power had to shoulder the blame. Although 1893 was politically an " off-year," wherever men had a chance to vote, they tended to vote Republican. In New York State the Democrats just managed to squeeze in their candidate for Governor, but the Legislature became Republican once more.

Platt was now ready to cash in politically on Dr. Parkhurst's propaganda. So, early in 1894, the Legislature passed a bill appointing a Committee headed by Senator Clarence Lexow to investigate the charges of political and moral corruption which had been brought by various reform organizations.

Then followed a political squabble which disclosed the latent clash between State and metropolis. Governor Roswell P. Flower, a prominent New York Democrat, vetoed the bill in terms which scathingly denounced the measure as a partisan manoeuvre and vigorously upheld the city's right to " home rule."

For a while it looked as though Platt's game was blocked, because the Republican Boss did not have enough legislative votes to re-pass the appropriation bill for the Committee's expenses over Governor Flower's veto. But at this juncture a group of wealthy New Yorkers guaranteed the funds; whereupon the Legislature passed a Resolution appointing a Committee to serve without pay. The Lexow Investigation was thus assured.

This unexpected outcome filled New York's Tammany rulers with secret consternation. At first they had not taken the Parkhurst crusade seriously. When the noted preacher had uttered his declaration of war, Mayor Grant issued a statement challenging Parkhurst to prove his assertions;

and *The Tammany Times*, Croker's organ, said derisively:
" A ' loose ' idea in a man's head is a serious thing. Every
once in a while an idea probably forms in Dr. Parkhurst's
head, and then it gets loose and rattles around at such a
great rate that it drives the poor man crazy. It keeps rattling
around until the next idea forms and drops off, and that is
the reason he seems to be crazy all the while."

The Democratic tidal-wave of 1892 and Gilroy's election
as the new Tammany Mayor made Parkhurst's denunciations
seem, for the moment, of small account.

However, the Doctor and his colleagues persisted. Bit
by bit, they backed up their vice charges by very specific
evidence. Meanwhile, the political reformers had been un-
earthing election frauds of startling magnitude. And now
the Fassett Committee was to sift all these charges!

To Richard Croker the trend of events looked ominous.
His unerring intuition warned him that trouble was ahead;
just as the falling glass tells the mariner of the approach
of a storm.

Croker knew all the signs — he had lived through the
political hurricane which had wrecked " The House that
Tweed Built." The current unrest due to hard times, and
the nation-wide Republican swing in the recent elections
had put him on his guard. The aggressive mustering of his
varied enemies was further evidence of impending danger.
And his uncanny political sixth-sense whispered that, after
so many years of unbroken Tammany rule, the people were
ripe for a change — if only out of idle curiosity. The popu-
lace of a great city, fickle and emotional, gets that way every
once in a while.

Watching and weighing the situation, the Boss saw matters
go from bad to worse. The revelations before the Lexow

Committee were startling, and they evoked a formidable popular response. The political barometer was falling faster and faster. It *was* to be a hurricane!

Silent and motionless, as was his wont at crucial junctures, the great Boss sat and thought the matter through:

Tammany would be beaten in November by a coalition pledged to reform. Whoever led Tammany on that melancholy occasion would be discredited. And Croker had no mind to "take the rap." Therefore he would presently resign the titular headship of Tammany Hall.

But his resignation would have a string to it. The new "leader" should be his deputy, so circumstanced that he could not grasp the substance of power. Behind the scenes, the real Boss would await his hour.

And that hour would surely strike. For hurricanes come seldom — and cannot long endure. Imagine "York" of the Gay Nineties tolerating more than one dose of "reform"!

Meanwhile, he was rich; he loved his race-horses; he needed rest and change of scene. It would all work out in the long run.

So the Boss promptly dropped out of the political limelight, and presently rumors began to circulate that he was again in poor health and might resign. Early in May, Croker went to Washington, where he had a confidential talk with his friend Senator Murphy; and on his return to New York, he formally tendered his resignation as Chairman of the Finance Committee of Tammany Hall. A month later, he slipped away for Europe so quietly that no one outside the inner circle knew, until he was gone.

The hostile press descanted knowingly upon Croker's "flight"; his foes jeeringly prophesied that he had gone for good; even the Braves grumbled a bit, feeling "let down" by their Big Chief on the eve of a dubious campaign.

Croker did not seem to care. His colors flaunted on the British turf. His revenues were ample. His was a very voluntary exile.

But back in New York, the glass fell ever lower, and the hurricane winds began to blow. All Tammany's foes sunk their respective differences and staged a big "get-together" meeting in Cooper Union, where a Committee of Seventy was formed to direct the campaign.

On that Committee every anti-Tammany element was represented. There were political reform organizations like the City Club and the Citizen's Union, moral reform organizations such as Dr. Parkhurst's Society for the Prevention of Crime, and anti-Tammany Democrats of various shades. The "Fusion" coalition soon found a suitable candidate for Mayor in William L. Strong, a wealthy merchant of unblemished reputation and a Republican of independent views.

With a well-balanced ticket, the Fusionists sought the endorsement of the local Republican machine, and were told to "see Platt." This they did — and found that gentleman in a very mixed state of mind.

Platt's wily soul was troubled by the trend of events. This Fusion movement, pledged to a non-partisan reform administration, filled him with secret dread. Tammany could be beaten in November, right enough; but where would he and his Republican "regulars" come in? These Fusionists denounced the Spoils System and prated loudly about Civil Service Reform. But, if there were to be no spoils, both the old machines might soon, as Plunkitt put it, be near the "bustin' point." A "deal" with Tammany would be better than that!

Platt was sorely tempted. But he did not quite dare, because of two special factors: (1) the Mayoralty candidate; (2) public opinion.

By nominating a Republican (of sorts) the Fusion leaders had cleverly spiked Platt's guns. Of course, they had not fooled Platt. In his eyes, an independent Republican was no better than a Mugwump. Nevertheless, Mr. Strong *was* a registered Republican, and if Platt were to "knife" him, the blow to the principle of party regularity might entail worse consequences than a dearth of spoils. Such fine-spun tactics would be quite above the heads of the partisan rank-and-file.

As for the second factor: Platt, like Croker, realized that the metropolitan public was in a hyper-excited mood. To stand in the path of this emotional tornado would be too risky. Better let the public blow off steam and get its fill of reform, reasoned Platt. Then things would become "normal" again.

Platt sadly realized that his Lexow Investigation had started something beyond his control. What he had hoped to unearth were some good old-fashioned election frauds — strictly Democratic, of course.

But the investigation had gone much further; it had ripped the lid off the whole metropolitan vice situation. And "Platt was not particularly interested in the revelation of sin, for he had his private experiences with it, and the revelation of some of them by his political opponents, who had climbed up to a window in the Delavan House in Albany to make their investigations, had caused him some embarrassment." [7]

Furthermore, the Lexow testimony had proved that many illegal practices in the metropolis were " protected " by the police. And that did not please Platt either; because the Police Department of New York City was run by a bipartisan Board of Commissioners, and the Republican member (McClave) was obviously smirched by the abundant graft that was going around.

So Platt was determined to stand on the side-lines and let things take their course.

The Fusion campaign was a genuine crusade. A novel enthusiasm stirred men's blood and fired their imaginations. The Protestant ministers marshalled their flocks and led them, *en masse*, to fight for the good cause. Some Catholic priests did likewise; among them, Father Ducey, an earnest social worker. And Dr. Parkhurst swept through the city like the trumpet of wrath.

Thousands of chronic stay-at-home voters rushed to the polls. Throughout the upper and middle classes, party lines melted in the heat of emotional contagion, and the tenement districts were affected as well. Toward the close of the campaign the trend grew so clear that it became the fashion to deride Tammany, and those persons who always like to be on the winning side proceeded to climb on the Fusion bandwagon.

Yet, though the very stars in their courses seemed arrayed against it, the Wigwam did its best. Like the seasoned veterans they were, the Tammany battalions went into battle with well-drilled precision, and fought doggedly to the last. Tammany's stock candidate, Hugh J. Grant, was nominated and " ran on his record." Much money was raised and was freely sent. All that the machine could do was done.

But the outcome was a foregone conclusion. When the

battle was over and the votes counted, William L. Strong had been elected by over 45,000 majority, and practically the entire Fusion ticket had won. A real non-partisan, reform administration had been installed at City Hall — the first that New York had ever known.

Tammany was out of power; off the pay-roll; beaten and discredited. The Reformers had swept the town!

CHAPTER XVI

" THE ALLIANCE BETWEEN THE PURITAN AND THE GRAFTER "

MAYOR STRONG gave New York a model administration. Capable department heads were at once appointed, who staffed their offices with men of ability and intelligence. *Honesty and Efficiency* was the watchword; and those ideals were lived up to.

Even the Augean Stables of the Police Department were taken in hand by Theodore Roosevelt, who tackled the job with all the ardor of his strenuous youth. Backed by competent colleagues, Roosevelt reorganized the Department. Veterans like " Tenderloin " Williams were retired " for the good of the service," while younger sinners were retired from " juicy " precincts to quiet ones where opportunities for graft were few.

To be sure, graft was by no means extirpated. The New York Police Department has an inner life of its own. It has traditions which stubbornly resist the transient efforts of Commissioners who come and go, while " The Force " clumps stolidly on its routine way. But so long as *T.R.* was in command, graft kept coyly under cover; and gambling, vice, and " blind tigers " bowed their diminished heads.

The most striking improvement was in the Street Cleaning Department. From time immemorial it had offered the readiest field for graft, of both the " honest " and dishonest varieties. Contracts had nearly always been notoriously padded, while the Department payroll supported, in semi-genteel leisure, thousands of deserving party "workers." Into this restful scene broke Colonel George E. Waring, Jr. Thenceforth, not only were contracts written "straight"; the street-cleaners themselves were put into white uniforms, and were thereby made so conspicuous that every passer-by could tell at a glance whether one of "Waring's White-Wings" was soldiering on the job or loafing in a corner-saloon. The results were startling. For the first time in its history, New York's streets were kept clean.

The whole municipal program was conducted along similar model lines. New schools were built, new parks and playgrounds laid out, and many long-needed improvements of various sorts were planned and executed.

Such was the splendid record of the Strong administration. And yet, before it was a year old, it was manifestly unpopular, while at the next Mayoralty election it was emphatically repudiated amid the exultant cheers of the multitude.

Why did this happen? In the bitterness of defeat, many disillusioned reformers asserted that the bulk of New York's citizenry deliberately preferred bad, wasteful government.

But this is a very inadequate explanation. As a matter of fact, the average New Yorker, poor or well-to-do, enjoyed having clean streets, tidy parks, good schools and an efficient health department. Furthermore, the vast majority of the poor had no direct personal interest in municipal graft, since they could expect no "cut" on padded contracts and, obviously there were not enough city jobs to go round.

No, it was neither its honesty nor its efficiency which hurt the Strong administration with the metropolitan public. Other things, less prominent on the record, proved its political undoing.

From the embittered outbursts of Reform's disheartened friends, let us turn to the cynical verdict of its professional foes:

" These reform movements," remarked an East Side politician, "are like queen hornets. They sting you once, and then they die." In similar vein, George W. Plunkitt said condescendingly: " College professors and philosophers who go up in a balloon to think are always discussin' the question why reform administrations never succeed themselves. The reason is plain to anybody who has learned the A.B.C. of politics. . . Reformers are mornin' glories — look lovely in the mornin' and wither up in a short time, while the regular machines go on flourishin' forever like fine old oaks. . . The fact is, a reformer can't last in politics. He can make a show for a while; but, like a rocket, he always comes down."

There is a modicum of truth in these verdicts. Certain it is that, throughout New York's political history, no reform administration has ever yet succeeded itself. Yet even this rather begs the question. It states the facts, but it does not really explain.

One factor, however, is clear: the reformers play into the enemy's hands by internal dissensions, personal jealousies, and lack of organization. To a certain degree, this is inevitable. A " Fusion " movement is a coalition of diverse elements, each with its special objectives, and led by highly individualistic personalities. Such a loose coalition cannot compare in disciplined unity with a well-drilled machine.

Then again, the Strong administration was disliked by the Republicans almost as much as it was by Tammany Hall. Platt's worst fears were realized when Mayor Strong held firmly to his campaign pledge of a non-partisan policy. Deeply chagrined at the Mayor's disregard of party needs, the Republican Boss wrote indignantly: " Colonel Waring was put in charge of the Street Cleaning Department, and no organization leader could get a place from him." ¹ Determined to stop this sort of thing at all costs, Platt was now ready for a " deal " with Tammany, and his manoeuvres during the campaign of 1897 played their part in the Tiger's return to power.

Sydney Brooks, one of the shrewdest foreign observers who has ever written on our political life, says:

" The reformers set their standard high — and by that standard they are judged. The promised reforms are long a-coming, and when they do come are not always seen to work quite smoothly. Up goes an instantaneous howl of impatience and disappointment from the reforming press, and of derision from Tammany.

" Moreover, no reform administration has yet mastered the secret (which Tammany so perfectly understands) of ' team-play.' The heads of the various departments work far too independently of each other; they are too much like a company of star actors; they quarrel with one another and criticize each other's conduct with a publicity and freedom quite destructive of any real unity.

" All this the public sees. It is amusing and piquant enough for a time; but amusement ends by passing into boredom, and finally into disgust. There comes at last a period when to the ordinary citizen Tammany seems preferable to the discord and din of this jangling jealousy. Tammany has at least the precious and healing gift of working in silence." [2]

This analysis may explain machine success at the polls. But it does not account for the popular revolt which turned the reformers out of office only three years after the same public had installed them amid wild enthusiasm. Obviously, powerful emotional factors must have come into play, to have caused such a dramatic revulsion of public opinion. And those factors seem to fall under two main heads: (1) popular dislike or distrust of the reformers themselves; (2) popular resentment at some of the reform policies.

Sydney Brooks explains the first point when he writes: " The reformers were unable to conquer that social distrust of 'gentlemen' which one encounters so often and so unexpectedly in American, and especially in city politics. The average New Yorker dislikes to be governed by men of refinement, independent means, superior position. At a time of strong moral excitement he may vote for them; but he quickly wearies of their aloofness, exaggerates their detachment from the 'plain people,' and comes in the end to resent their pretense and activity as a sort of affront to democracy." [3]

Yet more was involved than dislike of " gentlemen " and " highbrows." There was also a widespread popular distrust of the ethics and motives of the wealthy bankers and business men who were so prominent in the Fusion movement. And on that score, no one has hit the nail on the head better than " Mr. Dooley," the literary creation of the celebrated Chicago humorist, Finley Peter Dunne.

Mr. Dooley undoubtedly voiced the latent feeling of the metropolitan masses when he said, shortly after the Lexow Investigation:

"This here wave iv rayform, Jawn, mind ye, that's sweepin' over th' counthry, mind ye, now, Jawn, is raisin' th' divvle, I see be the pa-apers. I've seen waves iv rayform befure now, Jawn. Whin th' people iv this counthry gets wurruked up, there's no stoppin' thim. They'll not dhraw breath until ivery man that tuk a dollar iv a bribe is sint down th' r-road. Thim that takes two dollars goes on th' comity iv the wave iv rayform. . ."

"'Jawn,' said Mr. Dooley.

"'Yes,' responded Mr. McKenna.

"'Niver steal a dure-mat,' said Mr. Dooley. 'If ye do, ye'll be invistigated, hanged, an' maybe rayformed. Steal a bank, me boy, steal a bank.'" [4]

Yet neither Mr. Brooks nor Mr. Dooley have given us the full explanation. Such popular dislike and distrust, while widespread and deep-seated, were generalized emotions. They could not, of themselves, have precipitated the popular revulsion of 1897.

The chief cause of that revulsion was that the people bitterly resented "strict enforcement" of laws against Sunday liquor-selling and gambling which was the policy of the Strong administration.

True, the reform officials merely applied existing statutes. But those statutes had been passed by up-State legislators, and had never before been consistently enforced in the metropolis. The metropolitan masses had never approved of this legislation, which ran counter to their ideas and habits. So, when the reformers began to put "teeth" into the laws, the New York public tossed its head like a mettlesome horse which first feels the curb, took the bit in its teeth, ran away, and tossed the driver into the ditch.

Today, thanks to our nation-wide Prohibition controversy,

we are learning about matters like *law* versus *custom*, and enforcement versus public opinion. In the nineties, such things were relatively new and localized. Yet the basic issue was the same; and its political consequences, wherever law and custom collided were practically identical. Those early New York reformers were read a lesson which many of their spiritual successors do not yet seem to have grasped: that laws repressing social habits cannot be imposed upon self-governing communities without arousing popular discontent which, in turn, produces not only political revolt but also public tolerance of wholesale graft and other corrupt practices.

As for those persons who, knowing all this, nevertheless persist in such policies; they simply abet that most paradoxical of political combinations: *The Alliance of the Puritan and the Grafter*.

That telling phrase was coined by Alfred Hodder, one of the few reformers of the nineties who possessed both sympathetic insight and a saving sense of humor. Hodder wittily exposed this "alliance," by which the Puritan got the applause, the grafter got the graft — and the public paid.[5]

Developing Hodder's idea, Sydney Brooks makes some reflections on American politics, so shrewd and penetrating that they may be read with profit by us of today:

"The ordinary American is, in politics, both a sentimentalist and a coward. He believes (or likes to pretend he believes) that legislation can cure anything. So when a zealot arises who demands that henceforth there shall be no Sunday drinking in New York City, no gambling, and no prostitution, he finds the State Legislature at Albany more than ready to meet him half-way. Pandering to the moral sentiment of the community is one of the daily necessities (or pastimes) of American political life.

"The consequence is that the most impossible laws find their way on to the statute-book. . . We are dealing, remember, with a cosmopolitan, feverish, pleasure-loving population, pagan in its tastes, its habits, its opinions; imbued with a mercenary view of politics; and always in more or less open revolt against the laws by which the State Legislature (largely elected and controlled by rural votes and notions) attempts to regulate its behavior. It is a population that takes instinctively to the ideal of: *A free-and-easy life in a free-and-easy town.*

"This is an ideal with which Tammany whole-heartedly sympathizes; and one which, for a price, it will undertake to translate into fact. New Yorkers, arguing that the fault is not so much in themselves as in the Puritanical lawmakers at Albany, will agree that it is better that the purveyors of 'pleasure' should pay blackmail to the police than that there should be no 'pleasure' at all. It is just here, of course, that they end by finding themselves in conflict with the stringent code and severer logic of the reformers — who do not remember that, though Americans respect law, they do not always respect laws. . .

"The law being on the statute-book, however, something must be done about it. To repeal it is hopeless; because no legislator will dare to have it said that he favors gambling or Sunday drinking or vice of any kind.

"Hence follow, especially among reformers, the most extraordinary devices for getting out of the pit of their own digging. Some will rigidly enforce the law in its minutest stringency, and so convulse the city. Others are for what they call 'liberal enforcement'; that is to say, they will punish serious and flagrant violations, and leave the rest alone.

"But this is a policy which creates as much ill-feeling and repulsion as the severer and more logical plan, and considerably more uncertainty.

"The reformers were unable to avoid the dilemma. The Mayor favored 'liberality' on the arguable ground that the extreme of the law is always the extreme of injustice. The District Attorney was first for altering the law (which proved impossible) and then for carrying it out to the letter — which proved more impossible. In the end, between the two of them, the saloon-keepers, the Germans, the Irish, the extreme temperance party, and the average citizen were about equally alienated.

"The Tammany method is, after all, the most consistent and the easiest. To the saloon-keeper and other purveyors of pleasure, Tammany, through the mouths of its police officers, simply says: 'Pay me so much per month, and I will protect you.'

"In the result, everybody is contented. The law remains on the statute-book, a glowing testimony to the 'morality' of New York; it is not enforced, so nobody feels its inconvenience; and Tammany grows rich out of the proceeds.

"A league with vice? Yes; but a league that the idealism and hypocrisy of American politics have combined to make all but inevitable." [6]

What undoubtedly angered New Yorkers most was the enforcement of the Sunday liquor law. If the moral reformers who urged Mayor Strong strictly to prohibit Sunday liquor-selling had only read the history of their own town, they might have realized the trouble they were laying up for their administration. New York had kicked over the

traces before on the liquor issue. Away back in 1854, when
up-State New York was swept by a temperance wave, the
Legislature had passed a "Dry Law" of a very arid
character.

Instantly, the metropolis was up in arms against "hayseed
tyranny." Many persons were seriously alarmed at the outlook. "The cautious laid up supplies against the dry day.
Those who boasted not cellars threatened to flee the State
before July 4th, 1855, when the new statute, entitled: 'An
Act for the Prevention of Intemperance, Pauperism, and
Crime,' was to go into effect. The Fourth of July had been
chosen because it marked, in the language of the Drys, a new
birth of freedom — freedom from the Demon Rum." [7]

In this hectic hour a clever politician stepped forward to
calm popular fears. He was Fernando Wood, the new
Mayor. In a series of proclamations he made it clear that
New York City would never be "dry" so long as he was
Mayor.

Result: Fernando Wood was hailed as a deliverer; and
on this wave of popularity he rode securely into his grafting
régime.

One of the most unfortunate results of repressive liquor
legislation was that it made the foreign-born citizens vote
on this one burning question, to the exclusion of all other
issues.

The Germans, for instance, were a thrifty, self-respecting,
law-abiding folk, who under normal circumstances would
have ranged themselves on the side of civic betterment and
political reform.

But the moral reformers would not have it so. In the
late sixties, the Legislature passed an Excise Law forbidding
the Sunday sale of intoxicating drinks. This deprived the

Germans of their chief pleasure — a Sunday outing at a beer-garden, which the Legislature (legally) abolished with a stroke of the pen.

The irate Teutons, however, declined to submit and bitterly opposed the new Law. Determined to have their Sunday beer they first tried to gain their end legally by having the statute declared unconstitutional.

The Germans failed in their legal endeavors. The Excise Law was not only declared constitutional; it was further sharpened. By the nineties, liquor-selling on Sunday, and gaming at all times, were legally prohibited in New York City, under heavy penalties.

But — gambling-joints continued to run by the hundreds, while the Germans still had their Sunday beer!

Then Mayor Strong appointed Theodore Roosevelt Police Commissioner. " Roosevelt was young, ambitious, and filled with a large sense of his own righteousness. He enforced the Sunday closing law vigorously, and the result was that he became a terror to pinochle players in the back rooms of saloons. The small joys began to disappear from daily life, and their place was taken by that abstract ghost, *The Law*, which, try as hard as they could, people who liked sex, beer, and cards could neither see, taste, nor touch." [8]

The moralists were delighted, but many other persons voiced different opinions. So loud grew the chorus of discontent that the Democrats made *A Liberal Sunday* and *Personal Liberty* the chief planks in their platform during the campaign next year (1895).

On the other hand, the Republicans, angling for the rural vote, prophesied *Free Whiskey and No Sunday*, if the Democrats won. The up-State voters apparently feared this, for they elected a Republican Governor and a legislative majority.

Below the Bronx, however, things went just the other way. New Yorkers had no chance to elect a new Mayor that year. But there were the County offices to vote for; and the metropolitan masses, swarming to the polls, voted heavily for Tammany. The turn of the tide was plain.

The unexpected complications which arise from legislation attempting to regulate social habits are strikingly exemplified by the so-called *Raines Law.*

Senator Raines, an ardent " Dry," thought he was hitting the saloon hard when he framed his famous Bill providing that hotels only could serve liquor on Sunday. It was on Sunday that the saloons were busiest; for then, men had both time to kill and money to spend. Senator Raines and the moral reformers intended to stop this.

The Senator fondly believed that he had dealt a body-blow to the Demon Rum. But what actually happened was that every saloon leased the floor above, and became a " hotel." To pay the extra rent, the rooms were let to transients — and no questions asked. The net result of the Raines Law, therefore, was that the saloons continued to do business (on a more immoral basis), while prostitution was greatly extended, and opportunities for casual fornication were made cheaper and easier than ever before.

Commercialized vice was, in the nineties, as thorny a problem as that of liquor; and legislative efforts to stamp it out were equally futile.

In order to understand the reason for this, we must try to grasp the spirit of the times. And that is not easy; because, while New York's attitude toward liquor has not altered, its attitude toward prostitution has greatly changed.

Yet the basic reason for this change is, not prohibitory laws, but the processes of social evolution.

Today, factors like the economic emancipation of woman and what has been wittily termed *The Amateur Competition* have so diminished the demand for public prostitutes that commercialized vice is no longer a major problem. As we know, public opinion in New York now favors (or, at least, acquiesces in) laws against street-walkers and disorderly houses; whereas it is emphatically not behind the liquor laws.

In the nineties, tradition deemed " the red lights " as inevitable as saloons. Most men then believed that the segregation of vice in a " red-light district " was the only feasible method of control.

Richard Croker undoubtedly voiced the majority opinion of his day in a newspaper interview regarding Dr. Parkhurst's activities. When asked what he thought about the celebrated preacher's crusade against vice, Croker answered slowly:

" I have never said anything against Dr. Parkhurst, and I have a good deal of respect for any man who tries to do what he thinks is right. His methods are simply a matter of opinion. Personally, I don't believe they are wise.

" Of course, he knows, and everybody else knows, that no man or set of men can eradicate the social evil. All that anybody can do is to prevent it from annoying and contaminating respectable people. I don't believe Dr. Parkhurst's methods can accomplish that object. The indiscriminate closing of all places, regardless of their location, simply spreads the evil all over the city. It does not restrict it. It expands it." [9]

Here, as usual, Croker was a realist. He knew that Little Old New York was a free-and-easy metropolis, bent on its time-honored pleasures. A popular song of those days ended with the refrain: *I want what I want when I want it!* That exactly voiced the spirit of the Gay Nineties — and of the early Twentieth Century as well. The reformers had tried to close up things that the metropolis wanted left "wide-open." And New Yorkers showed what they thought of those tactics at the very first opportunity.

The Strong administration, a model of honesty and efficiency, might under other circumstances have won enthusiastic popular support. But it had committed the cardinal blunder against which "Old Mike" had warned Big John Kennedy: It had "got between the people and its beer!"

CHAPTER XVII

" THE RETURN FROM ELBA "

THREE years was the term of Richard Croker's voluntary exile, from the time he formally resigned his strategic Chairmanship in the spring of 1894 until his dramatic return from England in September 1897, on the eve of the most momentous Mayoralty campaign New York City had ever known.

Three years is a long time, politically. It was doubly long in Croker's case. For the Boss-ship of Tammany Hall is such a personal affair that absentee rule demands great dexterity. Nothing, indeed, so attests Croker's political genius as the way in which he kept his hand on the machine from overseas.

During his exile, Croker metamorphosed himself into an English sportsman. Besides a town house in London, he had an establishment near his racing-stables at Newmarket and a country seat at Wantage, Berkshire. Thither he went to escape from worry and to indulge his sporting fancies. Before long, Croker knew everybody worth while in the neighborhood, and seemed perfectly at ease with the racing nobility.

Wantage was much like the country seat of any well-to-do English gentleman. The house itself was surrounded by a moat, and there were extensive grounds. In his drawing-room, Croker had an electric piano. This was connected

MR. CROKER AT THE RACES

with his bed chamber, so that he could play it if he wished at any hour of the day or night. A fine billiard room with tables by Roberts intrigued that great player to visit the great politician.[1]

Croker insisted upon driving a good horse, which meant to him a fast trotter. Promising foals and race-horses stood in his stables, with celebrated trainers in charge.

Here, Croker was like a boy out of school. One foal he himself brought up by hand. He would talk by the hour to *Dobbins*, his favorite race-horse, as if he really believed the splendid stallion understood. Two bulldogs: *Rodney Stone* (world's champion) and *Bromley Crib*, were especial favorites. But perhaps Croker's greatest fun was feeding the pigs. These he had named after New York politicians whom he knew to be crooked and greedy.

All this time, the Boss was awaiting the psychological moment to return to the political fray. Secret agents at home served him well, and their confidential reports kept him in close touch with all that happened.

And much did happen during those three years: notably, one event which radically altered the entire metropolitan situation. The Legislature had passed the "Greater New York" bill, enlarging the city to its present size. Instead of merely Manhattan and the Bronx, New York was thenceforth to include the Boroughs of Kings (Brooklyn), Queens, and Richmond (Staten Island). By a stroke of the legislative pen, New York was thus trebled in size and nearly doubled in population. Here, indeed, was a sweeping transformation, which might have incalculable consequences.

The Greater New York Charter was the work of political reformers, aided by the Republicans. Both had their special ends in view. The reformers wanted to add the great middle-class residential districts of Brooklyn to the metropolis, since these might be expected to balance Manhattan's tenement vote. Furthermore, in order to weaken the appeal of party regularity, the Bill provided that Mayoralty elections should fall in " off-years "; i.e., years when national elections for President or Congress did not take place. So the first municipal election under the new charter was slated for 1897; thereby (incidentally) giving the Strong administration an additional year in office.

The Republicans acquiesced in all this because Brooklyn had normally been Republican, while Queens and Richmond (then semi-rural) were even more strongly of that political faith. Since the Republican vote of Manhattan and the Bronx already averaged better than 35%, these reënforcements might turn the trick and make " Greater New York " a Republican metropolis. Thus reasoned Platt and his lieutenants. And, by the same token, Tammany looked askance at consolidation. But Platt had the votes at Albany, so the new charter went through.

An important change in the local Democratic situation should also be noted. Tammany always had been (and, for that matter, still is) a distinctively Manhattan organization. Even the Bronx Democracy, while usually amenable to orders from the Wigwam, was not technically part of Tammany Hall.

The extension of the city's borders introduced a new factor in the shape of a powerful, high-spirited Brooklyn organization, known as the " Kings' County Democracy." [2] A well-drilled machine led by a local Boss of real ability, the Kings' County Democracy was not disposed to take orders from any one, and would surely demand its say in all metropolitan decisions.

The leader of the Brooklyn Democracy, Hugh McLaughlin, was a Boss of the old breed. Born and reared in the hard school of poverty, McLaughlin, like Croker, had forged to the front by innate forcefulness and ability. Moreover, McLaughlin had ruled his bailiwick longer than Croker had Tammany; for he had dominated Democratic politics " across the river " since the close of the Civil War. The independent rôle played by Hugh McLaughlin and the Kings' County Democracy must henceforth be remembered as a constant factor in all Croker's political calculations.

While Croker was mulling over these matters, another political complication arose, different in character but even greater in scope. This was the rise of Bryanism. The radical tide which had been rapidly rising in the West overwhelmed the Democratic National Convention of 1896, and committed the party to the Free Silver heresy embodied in the famous slogan: 16 *to* 1!

The effect was catastrophic. The Democracy of the Eastern States was shattered. The conservative right-wing of the party bolted and put a special " Gold Democrat " ticket in the field. Many Democrats who did not formally bolt, either secretly knifed Bryan at the polls or exhibited a mere perfunctory regularity.

Among these latter were David B. Hill, the New York State Boss, and the leaders of Tammany Hall. Hill and Tammany had fought Bryan fiercely on the Convention floor. When " The Peerless One " had swept the Convention off its feet with his flaming oratory about the Crown of Thorns and Cross of Gold, a reporter asked Hill if he were still a Democrat. To which, the up-State Boss replied: " I am a Democrat still — *very still!* "

And so was Tammany; the result being that William

McKinley, the Republican candidate, carried New York City to the tune of 20,000 votes.

In the hurly-burly of the first Bryan campaign, Richard Croker was nowhere to be found. He had no desire to be mixed up in such a mess; so he remained abroad practically all that year, and refused to talk about anything but horses.

But from his English estate, Croker was watching every move of the Strong administration. Cannily he noted each mistake made by the reformers, and the resulting chorus of popular discontent over strict enforcement of the anti-gambling and liquor laws. To a close friend he remarked: "Roosevelt is all there is to the Strong administration, and Roosevelt will make it or break it." [3]

By the spring of 1897, Croker had about made up his mind that the time was ripe for his return to political life. He sensed the trend against the reformers and knew that if he led Tammany to victory in the coming Mayoralty campaign, it would be the greatest triumph in his career. This very point was being urged upon him by his close supporters. By early summer (1897) several of his old friends, such as William C. Whitney and Hugh J. Grant, came to England to argue with him. For a while, Croker asserted that he was definitely out of politics, but presently he told his intimates in confidence that he would return to New York by Fall.

On September 7, 1897, the Boss landed in Manhattan. Next day a New York newspaper thus describes what his admirers afterwards termed: *The Return from Elba.*

"Richard Croker, perceptibly grayer of hair and beard, and with a deep tan on his cheeks, stood in the bow of the S.S. *New York* as she steamed slowly up the bay yesterday morning. He was dressed in a plain blue serge suit, a blue

cravat was snugly tied at his low collar, a white Alpine hat
was crushed down over his grizzled hair, and he leaned on
a cane.

"His eyes were keen and lively. From under the shaggy
brows he shot furtive glances at the jagged profile of the
great city ahead, the outline of which was just beginning to
be defined as the morning mist drifted away. Those who
gazed at the Tammany chief knew that his brain was busy,
and the hard, set expression of the face was some index of
the thought.

"Mr. Croker's homecoming is fraught with great concern
to Tammany Hall. None of the Braves ventured down the
bay to meet him, and there was no noisy demonstration of
welcome. This was in accordance with Mr. Croker's wish.
He wanted to come back quietly and unobtrusively. But it
is safe to say that there is not a member of Tammany Hall
(not to mention those outside the organization) who has
not asked himself: 'What is Croker going to do?'"[4]

The returned Boss was faced with a very complicated
situation, especially within his own party. He knew that
only by clever tactics, combined with an iron will, could he
master the difficulties which beset his path.

Croker's return made a considerable stir, and all sorts of
rumors were afloat. But to all inquiries Croker maintained
his canny silence, intimating that he was still "out of politics" and adopting the air of a retired statesman. In fact,
after conferences with some intimate friends, he left the city
for his stock-farm at Richfield Springs, and did not return
to town until the end of September.

Croker knew that before the Mayoralty campaign got
fairly under way, he must be once more the undisputed master of Tammany Hall. This would not be easy; because,

during his long absence, the organization had begun to get out of hand. Three years off the pay-roll had left the tiger hungry — and hungry tigers are proverbially hard to handle. The ranks were a-grumble with sullen discontent, while the officers' corps was mutinous. All in all, it was a pretty ticklish situation.

Tammany's nominal head was John C. Sheehan, installed by Croker as his deputy. Sheehan was not a New Yorker. He was a Buffalo politician who had moved to the metropolis some years before. Though his rise in Tammany had been rapid, Sheehan lacked those local roots which anchor the average district leader in the loyal affections of his " home ward." That, however, was probably the main reason why Croker had made Sheehan his deputy. With no sure base save Croker's favor, Sheehan had seemed an ideal chair-warmer, to be unseated at the Boss's good will and pleasure. Furthermore, Sheehan was weak and vain — added reasons for his " promotion."

Yet Croker had made one miscalculation. Being vain, Sheehan loved even the shadow of power which brought him public prominence and political lip-service; being weak, he might be cajoled by others, stronger than he, who aspired to the half-vacant throne. For the headship of Tammany, remember, is not an appointment, but a growth; and a stern survival of the fittest is forever at work adjusting authority to reality.

So, during Sheehan's vice-royalty, ambitious district leaders had dreamed dreams — and had unobtrusively prepared against future eventualities. Strongest among these embryo pretenders to the seat of power stood the burly form of " Big Tim " Sullivan, liege-lord of the lower East Side, who for years had been quietly cementing alliances with neighboring district leaders and was now (next to Croker) the most powerful personage in the Tammany organization.

Big Tim's agents had not failed to whisper in Sheehan's ear that the days of his vice-royalty were numbered, now that Croker was returning; and they went on to ask pointedly how he liked the prospect. And Sheehan had shown by his attitude that he did not like it at all.

We have already said that Croker's secret agents served him well. So we may be sure that all these doings were known to Croker in his exile. Yet mere knowledge did not solve the problem; and it was presumably this which, during the homeward voyage, made the Boss pace the deck, aloof and silent, during the long watches of the night.

Once landed, Croker did not waste a moment. His disinterested pose concealed a fierce activity that knew no rest. Those quiet conferences with trusted intimates were the first steps in a subterranean campaign during which every man in Tammany Hall was weighed and evaluated. The balance-sheet was none too favorable. A majority of the district leaders were clearly disaffected; Big Tim Sullivan was the redoubtable chief of the threatened mutiny; and Sheehan would not tamely resign.

But numbers are not everything. The hostile coalition was still poorly cemented. Sheehan was a poor crutch for Big Tim to lean upon. And the Boss was a host in himself.

So one fine autumn afternoon, Croker set out for Tammany Hall. A meeting of the Executive Committee had been called and word had been passed that a " showdown " was at hand. Wherefore, the Wigwam was crowded with leaders and followers, feverishly waiting. What would transpire?

Just five minutes before four o'clock (the appointed hour)

the familiar thickset figure with the scrubby beard and the steel-trap jaw walked jauntily up the steps of the Hall, accompanied by James J. Martin, the Committee chairman. The Boss was dressed in the height of fashion: black frock suit, satin cravat, and high silk hat with a broad black band, English style.

A prominent journalist who was present on that memorable occasion gives us this vivid account of the scene that followed:

" The spirit of revolt was rife in Tammany. Twenty-one of the thirty-five district leaders, each as powerful in his own local sphere as the Tammany Boss had been in the general sense, were arrayed against him.

" His reappearance at Tammany Hall was as dramatic a spectacle as I have ever seen. He walked through a long lane of scowling and unfriendly leaders and their henchmen, but seemingly paid no attention to their presence or their mood. A long black cigar clenched tightly in his teeth, his head erect, his broad square shoulders thrown well back, his face absolutely expressionless, his step elastic, and his whole personality suggesting indifference, he threaded his way through the hostile crowd in the public room and passed into the council chamber. Thence he sent a peremptory order to all the district leaders to come to him. Following the blind, unreasoning instinct of obedience, which is the law of organization discipline, they came.

" The door of the council room was closed. Croker, still puffing at his cigar, talked to the district leaders for ten minutes, calmly and without apparent personal interest. He spoke without emotion, and addressed himself directly to the men lined up in front of him. He heard that some of the leaders had complaints to make. What were those complaints? None? Well! He just wanted to say that he was tired of hearing that certain leaders were dissatisfied.

" ' Tim Sullivan, are *you* dissatisfied? ' Croker glanced keenly at the man as he shot the inquiry; gruff, direct, with a challenge in it to the most powerful individual of them all. Sullivan declared he was not dissatisfied.

" ' Very well, then,' calmly continued Croker, ' there is no dissatisfaction. Now I want you men to go back to your districts and get to work. If you don't, I'll put men in your places who will work. We have a show to carry New York this time, and if you go about it right, we'll do it. But I don't want to hear any more growling. We'll meet here next Tuesday to perfect plans for the campaign.'

" Then Croker came out into the general committee room, where a portrait of John Kelly, his predecessor and mentor, hangs in the place of honor. Croker's appearance was the signal for such an exhibition of abject servility as I have never witnessed at a political assemblage. Men who had been loudest in their denunciation of him were the most demonstrative in their sycophantic assurances of loyalty.

" Calm, imperturbable, Croker stood in the centre of the crowd and listened to their protestations of friendship and obedience, even though he knew, as he told me, that they were insincere." [5]

The embryo mutiny had been squelched. Sheehan was politely yet firmly deposed; Big Tim went back to the Bowery to get busy and obey orders; and " The Boys " went to work with a cheer.

The crisis was over, and the Boss was boss, indeed, once more.

CHAPTER XVIII

" TO HELL WITH REFORM! "

IN THE midst of a red-hot campaign speech, Asa Bird Gardiner, Tammany candidate for District Attorney, shouted: " To Hell with Reform! " And the crowd went wild!

That impromptu phrase at once became a campaign slogan which probably netted Tammany thousands of votes among the metropolitan masses, angered by Roosevelt's strict enforcement of the liquor laws. For, in their anger, the masses forgot all the good that the Strong administration had accomplished.

The Mayoralty contest of 1897 was a sizzling affair. And well it might be; for the stakes were enormous. The new charter had made the Mayor of Greater New York its almost absolute master, with official prerogatives hitherto unknown. Arbiter of the city's destiny over a four-year term, and with a wealth of patronage embracing 60,000 municipal jobs, the first Mayor of the enlarged metropolis would possess a power for good or for ill which was well-nigh incalculable.

No less than four candidates were in the race for this superlative civic prize. First in the field was the non-partisan ticket, sponsored by the Citizens' Union and other reform bodies, and headed by Seth Low. In the eyes of his supporters, Mr. Low was the ideal candidate; for he was a man of high character, broad intellect, and wide political experience. He was then President of Columbia University, and had made an excellent Mayor of Brooklyn some years before. A broad-gauge Republican, Low might count on drawing the liberal elements in both parties who were ready to ignore " regularity " in the common cause of non-partisan civic reform. As a matter of fact, many prominent Democrats endorsed Low's candidacy; among them, Edward M. Shepard, who, four years later, was to be the Tammany nominee.

Next in order was the Tammany ticket, headed by Judge Robert C. Van Wyck. The Tammany candidate could in no way compare with Seth Low. A rather obscure Judge, with an undistinguished record, Van Wyck was plainly a " machine man " who, if elected, would do as he was told by his political superiors. Tammany was frankly out to win the greatest prize municipal politics had ever offered; and anybody who blinked at that fact was either a human ostrich or a fool.

The third ticket in the field was that of the so-called " Jefferson Democracy," the character of which can be judged by its Mayoralty candidate, Henry George. It was, in fact, a coalition of radical elements; chief among them being the rump of George's Laborites who had made such a stir in the Hewitt campaign of 1886, together with extreme Bryan Democrats seeking revenge for Tammany's knifing of their leader in the Presidential contest the year before. The Jefferson Democracy was thus an anti-Tammany organization, since most of Henry George's support would come from sources normally Democratic.

The tantalizing riddle in the campaign's early days was the attitude of the Republican machine. Would it endorse

Low as it had endorsed Strong, or would it nominate a ticket of its own and thereby weaken the reform forces?

Pressure was put on Platt by influential Republicans to make him endorse Low. But those efforts were vain, for the " Easy Boss " was in a very adamantine mood. One non-partisan administration was enough for him. If this pestiferous novelty got to be a habit, where would all " practical " politicians end? " Platt himself afterward admitted that ' for the doctrine of non-partisanship in local elections ' he had ' the sincerest and profoundest contempt,' and that ' the success of such an attempt would have a demoralizing effect on party organization.' " [1] And Edward Lauterbach, one of Platt's trusted lieutenants, frankly confessed that " he and his Republican associates would rather see a Tammany man elected Mayor than have a non-partisan succeed in getting office." [2]

There can be no reasonable doubt that Platt and Croker had made a definite " deal." And its first result was the nomination of a full Republican ticket, headed by General Benjamin F. Tracy, who was notoriously Platt's " man."

The political set-up was thus described by Dr. Albert Shaw, a noted authority on municipal government and editor of a leading review:

" The mayoralty of New York, under the new charter, is a dictatorship — one of the three or four most important autocracies in the world. . .

" Everybody in New York except persons of the most limited intelligence have been made fully aware that their choice of despot for the next four years must be made from a list of four men, viz.: Seth Low, Henry George, Richard Croker (by proxy), and Thomas C. Platt (by proxy). . .

" The real fight of the Republican machine is against Low,

who is himself a Republican and whose supporters are very largely drawn from that party. The fight of the Henry George forces is directed against Tammany. As election day approaches, it becomes clear that the Republican and Democratic machines are, comparatively speaking, in sympathy with each other; and that, on the other hand, the Seth Low and the Henry George movements stand upon common ground in their vigorous opposition to the government of non-resident Bosses. For it is to be remembered that whereas Mr. Croker lives in England, Mr. Platt lives and votes in the town of Owego, Tioga County." [3]

Croker's foreign residence and associates were stock arguments of his opponents, and the changes were rung upon this issue with a virulence far removed from the polite sarcasm of the dignified editor of *The Review of Reviews*. Croker was branded as having hob-nobbed on English race-tracks with "British snobs" — including, of course, the Prince of Wales. As one stump-orator elegantly phrased it: "He spends his time flocking with the lecherous sons of a rotten aristocracy." [4]

Henry George devoted most of his efforts to bitter attacks on Croker, saying that, if elected Mayor, he would cause a searching investigation into Croker's suddenly acquired wealth; and Mr. George went on to intimate that such an investigation would cause the Tammany Boss to end his career, like his predecessor, Tweed, with a trip to the penitentiary. The fiery Single-Taxer closed with those words: "The best thing Croker can do, if I am elected, is to take the first ship for England and join the Prince of Wales and his other snob friends."

To this, Croker answered next day: "I feel complimented that they (Henry George et als.) have made me their platform. It shows how utterly lacking they are in issues. If Mr. George is such a great lover of justice as he pretends to be, the Grand Jury room is open to him now, just the same as it would be if he were Mayor." [5] In other words, it looked like an old-fashioned, mud-slinging campaign.

When the contest was at its height, Henry George suddenly dropped dead of apoplexy. His son, Henry George, Jr., was promptly nominated in his stead. But the son was not the father, and the " Jefferson " movement quickly faded into the background. On election day it polled only 20,000 votes, and there is good reason to believe that thousands of men who had intended voting for the famous Single-Taxer switched back to their normal allegiance and voted Democratic as usual.

Meanwhile, Tammany was carrying on in the spirit of Gardiner's slogan: *To Hell with Reform!* The main line of attack was voiced by one of Tammany's spokesmen, who exclaimed: " Tammany serves notice tonight on the ignorant and incompetent administration which now governs this city that it has started a relentless warfare against the ' reform ' cabal, which will not end till that cabal is exterminated, root and branch, and New York City is redeemed from its domination. This ignorant set has made New York ridiculous in the eyes of the world, presenting the picture of Hypocrisy arm-in-arm with the ghost of assumed Virtue; watching Hope die in the arms of official Incompetence." [6]

When the campaign got fairly under way and the Tammany orators warmed up, their vitriolic flights knew no bounds. The reformers were denounced as " whited sepulchres " and " political howling dervishes " — not to mention such stock epithets as " snobs," " silk-stockings," and so forth.

The campaign was hard-fought and bitter. It was also

highly picturesque. That was the era of torchlight parades with gaily-uniformed marching-clubs, blaring bands, and rolling, booming drum-corps.

The most unusual spectacle of the campaign was undoubtedly "The Chicago Invasion." Carter Harrison, Mayor of Chicago and Boss of Cook County, was a close friend of Croker's, and had volunteered to do his bit in "whooping it up" for Tammany. A few days before election, the Chicago Boss and a delegation several hundred strong arrived in New York by special train, and that evening Tammany staged a big show to bid its allies welcome.

It was a grand occasion. By nightfall, 14th Street was jammed with a surging crowd, from Third Avenue to Union Square. Fireworks, three brass bands, and parading Tammany delegations enthused the crowd for hours. Then the embattled Cook County Democrats, headed by their own band and a gigantic drum-major, marched down 14th Street and into Tammany Hall. They were in gala attire: black frock coats, tall silk hats, and white gloves. The climax of the evening came when Carter Harrison and Richard Croker appeared arm-in-arm, and the big hall, packed to capacity, rang with frantic cheers.

The campaign drew to its close in a fever of excitement and a glare of red-fire. The contestants did their utmost amid torrents of oratory. Every voter in Greater New York was appealed to in every conceivable way, and was insistently urged to "do his duty" at the polls.

From the reform standpoint, the most disquieting factor was the suspected understanding between the Democratic and Republican machines. The newspapers devoted columns of space to "exposures" of the "deal" between Platt and Croker. Yet the indignation aroused by these exposures among liberal-minded men in both parties promised many votes for Seth Low. The reform elements were all solidly behind the non-partisan ticket and could be relied upon to work in harmony. The election would be a fair test of a metropolitan sentiment. The outcome was in the hands of the voters.

Election day came: the first Mayoralty contest of Greater New York. All over the metropolis, from Manhattan's congested East Side to quiet hamlets on the outskirts of Queens and Staten Island villages, the citizens flocked to the polls. Voting was heavy but orderly, and the day passed immemorably brawlless.

When the polls closed at nightfall, the general impression was that the outcome was uncertain. Van Wyck had obviously swept Manhattan, but Seth Low had run strongly in the other Boroughs. The reformers had good grounds for hope.

The first returns indicated a close race. Then, as the evening wore on, tremendous majorities came in from the Tammany strongholds. Van Wyck was in the lead! Before ten o'clock it was practically certain that he had won, and the rest of the Tammany ticket as well.

Then "Little Old New York" broke loose. The residential districts of Brooklyn might be dark and silent, but Manhattan gave itself over to exuberant rejoicings such as the metropolis had rarely seen. From the Bowery to 42nd Street, the town was in an uproar. Union Square, Madison Square, Herald Square, Broadway, and Sixth Avenue were jammed with milling, jostling throngs, frenziedly acclaiming Tammany's victory.

The din was tremendous. Staid-looking citizens, casting dignity to the winds, capered like school-boys, blew hoarse

CROKER'S TAMMANY HALL

blasts upon tin horns, or whirled ear-splitting rattles. Fireworks in Madison Square and the explosion of bombs in mid-
air vied with the tumult below.

From ten o'clock until long past midnight, the jubilation
went on. Every hotel, theatre, saloon, and dance-hall was
crowded to suffocation, and each election bulletin provoked
a fresh roar. Street-fakirs were everywhere selling their
miniature roosters, brooms, and tigers; *papier maché* tigers,
these, eight or nine inches long, which clung garishly to one's
frock or coat.

Around hotel bars, crowded five and six deep, total
strangers clapped each other on the back, and between drinks
vociferated hilariously: " We didn't do a thing to Reform,
did we? "

Asa Bird Gardiner's slogan was, in fact, the keynote of
the celebration. Impromptu parades started, with hastily
scrawled placards reading: *To Hell with Reform!* And
through the swarming crowds burst phalanxes of young men
in snake-dance formation, chanting endlessly the refrain:
" Well! Well! Well! Reform has gone to Hell! "

Borne on the foaming crest of this wave of popular re-
joicing, Tammany radiated triumph. In one of the spacious
parlors of the Murray Hill Hotel, Richard Croker, surrounded by jubilant admirers, received the election returns.
When asked by a reporter for a statement, the Boss glanced
up from a bulletin he was scanning and said laconically: " I
told you three years ago that when reformers got into office,
they tried to stand so straight that they fell over backward! "

As soon as Van Wyck's election was seen to be assured,
Croker proceeded to Tammany Hall. Ascending the rear
stairway, the Boss emerged quietly from the door at the back
of the stage and paused to survey the scene.

The vast, barnlike auditorium, draped with bunting, was a blue haze of tobacco smoke and shouting, stamping men. As the Boss paused in the doorway, Thomas F. Grady, Tammany's star orator, was in full swing. " If Mr. Croker —" shouted Grady, and then stopped, his voice drowned by applause. " If Mr. Croker," continued the orator, " returned from Europe to direct our politics, he made a good job of it —" (A voice: " You bet he did! ") Grady got no further, for at this moment the crowd glimpsed Croker as he walked slowly onto the stage.

Then pandemonium broke forth. Shouts, yells, cheer upon cheer, rent the smoke-laden air. Minute after minute, the ovation kept up, while the Boss, smiling and nodding curt acknowledgments, stood quietly and received the frenzied homage of his followers.

It was unquestionably the greatest moment of his career. He had led Tammany to supreme triumph. He had ensured the Tiger four years of unlimited power over the metropolis. Richard Croker was indeed Master of Manhattan.

CHAPTER XIX

THE MASTER OF MANHATTAN

THE DAY following Tammany's triumph, Mayor-elect Van Wyck stated: " I will be frank and plain as to the men I shall call to office. *Put None but Democrats on Guard!* shall be the motto of my administration."

Here was fair warning. Non-partisan reform was in the discard. Greater New York would begin its civic life under an out-and-out Tammany administration. That was what the voters had apparently wanted. And that was what they would surely get.

Furthermore, they would get government of, by, and for Richard Croker. No well-informed citizen could doubt it. Van Wyck was obviously Croker's " man." The Boss had plucked him from obscurity and had seated him in the Mayor's enlarged chair. Van Wyck was " machine-made." He would do as he was told.

Of this, Croker soon gave a convincing demonstration. Having refreshed himself from his campaign labors by a brief pleasure jaunt in the South, Croker took up his next task — the division of the spoils. In the Greater New York of tomorrow, the wealth of patronage would be enormous. And it must all be duly apportioned before the Van Wyck administration took office on New Year's Day. Of course, the charter provided that appointments should be made by the Mayor himself. But the law permitted this civic autocrat to take advice. And Mr. Croker now showed the public who Van Wyck's adviser would be.

Shortly after Thanksgiving, the Boss, with " his " Mayor, went to Lakewood, New Jersey, and established headquarters at the principal hotel. There, all who hoped for office must come to do obeisance to the Boss. And thither they promptly came. Every train for Lakewood was filled with politicians, great and small, and the big hotel was soon crowded with a bustling, expectant throng.

The New York newspapers called Lakewood " Croker's Court." And well they might; for the triumphant Boss gave himself the airs of a royal sovereign. His every act seemed deliberately designed to impress his followers with a sense of his autocratic power.

In the first place, Croker compelled them to come to him at a relatively remote place of his own choosing, not merely out of the city, but even out of the State. And from the moment they entered the hotel doors, they were made to feel the Boss's authority.

The stage-setting was perfect. The spacious lobby of the Lakewood Hotel was Croker's audience-chamber. Strolling back and forth, deep in low-voiced conference with successive leaders, the Boss held the centre of the stage. Every eye was continually upon him, while the throng of politicians, watching at a respectful distance, patiently waited their turn to be summoned to " the presence."

The audience-chamber was merely part of an elaborate court ceremonial, rigidly enforced. In the big dining-room Croker's table was conspicuously placed; and at that table, only the Mayor-elect was permitted regularly to sit. Even the most distinguished Tammany notables received occasional invitations to be Croker's guest.

The Boss's most extraordinary order was his decree of evening dress. At dinner, Croker always appeared in evening clothes, and he let it be known that those about him must be similarly attired, on penalty of his displeasure.

The results were startling — even ludicrous. Tammany roughnecks struggled into " boiled shirts," grew apoplectic over high starched collars, and tried to look at ease in " tuxedos" or swallowtails which, somehow, would not fit. Among this uneasy company sauntered the Boss — immaculately tailored by London's best. Croker fairly flaunted his English wardrobe, his English manners — even his English valet. And the very men who had most fiercely denounced " Anglomaniacs " swallowed it whole — and followed suit!

With leaders like Big Tim Sullivan gasping in amazement, the ordinary Braves were in a daze. If the Boss had appeared arrayed in crown and sceptre, they could not have been much more astonished. The wildest rumors concerning the Boss's foreign habits were afloat, and were apt to be believed. Perhaps the most amusing instance of this was the hoax played on three humble office-seekers. " They were told that every morning at sun-up Croker walked on the hotel lawn in his bare feet, and if they wanted to make themselves solid with the Boss they should follow his example. The misguided fellows adopted the suggestion next morning, notwithstanding the fact that a light snow had fallen during the night. Croker saw them through the window. ' Come in out of there,' he called to them. ' Do you want to catch pneumonia? ' " [1]

For over a month, Croker's court went on. By Christmas it was generally understood that " the slate " had been made up and every important office apportioned. Through it all, the Mayor-elect had played his part with the air of dignity gained on the judicial bench. The Boss treated Van Wyck with urbane politeness, and took care that the Mayor-elect received due deference. Everybody understood the realities of the situation, but appearances must be preserved, for the Boss's dignity as well as his deputy's.

Despite this lip-service, Van Wyck did not seem wholly happy; for, away from " the presence," he vented his irascible nature in occasional fits of spleen. In conference, however, his demeanor was flawless, and he never failed to give the Boss's "suggestions " his dignified *O.K.*

Adjourning his Lakewood " court " in the closing days of the year, Croker headed the Tammany host in its return to the metropolis, for Inauguration Day.

The evening before that momentous event, the Boss held a grand reception at which he shone in the height of his glory. As the press described it: " Anyone who desired to observe the Court of Croker should have paid a visit to the Murray Hill Hotel last night. The brilliantly lighted lobby of the big hotel swarmed with the Boss's adherents. Into the midst of his courtiers, now and then, strolled Mr. Croker, arrayed in a tuxedo, silk hat, and a big cigar. He didn't sit down at all, but leaned now against the counter and again sauntered over to the news stand, talking to whatever man or group might be lucky enough to secure a word from him. The politicians talked among themselves, but every eye followed the Boss's every movement." [2]

At noon on New Year's Day (January 1, 1898) the Strong administration went out of office and Tammany took over, not merely Manhattan, but all of Greater New York. The new régime burst in with much pomp and ceremony. City Hall blazed with light, effectually routing the gloom

of a foggy winter day. A band played, and the old building
swarmed with Tammany men, surging exultantly through
the flag-draped rooms and corridors. As soon as Mayor Van
Wyck had been inaugurated, he announced a long list of
municipal appointments amid salvos of shouts and cheers.

In the throng that attended the new Mayor's inauguration, only one prominent figure was absent — Richard
Croker. With his usual canny tact, he let Mayor Van Wyck
be the whole show on this occasion; perhaps, also, because
he, the Boss, thought it better for his own prestige not to
appear where he would necessarily occupy second place.

But that same afternoon, Richard Croker put on his own
show, where he could rightfully hold the centre of the stage.
This was at the opening of his new headquarters, the Democratic Club. There the Tammany cohorts, fresh from the
inaugural ceremonies, hastened in joyous mood. And that
mood the Boss had prepared to satisfy. For after a conveniently brief speech of welcome, the Club President, ex-
Governor Flower, smilingly announced: " Gentlemen, the
back room is ready for luncheon. The bar is open — wide
open. So walk in and help yourselves! "

Hungry — and very thirsty, the crowd needed no second
bidding. Croker's guests found his hospitality ample; for
in the " back room " was a long table laden with refresh-
ments; on the well-stocked bar were two huge punchbowls;
while for those with more plebeian thirsts there was a barrel
of beer.

The jollification lasted well into the evening. On this
occasion, ceremony was waived, Croker was the genial host,
and everybody had a " grand time."

Yet the reins, loosened a bit at fitting moments, were soon
tightened again. On the morrow of Inauguration Day,

Richard Croker, the genial host of the previous evening, had become the stern Boss once more. As for Mayor Van Wyck; having had his taste of the limelight, he assumed his proper place. Before the new administration was a month old, so temperate a critic as Albert Shaw wrote caustically: " The recent elevation of Richard Croker to a position of acknowledged authority in politics is absolutely without parallel in the history of the United States. Thus far, the government of our huge metropolis has been conducted personally by Mr. Croker quite as if he were a prince regent, with Mayor Van Wyck as titular occupant of the throne, but disqualified on the ground of infancy or mental incapacity." [3]

Croker's pose, indeed, befitted a royal personage. The court at Lakewood was a mere prologue to the court at the Democratic Club. The Club, itself, was virtually Croker's own creation. Before he took it in hand, the Democratic Club of New York City was a rather run-down institution, deeply in debt. Shortly after the November election, Croker announced that the Club was to be the social centre for the new administration and intimated that membership would be highly desirable for those prominent in the Party. That was enough! The Membership Committee was besieged with applications. By New Year's the Club had a waiting-list and blossomed forth in luxurious quarters on Fifth Avenue near Central Park.

Henceforth, the Democratic Club replaced the Wigwam as the rendezvous of Tammany's elect. Croker lived there most of the time and was usually present to oversee the proceedings. The code of etiquette promulgated at Lakewood continued to be enforced. Evening dress was the order after nightfall, and decorous conduct was exacted at all times. " It was really as good as a play to watch Croker every evening. He had a table near the centre of the dining-room, and only the chosen few were permitted to sit with him. . . Any one who wanted to stand well with the chief was expected to dine at the Club at least once a week. No one ever thought of going into the dining-room until Croker was seated. I have always believed that Croker regarded this as a huge joke and was continually laughing in his sleeve at his subservient followers. Frequently he would not go to the dining-room until very late, and the famished members would feel obliged to bear their hunger. Just as soon as Croker entered the dining-room there would be a grand rush. The majority of the diners would watch what Croker ordered, and then order the same thing. Croker, of course, pretended not to notice this, but he did. Frequently, to carry out his joke, he would order very little, and some of these brawny leaders who had large appetites would suffer because they were afraid to go any further than the chief." [4]

Croker did his best to make the Democratic Club a social as well as a political success. Every department was managed on a luxurious and elaborate scale. The cuisine was excellent, the bar was famous, there were entertainments galore, while Ladies' Day became a feature of New York life.

All these activities made great press-copy. One metropolitan paper featured a daily " Court Calendar " such as the London newspapers print. In this calendar, Croker was gravely referred to as *His Majesty*, the Tammany leaders were given high-sounding titles of nobility, and the Democratic Club became *The Palace*.

When Croker went to Europe (as he did every summer) his departures and homecomings resembled royal progresses. The pier would be jammed with thousands of the faithful, the Boss's stateroom would be festooned with magnificent floral offerings, and the liner would be escorted by a flotilla of private and municipal craft. On one occasion, a police boat preceded Croker's ship through the Narrows and fired a salute of twenty-one guns. "Why, that's the President's salute," smilingly remarked the Boss to a friend.

Croker's mastery over New York City was never more strikingly shown than in the famous banquet given in 1899 to commemorate Jefferson's birthday. The banquet was sponsored by the Democratic Club; and, acting on its behalf, Croker engaged the Metropolitan Opera House!

This may seem an absurd proceeding, since the Opera House had no cooking facilities. But it merely gave the Boss a chance to display his resourcefulness — and his power. A word from him, and two busy thoroughfares (39th and 40th Streets, between Broadway and Seventh Avenue) were closed to traffic for days. In those streets, improvised kitchens were erected and an elaborate dinner for 1200 covers was prepared.

The banquet was a huge success, especially for Richard Croker. At his entrance, the orchestra played *Hail to the Chief!* and all rose to do him honor. Besides the 1200 diners on the floor, the boxes were filled with ladies, who watched the scene below.

The main floor was a gorgeous spectacle. Thirty-two tables stretched its entire length, and directly under the proscenium were the two head tables — one for the speakers, the other for the Executive Committee of Tammany Hall, where Richard Croker had the seat of honor. These tables were a plain of roses, with tall white storks and graceful swans standing like sentinels. At either end were mammoth cornucopias pouring forth a profusion of fruits and flowers.

The banquet was orderly and harmonious, despite the fact that the diners drank 6600 quarts of wine, of which 3000 quarts were champagne.

The Boss was now enjoying to the full his power and his glory. No man, before or since, has ever been so much the master of America's metropolis. Not even Tweed attained this degree of undisguised authority. A writer of the day did not overstate the case when he wrote: "Seeing the powers of Croker, one almost believes that not a policeman walks his beat in New York City except by his grace; not a brick is laid on a public or private work that he may not impudently tear down if the contractor laying it withholds homage to the Boss; that not a wheel turns in any railroad, not a car moves up or down an elevator shaft in Greater New York but, by expressing an idle caprice, Croker may not stop them." [5]

Croker's regal dictatorship, which was a source of pride to his admirers and of amused curiosity to the metropolitan public, galled other men almost past endurance. As one distinguished opponent remarked bitterly: "It is no mere jest when people call Richard Croker the King of the City of New York." [6]

CHAPTER XX

THE BOSS MEETS A ROUGH RIDER

THE opening months of the year 1898 were for Richard Croker a veritable springtime of political hopes. New opportunities met his gaze, extending to State, and even national, horizons. Buttressed by his mastery over America's metropolis, what might he not accomplish?

Croker had left no stone unturned to make his metropolitan dictatorship secure. While his Mayoralty triumph was still fresh and his prestige at its highest, he had concluded a series of treaties with Hugh McLaughlin and the minor Democratic Bosses of the outlying Boroughs. By giving them good terms, Croker had impressed them with his generosity; and in return for concessions over patronage they had gladly acknowledged him as their suzerain. So long as these agreements remained in force, Croker could rest assured that the Greater New York Democracy would back him to any reasonable extent.

Sure of his home domain, Croker was now free to enter the realm of State politics. That, however, required circumspection. " Up-State " was, for the Tiger, a strange land, full of pitfalls for the unwary. More than one Tammany Boss had explored it, and had come to grief. This, Croker knew only too well; for he had been Kelly's right-hand man and had seen his stalwart chief broken in the attempt.

Nevertheless, the game was worth the risk. Croker knew that the only serious threat to his mastery of New York City was from Albany. If he could dominate State and metropolis, his rule would be unassailable. And the condition of both parties up-State was such as almost to invite his intervention.

The outstanding fact about the up-State Democracy was the decadence of the Hill machine. David B. Hill had built up the organization. But it was essentially personal, and it therefore rose and fell with his own fortunes. Hill was a master-politician. Like Platt, he was indifferent to wealth or society, his ruling passion being the game of politics. But, unlike Platt, Hill had an itch for high office, and he was unlucky enough to be badly stung by a " Presidential Bee." Hill's intrigues for the nomination failed dismally and cost him much of his prestige. Then, at the Democratic National Convention of 1896, he had stood forth as the arch-foe of Bryanism — and had been beaten. The result of these reverses was that he had made dangerous enemies within his own party. Though still the leader of the State Democracy, there were many waiting their chance to drag him down to political oblivion.

The up-State Republican machine was in equally bad shape. Platt's tactics during the recent New York Mayoralty campaign had landed him in serious trouble. His " knifing " of Seth Low had infuriated liberal Republicans throughout the State, and his dealings with Croker had heightened their anger. The entire liberal wing of the Republican Party was in a vengeful mood, ready to chastise the " Easy Boss " if opportunity offered.

Platt was thus in no position to wage aggressive war on Croker. In fact, his internal troubles made him disposed to prolong his confidential dealings with the New York City Boss and to trade favors in an unusually amicable way.

Croker's path seemed clear. And his immediate objectives were obvious: to over-ride or crush Hill, and seat a Tammany nominee in the Governor's chair. The Democrats had good prospects of electing a Governor that year.

Unfortunately for them, they could not reasonably hope to win the Legislature. Platt had rendered that almost impossible. Four years previously, he had engineered one of the cleverest *coups* in the annals of American politics. Taking advantage of temporary Democratic disorganization, the " Easy Boss " had dominated the Convention held in 1894 to revise the State Constitution, and had inserted several amendments which patently favored the rural districts as against the cities and especially the metropolis. With this legislative gerrymander safely locked into the Constitution, nothing less than a Democratic landslide could wrest the Assembly from Republican control.

Still, the Governorship was worth fighting for. Not unless a good Tammany man presided at Albany could Croker feel reasonably secure from some swift stroke of Platt's, designed to discredit the Tammany administration of New York City — as had already happened twice before.

However, for the moment, Platt's claws were clipped. So Croker could concentrate on his plans regarding Hill. During the early part of the year, the two Democratic Bosses manoeuvred for position in what looked like a fight to a finish — with Platt hovering about the combatants, apparently ready to aid Croker if Hill should gain any notable advantage. Then the duel was adjourned by the outbreak of the Spanish War. The public forgot local politics in the heat of war-fever; and Croker, realizing this, decided to take a holiday on the British turf.

By the time Croker returned to America at the end of

July, the war was over, and an important political event had occurred: Theodore Roosevelt was the hero of the hour!

Before the end of the Strong administration, the former Police Commissioner had become the Assistant Secretary of the Navy. And when the Spanish War broke out, Roosevelt resigned this Federal post to raise his famous regiment of " Rough Riders," and to cover himself with glory on the Santiago battlefields.

Already known as a staunch liberal, T. R. appealed strongly to the progressive elements in his party, who were incensed at Platt and his doings. Consequently, a popular cry arose to nominate Roosevelt for Governor — or take the consequences at the polls.

This was the news which met Richard Croker as he landed in New York, bronzed and jovial. When the reporters told him that Roosevelt was almost certain to be the Republican candidate in the autumn, Croker asked facetiously: " Has he been wounded yet? " And when answered, " No," the Boss continued: " Well, I'm afraid he won't do. No man is available as a war hero candidate unless he has been wounded — or killed. Better tell Mr. Roosevelt to get wounded." [1]

This jocularity, however, was camouflage. In secret, the Boss was deeply perturbed at the prospect of Roosevelt's candidacy. A keen judge of men, the Tammany chief recognized the young Republican's dangerous possibilities. In fact, Roosevelt made Croker almost as uneasy as he made Platt. Both Bosses saw in Roosevelt that most ominous type — a reformer who knew the political ropes and who had the art of winning the people. Such a man was highly dangerous to Bosses of every sort. If Platt had had his way, Roosevelt would have been frozen out of the political game.

As it was, " Roosevelt luck " in the shape of a brilliant war-record had forced Platt's hand.

But the Tammany Boss was still to be reckoned with. The lengths to which Croker went to prevent Roosevelt's nomination are sensationally disclosed by an " inside story " told by Chauncey Depew after Croker's death, many years later.

Mr. Depew (then President of the New York Central Railroad) had been asked to make the speech nominating Theodore Roosevelt for Governor at the Republican State Convention of 1898. The day before the Convention met, a prominent Democratic politician came into Depew's office and said: " I have a message for you which, personally, I am ashamed to deliver. Mr. Croker has sent me to say to you that if you make that speech nominating Mr. Roosevelt in the Republican Convention, he will resent it on your railroad."

To this ultimatum, Depew retorted: " I know Mr. Croker's power and the injury he can do the road. You can say to him that I am amazed at such a message coming from a man I have always found to be a square fighter, as this is a blow below the belt. I am going to make that speech; but before I make it, I shall resign as president and director of the New York Central Railroad. And when I put Mr. Roosevelt in nomination before the Convention of the State of New York, I will say why I resigned."

Depew's answer was effective, for within an hour the Boss's emissary returned to say: " Mr. Croker wishes you to forget that message. His own words were: ' It is withdrawn. I was very badly advised.' " [2]

This bit of secret political history opens the door to fascinating conjecture. By whom had Croker been " badly advised "? Was it Platt? Was this a last joint effort of the two Bosses to avert what they felt might be a grave misfortune to them both? Or had Croker's dictatorial power so unleashed his natural arrogance that he forgot his customary caution? Other acts of Croker's at this period lead us to surmise that the Boss was then in a mood betokening truculent over-confidence.

Within his own party, everything tended to feed his self-assurance and his pride. When Croker attended the Democratic State Convention at Syracuse, he received a tremendous ovation. " As the first section of the Tammany train, with 1500 Braves aboard, entered the city on its way to the station, the sidewalks were lined with men and women who cheered heartily for Mr. Croker and his army of tigers. He came like a conqueror. When he alighted from his parlor car, Mayor McGuire's bluecoats cleared a path for him, and with uplifted clubs drove the curious away. John F. Carroll preceded him to the carriage in waiting, and then the mob broke through the police cordon and crowded around the chief. In response to a volley of cheers, Mr. Croker doffed his hat, the cabman cracked his whip, and then began a triumphant gallop to the Yates House. The crowd ran before and behind his carriage, and when it reached the Yates a great cheer greeted the leader from the throng of delegates and sightseers gathered in front of the hotel. Again Carroll made way for the chief through the throng, and after persistent elbowing convoyed him safely to his room." [3]

David B. Hill was already installed at the Yates House, and the rival Bosses presently met, face-to-face, in the lobby. The throng of politicians waited breathlessly. But, to their astonishment, the rivals shook hands and vanished into a private parlor, in outwardly amicable conference.

The truth of the matter was that their mutual friend,

Edward Murphy, had been busy arranging a formal recon-
ciliation. He argued that, with so redoubtable an antagonist
as Theodore Roosevelt in the field, this was no time for factional quarrels. Murphy talked sense; so " the fight " was
postponed. When the Convention met next day, all was
" harmony."

Croker, however, won his main point: his " man " was
nominated for Governor. The Democratic candidate was
Judge Augustus Van Wyck, the brother of New York's
Mayor, and equally " dependable " in Tammany eyes.
With one Van Wyck presiding at City Hall and another at
Albany, Croker would have little to fear.

As Croker saw the situation, the chances were all in his
favor. The State Democracy would loyally back the Tammany candidate; Hill dared not do otherwise. On the other
hand, the Republican machine had been compelled to take
Roosevelt; so Platt would be lukewarm in his behalf. Furthermore, Roosevelt would not run well in New York City,
where memories of his strict enforcement policy as Police
Commissioner still rankled in many minds. The betting-
odds were decidedly on Van Wyck.

Then Croker made the mistake in political tactics which,
in the course of events, became a blunder of the first magnitude: he refused a renomination to Judge Joseph F. Daly.
Logically, this had nothing to do with the Governorship;
but, in practice, it proved to have a great deal.

Daly, a Tammany Judge, had twice defied the Boss. He
had declined to appoint a man recommended by Croker for
clerk of court; and he had refused to issue a judicial order
affecting the Boss's real estate interests, even after Croker
had informed him that it was a " personal matter."

After this, there was only one thing for the Boss to do:

"break" Judge Daly! In Croker's eyes, this was merely a bit of organization routine. Tammany was founded on disciplined obedience. Daly, a Tammany office-holder, had flagrantly disobeyed orders. Therefore, Daly must lose his job, if Tammany discipline were to be maintained. When the newspapers got wind of the affair in mid-October and began playing it up, Croker issued this statement, which he probably thought would settle the matter: " Justice Daly was elected by Tammany Hall after he was discovered by Tammany Hall, and Tammany Hall had a right to expect proper consideration at his hands."

Croker rested his case on the time-honored tradition of party regularity. But, unluckily for him, Croker had in this instance run foul of another time-honored American tradition: the independence of the judiciary. An upright judge was being "shelved" because he would not do the Boss's arbitrary bidding and grant him personal favors. To many men, Democrats and Republicans alike, this was intolerable.

Within a week, the "Daly affair" had become a major political issue. On October 21, a mass-meeting was held in Carnegie Hall, at which the Boss was held up to public condemnation. The star speaker was none other than Bourke Cockran, formerly one of the " Big Four " which had guided Tammany after Kelly's death, but who had subsequently quarreled with Croker and been thrown out of the organization.

Mr. Cockran had lost none of his " silver-tongued " eloquence. In telling phrases he depicted the Boss's autocratic power, and the perils thereof. " By an interview," cried Cockran, " he can send the stock of a corporation soaring above that mysterious line known as par, or sinking below those gloomy levels which evoke spectres of bankruptcy and liquidation." After a long survey of the Boss's arbitrary acts, the orator ended with a solemn warning that if the judiciary fell under Croker's sway, no man in New York City would be safe from his displeasure.

The disastrous Daly affair, as sudden as it was unexpected, filled Croker with angry amazement. His mind could not grasp the public's mood. How could good Democrats be stirred up over what he deemed a justifiable party act? The larger aspects of the situation escaped him, trained as he had been in the narrow partisan code.

But to his young Republican adversary, it was a glorious opportunity. T. R. knew just how to dramatize the situation and drive home the lesson in the popular consciousness. As Roosevelt himself said:

" My object was to make the people understand that it was Croker, and not the nominal candidate, who was my real opponent; that the choice lay between Crokerism and myself. Croker was a powerful and truculent man; the autocrat of his organization, and of a domineering nature. For his own reasons he insisted upon Tammany's turning down an excellent Democratic judge who was up for re-election. This gave me my chance. Under my attack, Croker, who was a stalwart fighting-man and who would not take an attack tamely, himself came to the front. I was able to fix the contest in the public mind as one between himself and myself; and, against all probabilities, I won." [4]

Roosevelt won by the narrowest of margins: a bare 18,000 votes. In Manhattan, the Tammany machine functioned perfectly and rolled up a huge local majority for its candidate. But the other Boroughs did not support Van Wyck so well; while Roosevelt swept up-State New York. The " Rough Rider " rode down to the Bronx with such a tremendous vote behind him that he just overtopped Van Wyck's big metropolitan lead. Theodore Roosevelt had been elected the next Governor of the Empire State.

The Tammany Boss's Albany invasion, like those of his predecessors, had failed. And the most serious aspect of this failure was that it came about primarily through a revolt in his own metropolitan domain. Croker had not merely lost his chance to dominate the State; he had lost prestige as well. A New York newspaper summed up the situation when it wrote, the morning after election: " The dream of a Crokerized State is shattered. There will be no second Van Wyck at Albany to protect the first Van Wyck in New York, whatever he may do." [5]

Thus, the year which had opened so brilliantly for Richard Croker ended in gloom. Yet his hold on the metropolis was still unshaken. His " man " sat in the Mayor's chair, and would continue to sit there three years more. Meanwhile, Tammany was making the most of its long lease of power. The Tiger was growing fat on patronage and graft — " honest " and otherwise.

And the Boss was getting his share.

CHAPTER XXI

"YORK": A WIDE-OPEN TOWN

ON THE wild night of Tammany's triumph, when Manhattan shouted itself hoarse yelling, "To Hell with Reform!" another slogan was heard on every side. That slogan was, *A Wide-open Town!*

For three years, New York City had been ruled by a reform administration pledged to the enforcement of laws against Sunday liquor-selling, gambling, and vice. That administration had been emphatically repudiated at the polls. So triumphant Tammany, noting the popular rejoicings, proceeded to give the people what they had apparently voted for.

Mayor Van Wyck's appointment of William S. Devery as Chief of Police gave due notice that, for the next four years, the metropolis would be run on free-and-easy lines.

"Big Bill" Devery was a brawny product of "the sidewalks of New York," who boasted that he had carried his father's dinner-pail when the elder Devery was laying the bricks of Tammany Hall. Starting as a humble patrolman, Bill Devery had worked his way up from the ranks. He knew the seamy side of New York life much better than he did an open book, and towards it he had the policeman's "hard-boiled" attitude. Liquor, gambling, vice were here. They were here because people wanted them. They made big graft. And the police, who were deputed to look after such matters, should get their share of whatever was going 'round. Big Bill's philosophy was simple. He saw nothing wrong with his code. Reformers were ignorant busybodies vainly striving to change the inevitable, and therefore merited contempt.

Devery made the orthodox police distinction between *Vice* and *Crime*. Vice was to be tolerated, within recognized bounds. Crimes (save when committed by exceptional persons with a strong political "pull") should be sternly dealt with. The murderer, the burglar, the hold-up man, and other offenders against life or property must be hunted down and brought to justice.

To do this, "The Force" must be kept efficient. So Devery was a stern disciplinarian. Any patrolman a block "off post" or found by his roundsman fuddled with drink would be haled before "the Chief," given a merciless tongue-lashing, and heavily "docked" in pay. At such times, the big, red-faced man with the bull-neck and the stage-policeman's mustache would grow purple with rage. His blue-grey eyes would stiffen and gleam until they seemed to pierce the very uniform of the trembling patrolman before him, and he would roar forth a storm of picturesque vituperation starred with oaths and phrases spicier than the newspapers dared to print.[1]

Big Bill was a "character"; a joy to every reporter's heart. He could always be counted on to give a "line" that would be the making of an interview. And Devery adored publicity. To him, notoriety was fame — the more of it, the better. His most treasured possessions were thirty-six big scrap-books, filled with press-clippings and cartoons about himself and his doings.

Such was the man whom the new Mayor appointed to look

after the manners and morals of " Little Old New York."
Small wonder that, within a year from the time Van Wyck
took office, New York City was known from coast to coast
as a very wide-open town. Anybody in search of a " good
time " was sure to find just what he wanted, with no trouble
or delay. Sunday thirsts became a dim memory; gambling-
joints flourished openly; while the red-lights blazed from
dusk till dawn. Of course, the law was still there. But,
with Big Bill Devery Chief of Police and Asa Bird Gardiner
District Attorney, what were a few statutes between friends?

A revealing picture of New York life in this wide-open
period is a survey of its " Underworld " made by Josiah
Flint, a keen observer of social conditions in his day. Flint,
who had spent years consorting with tramps and criminals,
and who knew how to gain their confidence, made an extended tour of the city under the competent guidance of a
" crook " friend of his — a little English " Moll-buzzer "
— in polite language, a snatcher of women's handbags and
purses.

Together, they visited many saloons and " joints " which
were the favorite hangouts of crooks. So unconventional
were the antics in some of these places that they shocked the
Moll-buzzer's moral sense. At length, as they sat in *The
Black Rabbit*, a notorious resort on Bleecker Street, the little
Englishman burst out: " There ain't no use talkin', this is
dead tough. I wouldn't allow this, 'f I was the Chief; I'll
be damned if I would. I like an open town where everything
goes, but I'd douse the glim here."

After a thoughtful silence, the Moll-buzzer went on:
" I'd like to see this town run by thieves once. 'Course
they'd graft — couldn't help it; but not more'n the
police do."

Richard Croker was a subject of never-failing interest for New York's underworld, which discussed him and his activities quite as intelligently as politicians and newspaper men. The crooks well understood his power in the city and considered him the chief Mogul.

Yet the Underworld asserted that, with all his power, the Boss could not "scrub out" the grafting conditions which then prevailed. "No one, not even Mr. Croker himself, was considered powerful enough to order the town shut, and enforce the order. One man with whom I talked about this matter said: 'Croker might order the town shut, and it might stay shut for a night or two; but if the boys thought that his Nibs was in earnest, they'd turn him down. Croker is Boss on the strength of the understandin' that York is to be open and that Tammany is to get the benefit of the police graft. If he should go back on his promises to the boys, he couldn't remain Boss a week.'"

Flint's informants placed the ultimate responsibility for current conditions squarely at the door of the average citizen. The Underworld believed that the people wanted an "open" city, and would be the first to complain if it were closed.[2]

While Bill Devery "shook down" the vice graft and Tim Sullivan syndicated gambling into a closely welded "ring," the Boss was making his big profits in Wall Street and through his hold over local corporations. It was dangerous for even the largest companies to incur the Boss's displeasure, as was dramatically shown by the case of one of the great public service corporations.

Late in the year 1898, the municipal authorities began a sudden attack on the Manhattan Elevated Railway. Almost every branch of the city government took part in this concerted assault. The Health Department declared several hundred points on the Elevated structure to be unsafe, and served notice that repairs must be made forthwith. The Park Department ordered the company to remove its tracks from Battery Park immediately, citing an obscure clause in the original franchise. The Board of Aldermen threatened to pass a series of ordinances which would cost the company millions of dollars.

For a while, the public was mystified at this savage (and apparently purposeless) series of blows at the " El." Then, on February 5, 1899, *The New York Evening Post* published " an account of what passed between George Gould and Richard Croker, from a source which can be depended upon as entirely accurate."

The account stated that Croker had called upon Mr. Gould (the President of the Manhattan Company) and had demanded, on behalf of a corporation in which the Boss was heavily interested, the privilege of attaching its compressed-air pipes to all the Elevated structures. Mr. Gould said he would consult his chief engineer as to whether the structures would carry the load, and would also ascertain whether he had the legal right to grant such permission.

Thereupon, the Boss had exclaimed: " Oh, hell! I want those pipes put on, and I don't want any circumlocution." And when Mr. Gould further temporized, Croker added: " We want these pipes put on, and we don't want any fuss about it." At this point, Mr. Gould retorted: " Under the circumstances, Mr. Croker, I will settle the question now, without referring it to my officials. We will not permit you to attach your pipes to the Elevated structures." Immediately after this stormy interview, the attack on the Manhattan Company began.

Croker angrily denied the truth of the story, but there seems little doubt that it was correct. Had the account been false, Croker would have been clearly entitled to sue the *Post* for libel — which he never did.

Furthermore, there were rumors in Wall Street that Croker, before launching his assault, had sold a big block of Manhattan stock " short," and had thereby cleared a large profit; for the stock went down rapidly as soon as the " El " came under fire. Croker was asked about this transaction during the Mazet Investigation, but declined to answer, on the ground that it was his " private business."

Croker had thus made a financial " killing " and had taught all local corporations a lesson in obedience, at one and the same time!

That was a halcyon epoch for Tammany, when everybody connected with the organization, from the Boss and the Mayor to ward heelers, was making " easy money." But those golden days were interrupted by a chill wind blowing from the north. The danger against which Croker had endeavored to provide by electing a Tammany Governor came to pass. Albany appointed another Legislative Committee to investigate New York's Tammany administration.

In 1899 the Mazet Committee opened its sessions in New York City. For nearly a year, the investigation went on; and the enormous mass of testimony, published in five large volumes, throws a flood of light on the conditions of the period.[3]

The findings of the Mazet Committee were thus summarized in its majority report:

" The one clear and distinct fact brought out by this investigation is that we have in this great city the most perfect instance of centralized government yet known. . . We see that government, no longer responsible to the people, but to a dictator. We see the central power, not the man who sits in the mayor's chair, but the man who stands behind it. We see the same arbitrary power dictating appointments, directing officials, controlling boards, lecturing members of the Legislative and Municipal Assemblies. We see incompetence and arrogance in high places. We see an enormous and ever-growing crowd of office-holders with ever-increasing salaries. We see the powers of government prostituted to protect criminals, to demoralize the police, to debauch the public conscience, and to turn governmental functions into channels for private gain. The proof is conclusive, not that the public treasury has been directly robbed, but that great opportunities have been given, by manipulation of public offices, to enable favored individuals to work for their own personal benefit. The enormous increase in the budget of the city of New York, the inefficiency and wastefulness in the public service, the demoralization of many of the departments are due absolutely to this abdication of power by the officers of the people to an organization, the ruler of which, an autocrat, has testified that he was working for his own pocket all the time." [4]

The Mazet Investigation made a profound sensation. Yet its immediate effect was not what, perhaps, might have been expected. Reformers were horrified, and the metropolitan press teemed with bitter editorials and biting cartoons. But this was " preaching to the converted." The Mazet Investigation informed good citizens officially of what they already knew through the newspapers or from their own personal observation. The metropolitan masses were not deeply moved by sensational details of graft and illegal practices. The average New Yorker might not approve of them; but he preferred them to " strict enforcement," and he felt that he could not enjoy forbidden pleasures and have civic purity as well.

Furthermore, the Mazet Investigation, like its predecessors, was tainted with politics. It had been appointed by the Republican machine, and of its seven members only two were New York City Democrats. Those two members had tried vainly to broaden the scope of the inquiry by urging that Platt and other Republican leaders be put on the stand — which the Republican majority curtly refused to do.

The pair therefore issued a heated minority report, assailing the Committee's findings as " grossly unfair, conspicuously partisan, coarse in language, vituperative in temper, and absolutely unjustified, except by reckless disregard and perversion of the proof adduced." The dissenting report ended by stating: " There will always be serious political differences dividing our citizenship; but let us hope there will never again be so contemptible an exhibition of the depths to which partisan bigotry can descend." [5]

These violently controversial and contradictory reports naturally aroused party feeling and tended to discredit the majority's findings in Democratic minds. Relying upon partisan loyalty, Tammany marched stolidly forward, with no perceptible change in administrative policies or methods. Mayor Van Wyck publicly lauded Devery as " the best Chief of Police New York City ever had "; while Croker appealed to all good Democrats to stand fast against the attacks of " a combination of Republican wolves and disappointed office-seekers."

However, in April 1900, toward the close of its sessions, the Mazet Committee unearthed one matter which was destined to have momentous political consequences. This was the notorious " Ice Trust " scandal.

The Committee exposed a series of confidential agreements between the Tammany administration and the American Ice Company, which gave that Company a practical monopoly on the sale of ice in the metropolis.

The American Ice Company was a consolidation of several previously independent concerns, brought about by Charles W. Morse, an unscrupulous financier of dubious reputation. In order to ensure the combine its monopoly, the Van Wyck administration agreed to shut off outside competition by giving the company exclusive privileges to land ice at the municipal docks.

And it was further proved that, before this agreement was signed, the Company had presented blocks of its stock to practically every important Democratic politician in Greater New York. All the " big fellows " were in the deal; from Croker and the Mayor to Hugh McLaughlin, the Brooklyn Boss, and some of his friends. The value of these " gifts " can be judged by the fact that Mayor Van Wyck's stock, alone, was shown to have been worth nearly $700,000, before the Mazet Committee's disclosures knocked the bottom out of the Ice Trust and sent its shares kiting downward on the Stock Exchange.

The Ice Trust disclosures were the most disastrous blow to Tammany since the days of the Tweed Ring. Here was something which stirred not only moralists and civic reformers but the common man as well. Ice was a necessity of life, even to the poor. And the evidence proved conclusively that the result of the new monopoly would have been to raise the price of ice in startling fashion.

Once more the newspapers came out with scathing editorials and cartoons.   And this time, they struck home.   For, as spring merged into summer, and heat-waves set the tenements stewing, the masses realized what had been afoot. Tenement mothers hushed crying babies while scanning a cartoon of Boss Croker, garbed as a burly iceman and holding by the tongs a cake of ice in which a diminutive Van Wyck sat congealed.   Perspiring workmen reckoned grimly the hole which the proposed ice-schedules would have made in their wages.

That hurt — and hurt hard.   To graft off the rich and the pleasure-seekers was one thing; to graft off the poor was quite another.   The poor sometimes have long memories. The foundation had been laid for an emotional reaction against Tammany rule which, given further stimulus, might sweep the Tiger once more from power.

The people had begun to murmur.   But the next Mayoralty election was more than a year away, and much might happen before then.   At present, Tammany was in the saddle, and could not be unseated.

As for the Boss, he had other things on his mind.   He was taking a hand in national politics.

CHAPTER XXII

THE BOSS BACKS THE WRONG HORSE

No PHASE of Richard Croker's career is more dramatic than his sudden emergence as a leader in national affairs. During the Presidential campaign of 1900, the Tammany Boss became one of the great powers in national politics. At moments, his burly figure loomed so large that, in the Democratic camp, he stood second only to William Jennings Bryan, the Presidential candidate.

Before this, Croker had shown scant desire to play a part in the affairs of the nation. His spectacular appearances at National Conventions, heading Tammany parades, were simply moves in the game of New York City politics, designed to affirm Tammany's regularity and thus win a tactical advantage over factional foes. With Presidential candidates and platforms, Croker was not then directly concerned. Whatever a Convention should decide; that, Tammany would loyally support.

This was Croker's policy until the first Bryan campaign of 1896. What his attitude would have been on that occasion, had he then been active in politics, is problematical. Since that campaign was fought during his " exile," Croker carefully avoided committing himself, stayed abroad, and maintained a sphinx-like neutrality.

Croker's " Return from Elba " and his extraordinary victory of 1897 mark the change in his attitude. Vastly heightened in power and prestige, the triumphant Boss began to display an interest in both State and national politics such as he had never shown.

His first attempt to dominate State politics failed when Roosevelt defeated Van Wyck for Governor in 1898. But the Tammany Boss had failed only by an exceedingly narrow margin, and he had clearly established his primacy within his own party over his up-State rival, Hill. Croker did not deem his defeat final, and showed no signs of abandoning his larger plans, in either State or nation.

Before Croker could play a major rôle in national politics, one thing was vital: he must control the State Democracy. In those days, New York, with its big block of electoral votes, was the " pivotal State " of the Union. Sure beforehand of the " Solid South," the Democrats could always hope to elect a President, if they could carry the Empire State; whereas, without it, they stood no chance whatever. So, a New York Democrat, if he dominated both State and City organizations, could speak at the National Convention with an authority that would go far towards determining both the choice of the candidate and the drafting of the platform. He would stand before his party in the majestic rôle of War-wick, the King-Maker.

Richard Croker had probably never heard of Warwick. But he knew what he wanted, and how to get it. This was by crushing David B. Hill. We have seen that, in 1898, the rival Bosses had patched up a truce, through the good offices of Senator Murphy, their mutual friend. The Sena-tor, in fact, occupied a key position in up-State politics, and Croker now set out to win Murphy.

In this, he succeeded. Murphy was bound to Croker by warm personal friendship. Between Murphy and Hill, there were no such intimate ties. In fact, Hill had no real friends. Cold, aloof, and cynical, the up-State Boss commanded men's allegiance by self-interest, not by affection.

The struggle between Hill and Croker reached its climax during the autumn of 1899. Before the campaign began, a meeting of the Democratic State Committee was called at the Hoffman House, in New York City. Croker, master of the situation, sat on one side of the conference-room, flanked by Senator Murphy and by Patrick McCarren of Brooklyn, avowedly Croker's allies. Across the room sat Hill, almost alone. Croker ran the meeting with a high hand. He sneered openly at Hill's angry protests and vociferous objections. Hill was beaten at every point.

When the meeting was over, the up-State Boss, broken and dispirited, made no attempt to conceal his defeat. " The inevitable has happened," he said wearily to the waiting reporters. " The City has at last dominated the State. The State organization has been Tammanyized."

The reaction of Croker's victory on national politics was self-evident. Indeed, at this same meeting, the Tammany Boss took a definite stand on national issues. Though the Presidential campaign was still a year away, he committed the State organization to a declaration favoring Bryan's renomination. This stand of Croker's was the culmination of a curious series of events. It was literally a political somersault, which mystified many observers at the time.

Croker had been personally neutral during Bryan's first campaign in 1896. But Tammany had not been neutral. It had fought Bryan's nomination in the National Convention, and its thinly disguised hostility during the ensuing campaign had caused New York City to go Republican. Nearly all the big Tammany men were " Gold Democrats " at

heart, precisely like Hill and the other conservative Democrats of the Eastern States.

When Croker began to take an active interest in national
politics, therefore, he was half-committed against Bryan.
And, until the late summer of 1899, he stood with most of
his colleagues, on the conservative side.   Indeed, when he
sailed for England in April of that same year, he gave out
a_press interview which apparently aligned him definitely
with the anti-Bryan group.   In that interview, Croker stated:
" The time has gone by when the Democrats can accept the
doctrine of 16 to 1.   I feel sure that the Democratic Party
will nominate some one else as their candidate in the next
Presidential campaign."

In August, Croker returned to America and promptly
staggered even hardened reporters by calling Bryan "a
great leader" and stating that Free Silver was a complicated
matter which ought to be left for Congress to decide.   A
lightning change had taken place in less than four months
abroad, seemingly on a racing holiday!

Croker's " 'bout face " was the political talk of the town.
Yet he refused to enlighten persistent inquirers concerning
the reasons for his new stand.   " Those are my views," he
said stolidly, when interviewed next day at the Democratic
Club.   " I have nothing to add or retract."   He hedged only
when asked point-blank about his attitude toward Bryan's
renomination.   Here he was enigmatic: " I have not declared
for Mr. Bryan.   I am committed to no one."   Yet, a few
weeks later, Croker aimed the crushing blow at Hill by getting the Democratic State Committee to favor Bryan's
renomination.

What was the secret of Croker's amazingly rapid change
of front?   We believe it was due to two strangely contrasted

reasons: (1) his ability to sense the popular trend in New York City; (2) his inability to appraise the broader tide of thought and feeling in State and nation.

Richard Croker was a superlatively shrewd judge of local public opinion. So quick was he to detect a shift in sentiment that he realized what was in the wind before other politicians knew that something was astir. Only on rare occasions, as in the Ice Trust scandal, did Croker run foul of the metropolitan masses — the basis of Tammany's power.

During the summer of 1899, the Boss seems to have concluded that the popular trend in the metropolis was setting strongly towards Bryan. Even in his first campaign, Bryan had awakened considerable New York support. But at that time he was a stranger to most Easterners, and the intensive propaganda of his enemies (Gold Democrats as well as Republicans) had succeeded in arousing popular fear of himself and his ideas.

As time passed, however, Bryan's insistent championship of " the plain people," and his eloquent indictments of wealth and privilege, had their effect. Tammany itself was threatened with trouble, for the conservative-minded leaders were being confronted by an increasing Bryanward swing in the ranks.

Of all this, Croker was well aware. While in England, his secret agents advised him of each new development. His very remoteness from the scene of action possibly sharpened his perception. At all events, he returned to New York at the end of August with his mind virtually made up to go with the popular tide. Perhaps the fact that his rival, Hill, was irreconcilably hostile to Bryan helped his decision.

That decision once made, Croker threw himself heart and soul on Bryan's side. In the decisive battle at the National

Convention of 1900, the Tammany Boss was the most conspicuous figure, next to Bryan himself. Croker it was who
sent down to humiliating defeat the Eastern conservatives,
headed by Hill; and it was Croker, again, who inserted the
Free Silver plank, which might otherwise have been kept
out of the Democratic platform.

Richard Croker was thus pledged to Bryan unreservedly.
In racing parlance, he was sure his horse would win, and
backed it for all he was worth. The stakes warranted it.
Bryan was so indebted to Croker that, if he won the Presidential race, there were almost no limits to what the Tammany Boss might expect as his just due. On the other hand,
if Bryan lost the race, Croker would be out of national
politics, and would be gravely threatened in his own domain
as well.

How was it that Croker threw his wonted caution to the
winds and " backed the wrong horse " to the limit? The
wisest political prophets were then predicting that Bryan
had even less chance of winning than he had four years
before.

After the election, Croker tried to justify himself by intimating that the popular demand within Tammany itself
had forced him to back Bryan. One of his friends cites a
campaign anecdote to prove this. On the night of Bryan's
whirlwind tour of the metropolis, shortly before election,
the Boss pointed to the frenzied crowds acclaiming " The
Great Commoner," and said: " If I had not come out for
Bryan, the rank-and-file would have taken Tammany away
from me." [1]

Yet this is not an adequate explanation. Croker was too
canny not to have known how to cover his line of retreat,
if he had had his doubts. He would never have thus com-

mitted himself unless he had been sure of victory. It was a sublime ignorance of national affairs which betrayed one whose knowledge of local politics had no superior.

Croker's ignorance, not merely of national issues, but of the ideas and culture of his time, was colossal. This half-illiterate dictator of America's metropolis, who could scarcely speak grammatical English and who rarely read a book, was simply unaware of nearly everything outside his sphere. Now and then, he would reveal his intellectual shortcomings by some remark that would astound his hearers. During the second Bryan campaign, Croker, after listening to a heated controversy between some friends of his over Free Silver, broke in impatiently: "What's the use of discussing what's the best kind of money? I'm in favor of all kinds of money — the more the better! "[2] Obviously, economics were not in Croker's line.

Even in the field of national *politics*, in the restricted sense of the word, Croker more than once betrayed a ludicrous lack of the most elementary knowledge. A striking instance of this occurred during the winter of 1898, when a number of prominent Democrats, including the famous Kentuckian, Henry Watterson, were discussing Presidential possibilities at the Democratic Club. Admiral Dewey had just refused to be a candidate, and this " had a rather gloomy effect upon all present, except Croker. ' I'm glad he won't run,' said Croker, to the astonishment of his guests. ' I have a much better candidate — a man who will suit the Southern Democrats.' ' Who is it? ' asked Colonel Watterson. ' Who is it? ' ' General Nelson A. Miles,' said Croker, with a self-satisfied air. ' Good heavens! ' shouted Watterson. ' Man alive, don't you know that Miles is the man who put the shackles on Jefferson Davis? ' At this time, Croker was absolutely

ignorant of American history or the biography of our leading statesmen." [3]

While the Presidential race was on, Croker enjoyed himself to the full. Never had he appeared more buoyantly
self-confident than he did at the height of this campaign.
First of all, he methodically crushed opposition to his
supremacy in New York State. The liberal elements in the
State Democracy were backing a likely aspirant for the
Governorship; a young man who was making a brilliant
record as Comptroller of New York City — Bird S. Coler.
But his record had made powerful enemies. Though elected
on the Van Wyck Mayoralty ticket, the young Comptroller
had shown his independence, had blocked several political
" grabs," and had recently capped the climax by writing an
article for a leading magazine,[4] which severely criticized the
Boss and his political code. Thenceforth, the Comptroller
was on Croker's blacklist; and when David B. Hill came
out for Coler's candidacy, the irate Boss was doubly determined to block the young man's nomination.

Shortly before the State Convention, Hill and Croker engaged in as bitter an exchange of personalities as New York
politics had seen in a long time. On Labor Day, the up-
State leader delivered a speech at Troy, in which he denounced " political bossism, ignorant, corrupt, and arrogant,
which tolerates no criticism, knows no prudence, and accepts
no suggestions; which first dominates wards, then cities, and
afterwards reaches out for the control of States, and governs
its cringing sycophants through patronage and the cohesive
power of public plunder."

Hill's scathing words, so obviously aimed at the Tammany
Boss, sent Croker into a towering rage. Standing in the
lobby of the Hoffman House, he growled to the assembled

reporters: "Did you read Hill's speech at Troy? Well, Hill attacked me indirectly. That's his way of doing business. Hill never comes out in the open. He always hides behind something, and leaves a loophole to crawl out of. He is deceitful, tricky, and couldn't tell the truth if he wanted to. He is a picayune politician, a peanut politician, and he wouldn't be a district captain if he lived in New York City. Tammany Hall wouldn't have a deceitful, untruthful sneak like 'Dave' Hill in the organization. And Coler is just like Hill. He did the same in his article." After this tirade, the Boss thrust his hands deep into his trousers pocket and paced the hotel lobby, infuriated.[5]

A week later, the angry Boss had his revenge. At the State Convention, Croker rode rough-shod over Hill and the liberal opposition, decisively defeated Coler, and nominated his own candidate, a machine hack named Stanchfield.

Croker's ruthless tactics and his nomination of a weak candidate to satisfy his own personal grudges evoked a chorus of indignant protest from his own party, which should have made him reflect. The leading Democratic organs in New York City criticized Stanchfield's nomination in no uncertain terms. The *World* asserted: "The prospect of a Crokerized State is a deadly weight which no enthusiasm for Bryan can overcome." Up-State Democratic newspapers were even sharper in tone. *The Elmira Gazette* went so far as to say: "It is time to beat certain facts into the hard head of Richard Croker. It should be pounded into his cranium that the rural vote is stampeded by too much Croker. Voters throw down their hats and flee in terror even into Tom Platt's camp." Far beyond the boundaries of the State, leading Democratic papers took flings at the Tammany Boss and his doings. *The Nashville American*, voicing Southern

sentiment, wrote: " Croker may be able to control New York
and hold Hugh McLaughlin in line, in his fight on Coler;
but he is not going to convince the Democracy of the nation
that he is anything more than a vulgar, ignorant, overbearing
political charlatan who cares nothing for parties or politics
except as it may profit him." [6]

Perhaps it was this swelling chorus of disapproval; perhaps a dawning suspicion that all was not well with Bryan's
Presidential prospects, which soured Croker's temper and
made him increasingly irritable as the campaign drew toward
its close. The fact itself was so evident that veteran newspaper men remarked upon it, contrasting the Boss's angry
loquacity with the grim humor or grimmer silence of former
days.

Early in October, Croker seized upon Mark Hanna's sar-
castic comment that Croker was "Emperor of New York
City," to exclaim: "Called me emperor, did he? I only
wish I was emperor for a while. I'd make Hanna and his
gang step around lively." And Croker paid his respects
to Theodore Roosevelt by saying: "Look at that wild man
the Republicans have nominated for Vice-President. He's
going screeching over the country, bellowing about the Ice
Trust." [7]

By the last days of the campaign, Croker was plainly worried, and in a surly mood. It was then that he gave out the
famous interview, so often cited, in which he declared hotly
that Bryan would be the next President of the United States
unless the Republicans stole the election, and then went on:
" I advise all Democrats to go to the polling places on election night, count noses, and see that they get counted. If
the vote doesn't tally, let them go in, pull out the fellows
in charge, and stand them on their heads. I want you to

print this — " Croker concluded, shaking his finger at the reporters.[8]

As a matter of fact, that same day, Chief Devery issued a provocative order which hinted at police partisanship at the polls. Governor Roosevelt promptly wired Mayor Van Wyck that he would be held responsible for any election disorders which might occur. Thereupon, Devery's order was rescinded, and the election passed off quietly in the metropolis. Bryan carried New York City handsomely, but the State and nation went heavily for McKinley and Roosevelt. For the second time, "The Great Commoner" had been badly beaten.

Croker's "favorite" had lost the race! He had backed the wrong horse, and must now pay the forfeit.

CHAPTER XXIII

THE BOSS CONFRONTS THE RISING STORM

WHEN Richard Croker surveyed his political prospects the morning after Bryan's defeat, the horizon of his future was dark with gathering clouds. His dream of national leadership was hopelessly shattered. His control of the State Democracy was gravely compromised. Most serious of all, his grip on the metropolis was shaken; for New York echoed to the stir of mustering foes. Nowhere could the Tammany Boss discern signs of cheer.

Of course, the docile Van Wyck was still Mayor, and the city government was staffed by his henchmen. But the sands of the Van Wyck administration were running low. Just one year hence, a Mayoralty election was due; and the present régime was becoming increasingly discredited. The Ice Trust scandal had been merely the most glaring of a series which clearly revealed the extravagance, inefficiency, and graft entrenched at City Hall. The sensational exposures of the Mazet Committee had not only roused reformers to fresh activity but had also given New York much bad publicity. Substantial business men, hitherto indifferent, had come to fear for the city's continued prosperity and were convinced that a municipal overhauling was needed. Lastly, the masses, disgruntled by the Ice Trust, were further stirred by the prevalence of commercialized vice and organized crime, which in many ways bore hard on the home life of the self-respecting poor. The omens thus portended a civic awakening in the campaign of 1901, much like that of 1894, which had driven Tammany from power.

The reform forces began their attack without delay. Immediately after the Presidential election, a group of influential citizens, headed by the Episcopal Bishop of New York, wrote an "open letter" to the Mayor, denouncing the vice and crime which was rampant on the East Side, and backing up their assertions by specific evidence which involved both the Police Department and Tammany notables.

Other complaints of a similar nature had been previously made, with no tangible effect. Now, however, matters were different. New York was astir with discontent, and Bishop Potter's open letter to Van Wyck evoked a salvo of applause from the public.

No one knew better than Richard Croker that the political atmosphere was changed. Tammany, thrown on the defensive, must take precautions. And the Boss knew that the most effective tactics would be a counter-move against vice. Were Tammany to take a positive step towards cleaning up the scandalous conditions which had aroused the moral sentiment of the community, it would tend to quiet popular excitement and at least partially parry the reformers' keen-edged thrust.

Accordingly, less than a week after Bishop Potter's letter, Croker appointed a Committee of five well-known Tammany men, headed by Lewis Nixon, to investigate and report upon the vice situation.

New York was agog at the news that Tammany had apparently started in to "clean house." Many persons, of course, dismissed the announcement with a cynical smile, as being sheer bluff. Yet certain aspects of Croker's surprising

move made his " Reform " Committee appear sincere. The
Chairmanship of Lewis Nixon was evidence that the Committee intended to do some real investigating. Mr. Nixon
belonged to the " kid glove " wing of Tammany Hall. A
Virginian by birth, and a graduate of Annapolis, he was a
man of wealth, education, and good standing, who would
not allow himself to be made ridiculous as the dummy head
of a Committee appointed solely for " whitewashing " purposes.

Croker himself had instructed his " Committee of Five "
to report their findings fearlessly. Furthermore, at a meeting of district leaders, he had stated in vigorous language
that if conditions were actually as black as they were painted,
they must be bettered at once. When, at this point, murmurs broke forth and one man, bolder than the rest, asserted
that nothing effectively could be done, Croker bounded from
his chair, strode over to the man, and shouted in his face:
" You say you don't know what you can do? What you
want to do is to act, and try to do something, anyway. You
can't stop it, you say. If you do nothing except say what
you can't do, you can never stop anything. But if the people
find anything is wrong, you be sure that the people can put
a stop to it, and will! " [1]

This angry outburst gives the key to Croker's sudden reforming zeal. The grizzled veteran, who had witnessed the
fall of Tweed and who had himself bowed low beneath the
political typhoon of 1894, had read the signs aright. He
knew that only drastic measures could save Tammany from
defeat the following year. The evidence, therefore, clearly
indicates that Croker had resolved to abate the worst aspects
of commercialized vice, and that his Committee was a genuine first step along this line.

But the Boss was now to learn the distinct limits to his autocratic power; for he was soon faced with opposition in Tammany itself. So sullenly determined was resistance to his commands that it taxed his strength to the utmost, and even threatened his throne.

The reasons for this are not far to seek. The Boss was rich, and was full of years and honors. But there were other leaders in the organization who had not yet " made their pile," and who, regardless of Mayoralty prospects, were still " working for their own pockets all the time." To those leaders, the tribute gathered from " protected " vice and crime was the main source, alike of their wealth and of their power. They proposed, therefore, to fight "reform," of any brand. If this hurt Tammany's chances in the future, it was just too bad; but they intended to " get theirs " while the getting was good. And the head of this unregenerate faction was " Big Tim " Sullivan.

Big Tim (otherwise known as " Dry Dollar " Sullivan, and " The Big Feller ") was a dangerous foe to whoever crossed his path. For, despite certain genial qualities, Tim Sullivan typified all that was worst in Tammany Hall. The story of his rise from slum squalor to the overlordship of the East Side is a picaresque romance of debased politics.

Born in an East Side tenement during the Civil War, Tim began his career at the age of eight, selling newspapers. That he had a keen eye to the main chance is shown by the boyhood anecdote which gained him his nickname, " Dry Dollar." One day, Tim was discovered back of a saloon, drying off the big green revenue-stamp which had been affixed to a brewery keg, under the fond impression that it was a dollar bill!

Young Sullivan entered politics early, and affiliated himself with the "Whyo Gang," one of the most desperate criminal organizations of the day. Largely through its influence, Sullivan was elected to the Legislature, on an anti-Tammany ticket, when only twenty-three years old.

At Albany, Sullivan met Tom Foley, an East Side Tammany leader; and Foley, noting the young man's aggressive ability, induced him to join the organization. Thereafter, Sullivan rose rapidly in politics, and in 1890, Croker made him leader of the Bowery district, just north of his old bailiwick, the Five Points.

Croker put Tim in charge there, to handle a perplexing situation. The Bowery district comprised not merely that notorious thoroughfare but also a large tenement area which had recently been overrun by the newer immigrant stocks, especially Jews and Italians. These new groups were beginning to worry Tammany, because it found them hard to manage. Tammany could handle the Irish to perfection, and the Germans fairly well; but the average old " leatherneck" district leader was too set in his ways to manage folk he did not in the least understand. A younger man with a more flexible mind was needed, and the Boss picked Tim Sullivan as just the lad for the job.

Croker had chosen well, for the new leader took the situation in hand with consummate skill. Both the Bowery itself and the adjacent tenement neighborhoods, though presenting widely different problems, were admirably administered — from Tammany's point of view.

The Bowery, when Tim Sullivan took charge, was not a flourishing Tammany district. It was a region of cheap amusement resorts and cheaper lodging-houses inhabited by a transient population of vagrants, petty criminals, and casual

laborers. Few of these men were registered voters or had
any interest in politics.

Tim Sullivan took in the situation at a glance. Here were
thousands of potential votes going to waste! Tim soon
remedied that. The lodging-houses were so " fixed" that
they regularly voted every roomer — and often more besides. Even the outer fringe of bums and bar-room loafers
were trained into fairly dependable "repeaters." By the
mid-nineties, the Bowery was Tammany's banner district.
So close-knit was Big Tim's organization that when, in the
Presidential election of 1892, one of his precincts turned in
388 Democratic and 4 Republican votes, he reported to
Croker: " Harrison got one more vote than I expected there,
but I'll find that feller! "

Big Tim achieved these striking results by a judicious
blend of generosity and terrorism. To either of these policies there were practically no bounds. In the awe-struck
eyes of his Neapolitan and Sicilian subjects, " The Big Feller " appeared alternately in the guise of patron saint and
implacable chief of the Mafia.

Tim certainly knew his Italians. The political jollifica-
tions in " Little Italy " rivalled its religious *festas*. On such
occasions the whole district would be draped in bunting, glow
with electric lights, and glare with red fire. There would
be parades in which, amid a blaze of rockets and Roman
candles, and to admiring cheers from wives and sweethearts,
the embattled Italian-Americans would march in serried battalions led by precinct captains astride fat brewery-truck
chargers, and would proudly salute their liege-lord as he
stood, big and jovial, in the reviewing-stand.[2] Also, for
the faithful there was largesse unfailing — free coal, free
ice, wondrous outings, and municipal jobs. As for the dis-

loyal — they soon found it wise, for their business and even for their health, to " move out of the ward."

The Jews were not so easy to manage. Their political independence was proverbial. They liked to do their own thinking, and were sometimes stampeded by strange enthusiasms. One could never be sure that they would " stay fixed." Bred to persecution, they were liable to be stubborn, even under threats. Yet " The Big Feller " usually had his way with this " stiff-necked " folk. For chronic recalcitrants, he had his corps of professional gunmen.

Big Tim's mobilization of all the vicious and criminal elements of the lower East Side into a standing army, regularly employed for terrorism and wholesale repeating, in return for political " protection," was the special feature of his rule. Isaiah Rynders would have risen from his grave in sheer admiration, could he have seen how his amateurish efforts in this same region had been surpassed by his talented successor. Nothing approaching it had ever been seen before — at least, not in Little Old New York.

" The Big Feller's " standing army was organized into three grand divisions: the gamblers, the pimps, and the thieves. And this " army " was amazingly numerous. The number of gamblers, alone, in New York City was then estimated at nearly 10,000. Over the entire gambling fraternity, Tim's sway was absolute; for one of his choicest " grafts " came through his headship of the " gambling ring " which he had organized.

As for the pimps, they were legion. These human leeches (mostly young Italians and Jews) specialized in recruiting for the Red-Light Districts of the Bowery and the Tenderloin, their victims being mostly young girls of their acquaintance from the tenements wherein they themselves had been reared. Recruiting-sergeants for commercialized vice, they were aptly termed *Red-Light Cadets*. These wretches were a terror to every tenement home; and since the Cadets enjoyed political protection, bereaved parents could seldom obtain redress. Their depredations filled the hearts of numberless humble folk with suppressed wrath which was to be unleashed in the political uprising of 1901.

Less sordid, but more sinister, was the mobilization of thieves and thugs. At this stage, the old-time gangs of Croker's youth had almost passed away, and the name itself was being applied to much smaller, purely criminal groups, known among themselves as " mobs." In the late eighties, a young East Side Irish thug arose, whose organizing genius entitles him to rank as the master-criminal of his age. His name was " Monk " Eastman, and he swiftly welded the East Side " mobs " into a loose yet efficient federation; with diversified " rackets," all under the direction of their " Big Shot."

Tim Sullivan did not overlook so potentially valuable an instrument of political domination. Therefore, Monk and Big Tim came to an understanding. By the terms of their compact, the super-gangster's thugs could be depended upon to act as " shock troops " for the district leader's political needs, while Monk was assured of protection (within limits) for himself and his followers. And Monk's " regulars " amply proved their worth by yeoman service at the polling-booths — and in *other* ways.[3]

Those were the bases of Big Tim's power. And that power stretched far beyond his own district; for " The Big Feller " proved as apt at diplomacy as at administration. By a series of alliances, he bound several neighboring district leaders to his cause. Furthermore, he had secret supporters throughout Manhattan, since he was the natural champion of every corrupt politician, indifferent to everything save personal gain.

By the late nineties, Big Tim had established a veritable vice and crime empire, controlling most of the city south of 14th Street; or, as the Underworld put it, "below de line."

So ambitious and self-willed a personage as Tim Sullivan could not fail ultimately to match his strength against the Boss. Indeed, from the moment that Sullivan got his district in hand, he openly resented any outside dictation. Even before Croker's "retirement" in 1894, he and Tim Sullivan had more than one tense moment, and during the Boss's exile, Sullivan had headed a conspiracy which aimed at Croker's overthrow. Then came that dramatic "showdown" at Tammany Hall, when the Boss's iron will made even "The Big Feller" quail before him.

But the overlord of the East Side went unpunished for his disloyalty, and throve mightily during the ensuing years of Tammany rule. As the Van Wyck administration neared its close, Tim Sullivan was more redoubtable than ever before.

This was the man whom the Boss, by his "Reform" Committee, had defied. For it was plain that if East Side vice and crime were to be sharply curbed, Big Tim's treasury would be depleted and his power undermined.

Sullivan warned his chief deliberately and fairly. Scarcely had the Committee of Five been appointed than Big Tim called on Croker. "Boss," he said, looking Croker squarely in the eye, "Boss, them fellers have got to stay out of my district, or there'll be trouble." And "them fellers" stayed

out. Mr. Nixon and his colleagues did not include the
Bowery in their vice tour.

Big Tim was not Croker's only visitor. Other leaders
came to express their disapproval. " Is this a bluff? " one
of them asked Croker, " or is it on the level? " " It's on
the level," replied Croker. " Well," exclaimed his caller
disgustedly, " if it's on the level, just count me out of this.
I won't have anything to do with it, and I think it will do
us more hurt than good." [4]

Tammany Hall was buzzing like an angry hive when the
Boss announced that he was off for England on his annual
vacation. Several of his intimates besought him to stay on
the job; but Croker answered that he was fagged out and
must have rest and change of scene if he was to be in form
for the Mayoralty campaign the following autumn. The
bitter disappointment of Bryan's defeat and the anxieties
crowding thick upon him had undoubtedly taken their toll.
When he sailed, late in November, the reporters noted that
he looked far from well.

From his English country seat, the Boss watched — and
cursed Tim Sullivan and the vice cabal. For Tammany's
external foes were rapidly gathering strength for their attack.
Three distinct groups (the non-partisan Reformers, the Republicans, and the anti-Tammany Democrats), though not
yet formally allied, were working amicably together for the
same objective — Tammany's overthrow.

The first blow was delivered by Theodore Roosevelt. Although elected Vice-President of the United States in the
recent campaign, Roosevelt would be Governor of New York
State until his term expired at the end of the year. One
of Governor Roosevelt's last official acts was an executive
order issued late in December, removing Asa Bird Gardiner

as District Attorney for gross neglect of duty and appointing in his stead Eugene A. Philbin, an independent Democrat of excellent reputation. Mr. Philbin promptly cleaned out the District Attorney's office by discharging Gardiner's assistants and replacing them with men of his own kind.

Governor Roosevelt had struck shrewdly, both at the Van Wyck administration and at Tim Sullivan's vice ring. So long as Gardiner was District Attorney and Devery was Chief of Police, they could play into each other's hands and render law enforcement a joke. Now, however, the legal end of this precious combination was out; for the new District Attorney was eager to proceed against prostitution and gambling. Also, Mr. Nixon and his colleagues could prove their sincerity, because they could lay information with the District Attorney's office which would be acted upon.

A second blow against Tammany came in February, 1901, when the Republican Legislature ousted Devery by the simple expedient of abolishing the office of Chief of Police. And, besides this, District Attorney Philbin ordered a series of sensational raids against gambling establishments, apparently inspired by Nixon's Committee of Five.

That was flat defiance of Big Tim Sullivan. And Big Tim was not slow to take up the challenge. The wrath of "The Big Feller" knew no bounds. He had long hated Nixon, and now publicly denounced him as a "kid-glove carpet-bagger" and an interloper in Tammany Hall.

Other leaders of "vice districts," likewise threatened in their prerogatives, followed Big Tim's lead. One irate leader, after sneering at Nixon's Committee as "The Farcical Five," said sarcastically to a reporter: "Say, I'd like to get out of politics, but I ain't going to be driven out. I'm a reformer now, like all the rest. Why, I had a di'mond stud that flashed a red light, an' I gave it away! "⁵

Big Tim was out for blood. He cabled Croker that Nixon must go, and that Devery must, somehow, be reinstated. Meanwhile, Devery was growling threats that, if " let down," he would "spill the beans " and start a scandal that would rock Tammany Hall to its foundations.

Croker was in a sad quandary. If he let Sullivan have his way, he would lose prestige and his grip on the organization. If Nixon's investigation was called off, all hope of allaying popular discontent might as well be abandoned. As for Devery; the Boss's political intuition told him that this brutal braggart, with his continual " wisecracks " and his naïve defiance to respectability, would be just the " heavy villain " the reformers needed to dramatize the issue before the public in the coming campaign.

On the other hand, Big Tim meant business. His threats were no idle boasts. He had warned the Boss frankly that if Tammany was going into the reforming game, the powerful vice and gambling interests would refuse to " loosen up " when the hat was passed around for the campaign fund. Indeed, Big Tim went so far as to intimate that, under certain circumstances, " the interests " might knife Tammany at the polls. And such defections would spell almost certain defeat for the Tammany ticket, in any event.

Furthermore, Croker's Boss-ship itself was imperilled by his present attitude. For the moment, the vice cabal was a minority, since Tim Sullivan could not count absolutely upon more than ten or a dozen district leaders, while the Boss had more than that number pledged to follow him through thick and thin. But there were still other leaders, who deplored the situation and whose object was to save Tammany from the disaster which a factional war on the eve of a Mayoralty campaign would entail. If Croker stuck to his guns, and thereby split Tammany wide open, might not these moderates join the Sullivan faction to depose Croker, on the understanding that a neutral should be elected Boss, who would restore "harmony" and give Tammany a fighting chance?

The Boss thus wrestled with a dilemma that looked bad, whichever way he might decide. Croker chose what he doubtless considered the lesser of two evils: he bowed to Big Tim's ultimatum. The proof of this was Van Wyck's appointment of Devery as "Deputy" Police Commissioner.

The Sullivan crowd was jubilant, while Lewis Nixon was proportionately incensed. First learning of Devery's appointment through the newspapers, Mr. Nixon characterized it as "a shame and an outrage." "These people," he went on, obviously referring to Big Tim and his associates, "are capable of anything." [6]

Mr. Nixon at once cabled the Boss, and when Croker cabled back confirming the fact, Nixon knew that he had been "let down." So, two days later, "The Farcical Five" turned in a "Final Report" (not published) to the Executive Committee of Tammany Hall, and went out of business. The Boss's rôle of "practical reformer" was definitely at an end.

The effect of this backdown on public opinion was precisely what could have been foreseen. The reformers cried: "I told you so!" and denounced Tammany, not merely as an unrepentant sinner but as an arrant hypocrite.

Still more serious was the marshalling of anti-Tammany Democrats into a compact organization. In mid-April a rousing mass-meeting, held at Carnegie Hall, launched the

" Greater New York Democracy." At that meeting there were progressive Democrats like Bird S. Coler, old-line Democrats like Matthew S. Breen, and, of course, all Croker's personal foes, ex-Tammany men, some of whom had been waiting many years for revenge.

" Down with Croker! " was the slogan. Mr. Breen struck the key-note when he stated: " Tammany Hall's authority rests very lightly upon the Democrats of the Bronx, where I live, and upon the other Boroughs outside of Manhattan. There are thousands of honest Democrats who are sick and tired of being led around by the nose by Mr. Croker."

The Squire of Wantage must have been in a grim mood as he silently made ready to return and face the inevitable.

CHAPTER XXIV

THE BOSS FIGHTS HIS LAST CAMPAIGN

THE thick-set, scrubby-bearded man who landed in Manhattan one September afternoon was the Richard Croker of former days. Grim and reticent, he refused to be interviewed. " Nothing to say, boys! " was his laconic greeting to the eager newspapermen. Accompanied by two or three intimate friends, he at once escaped from the jostling throng on the dock and rode uptown to the Democratic Club. Obviously, he shunned publicity of any kind.

From the moment he landed, the Boss was engulfed by the raging torrent of Tammany politics. The local primaries were only two days hence, and the Democratic primaries of 1901 were unusually important. Several of Croker's most trusted lieutenants were being opposed for re-election by the Sullivan faction. The strife had been bitter, and the outcome would weigh heavily at Tammany Hall.

The fiercest, and the most vital, of these contests was that in the Second Assembly District, down on the lower East Side. It was traditional fighting-ground, for it was practically the old Fourth Ward, whose stormy politics had enlivened New York's early days. The Second District was an historic survival from the past. Although, by this time, the East Side had been re-peopled by newer immigrant stocks, " The Second " remained almost as Irish as it had been half a century before. For many years, this Celtic stronghold had been ruled by a Tammany leader aptly named Patrick Divver.

"Paddy" Divver, as everybody called him, was one of the old breed of saloon-keeping district leaders, governing his subjects in the rough yet paternal fashion of a Gaelic chieftain. They were his folk; of his own blood and faith. Together, they formed a compact clan, linked by the tight bonds of mutual understanding. Until this fateful year, no one had ever seriously challenged Paddy Divver's authority in his own domain.

But now, "Paddy" was fighting for his political life. The challenger was "Big Tom" Foley, while behind Foley loomed the even more impressive form of "Big Tim" Sullivan. And the real cause of this local war was "Paddy's" loyalty to the Boss.

Divver was Croker's staunch henchman. When nearly every other East Side leader had made terms with Big Tim, "Paddy" had stubbornly refused to divide his allegiance. The Second Assembly District had thus become a sort of independent enclave in the Sullivan Empire, within which "The Big Feller's" writ did not run.

And this was not "Paddy's" only offense against the overlord of the East Side. Too often he had heeded the plaints of parents anxious for the safety of headstrong daughters, and curbed the activities of Red-Light Cadets. "The Interests" indignantly protested to Big Tim, their protector; but so long as Paddy Divver ruled, they could not work freely in his territory.

The edict had gone forth, therefore, that "Paddy" must be overthrown. And "Big Tom" Foley was the man to do the job.

The primary contest which ensued was an amazing battle.

Every trick in the game of ward politics was played by both sides, and the humblest voter in the district was subjected alternately to blandishments, bribes, and threats. Sullivan money was flung around with reckless abandon. Divver, though less well supplied with cash, touched every chord of local pride and sentiment. The motto emblazoned on his campaign banners was: *Don't Vote the Red-Lights into the Old Fourth Ward!*

This was the situation which was put up to Croker the instant he stepped down the gang-plank. Divver at once begged Croker to come to his aid. Sullivan, on his side, let the Boss know that he was out to " get " Divver, and that if Croker stepped into the row, it would mean the open breach which the Boss had already done so much to avoid. Any one, no matter how exalted his station, who interfered south of 14th Street, did so at his peril. That was Sullivan's warning. And the returned Boss had less than forty-eight hours to decide!

Big Tim had delivered a second ultimatum. And again, Croker side-stepped. The Boss declared himself officially neutral, and Paddy Divver received only covert aid from headquarters. " Big Tim " was too big to be openly defied.

The crucial day, September 17, arrived, and throughout Greater New York the polling-booths opened at sunrise. But the Second District of Manhattan had been astir since long before dawn. Shortly after midnight, dark figures had begun to trickle furtively into the district, coming mostly from the Bowery, the nearby Sullivan stronghold. As they passed under the street-lights, one would have noticed them to be short-statured, swarthy fellows; and if he knew his East Side thoroughly, he would have recognized them as Italian gunmen — picked " repeaters " and the best " shock-troops" in Tim Sullivan's "army." Tim was taking no chances. He was sending Foley his "finest," commanded by the notorious gangster, Paul "Kelly"—born *Vaccarelli*.

By two o'clock in the morning, the invaders had formed in line before every polling-place. It was tiresome waiting —but there were compensations. For soon, commissariat wagons rolled up, laden with hot coffee and sandwiches, smokes, whiskey, and even benches to sit on. Like all great commanders, Big Tim appreciated the truth of the military maxim that an army travels on its belly, and saw to it that his troops were well supplied.

It was not long before Paddy Divver and his staff were informed of the invasion. Crimson with wrath, the old chieftain gathered his clansmen about him and made ready for the fray. The official opening of the polls would be the gage of battle.

Just before the "zero hour," platoons of police tramped heavily through the streets and took up their posts about the polling-places. This made no difference to the rival factions, and as soon as the polls opened, fighting began. Brawny Irish lads, overtopping the invaders by a head, rushed to break the waiting lines.

Alas! The Divverites found themselves everywhere outnumbered; and their foes, while small in stature, were veterans at the game. At nearly every point the invaders held their ground, and the Divverites were scientifically beaten-up or calmly blackjacked. Amid the riotous tumult, the bluecoated guardians of the peace stood impassive or looked elaborately the other way. They were Devery's men, and they had their orders.

By 9 A.M., a big Foley vote had been cast, while few Divverites had reached the polls. As the morning wore on, the clansmen were filled with despairing fury. Old-time residents of the district, surveying the scene, danced and gibbered with rage; but Big Tim's machine ground inexorably on.

In the forenoon, at a certain polling-place, Big Tom Foley and Paddy Divver met face-to-face. Turning to the election officials, Foley remarked sardonically: "Here's the man who said in the Democratic Club last week that you Inspectors would jump out of a ten-story window for him." "You're a liar!" shouted Divver, raising his fist. He got no further, for a flying-wedge of Kelly's gangsters tackled him and landed him out in the street. The incident was closed.

At noon, the commissariat again appeared, heavily guarded, and the gunmen were given a good lunch, with appropriate extras. About 3 P.M. rain began to fall on the Foley lines, and a few stragglers slunk off to nearby saloons; though the rest pulled down hats and turned up coat-collars, stolidly prepared to take a drenching. But Big Tim's commissary department had thought even of this contingency; for soon brisk lieutenants appeared on the run, bearing bundles of umbrellas.

Sometimes, however, the umbrellas never reached the lines; for in several instances lurking Divverites rushed the bearer and bore him to the sidewalk. Reinforcements from both sides would arrive at the double, and a free fight would ensue. In the mêlée, however, the umbrellas met their doom. "Snap!" "Crack!" and when the fight was over, all that was left was tattered black cloth, splinters of wood, and twisted wire.

The polls closed at nightfall, and it needed no prophet to foretell that Paddy Divver was undone. When the returns were tabulated, Big Tom Foley was declared the winner by a crushing majority of over three to one.

That evening, the Foley headquarters blazed with light, while in the Divver camp "Paddy" sat amid a circle of sorrowing friends and fluently cursed his enemies. To the reporters he said bitterly: "Foley beat me, but how did he do it? He brought in every crook he could lay his hands on, and even sent out of town for more. Devery was in the deal, and lined these repeaters up and protected them while they voted. Foley and Carroll rode around in the morning and handed out the stuff, so what could you expect? No, I won't do anything. It's up to headquarters. But mind you: it'll be Croker's turn next. This wasn't my fight; it was Croker's. That combine is reaching out to control Tammany. I was beaten by these people and by Devery's police. Croker will believe some things now that he didn't believe before."[1]

The downfall of Paddy Divver echoed through Tammany Hall. Everybody knew that the Boss's authority had been set at naught; that he had not dared to rescue a faithful henchman; that loyalty to the Boss no longer paid — at least, as against the Sullivan crowd.

The effects were clearly apparent. Men who had hitherto obeyed the Boss's slightest nod, now argued with him. Leaders who had never once questioned his mandate, frankly criticized his orders. Tim Sullivan was openly insolent. Shortly after his triumph over Paddy Divver, he brazenly told the reporters: "Croker ain't the whole thing!"

Up at the Democratic Club, the Boss ruminated upon the ominous trend, portending the disintegration of his power. Never a word did he speak. Chewing endless black cigars, he screened himself behind a mask of silence.

Yet behind this veil of inscrutability, the Boss was thinking — and acting. Only a fortnight, at most, remained before the "slate" would be made up and the Mayoralty candidate chosen. In the framing of the ticket, the Sullivan faction obviously planned to have their say; and Croker, by himself, might be unable to block their game. So the Boss turned to his colleague "across the river," Hugh McLaughlin. With Tammany Hall divided against itself, the powerful Brooklyn Boss and his Kings County Democracy were called in to redress the balance.

Croker found the Kings County Democrats in a receptive mood. They had no use for Tim Sullivan and his crowd. They realized that the vice issue was rousing the people, and that if the Sullivan faction dictated the Democratic ticket, disaster would follow which would involve the Brooklyn Democracy as well as Tammany Hall. So when Croker told McLaughlin to suggest a Mayoralty candidate, the Brooklyn Boss named one who measured up to specifications.

McLaughlin's nominee was Edward M. Shepard, a prominent Brooklyn lawyer. Mr. Shepard was undoubtedly the best candidate available, under the circumstances. Not only was he a man of unblemished personal and professional standing; he had always been considered a practical reformer. Mr. Shepard had advocated reform measures like the Merit System and the Australian Ballot; he had helped to purge Kings County of political corruption, and he had supported Seth Low, the Fusion candidate, four years before. His scathing denunciations of Tammany on that occasion were on record, and indicated independence of Tammany control. Being a resident of Brooklyn, he was not involved in Tammany's domestic feuds, and therefore was in no danger of being knifed by a disgruntled faction at the polls. Furthermore, he would not merely have the Kings County organization solidly behind him, but he might also be expected to run strongly in the outlying Boroughs, which had become restive under Tammany rule.

This last feature was vital to Democratic success. In the previous Mayoralty campaign, Manhattan had been the decisive factor, and the tremendous plurality it had rolled up for Van Wyck and the entire Tammany ticket had ensured victory. Now, however, conditions were almost reversed. In Manhattan, Tammany feuds and discontent in the tenements made the local outlook uncertain. Unless the other Boroughs came through well, the Democratic ticket was beaten, and Fusion would win.

For " Fusion " was a certainty. An impressive coalition had been formed, including the Republicans. Platt and the local machine hacks had learned their lesson. Their betrayal of Seth Low at the last election had almost disrupted the party. Furthermore, McKinley's assassination by a crazy fanatic had made Theodore Roosevelt President of the United States. And Roosevelt, the militant reformer, kept a hand on New York politics. Like Croker, Platt had made the sad discovery that his Boss-ship was on the wane.

Seth Low was again the Fusion nominee, and his candidacy had the same strength — and limitations. Mr. Low was the ideal of municipal reformers. He spoke learnedly and incisively on abstruse subjects like budget-planning and tax-rates, in a fashion that moved a polite audience to decorous applause. But at a popular mass-meeting, when the crowd yearned for oratorical fireworks, he never got a " big hand." In short: Seth Low was very competent, very dignified — and rather dull. Devery, the eternal " wisecracker," made

New York grin when he dubbed the Fusion nominee, *Little Eva!*

Fortunately for the Fusionists, their candidate for District Attorney, William Travers Jerome, was a " live-wire " who made up for Mr. Low's deficiencies in personal magnetism. Jerome, a Justice of the Court of Special Sessions, had been one of the first to enlist in the crusade against commercialized vice. Long before the campaign, he had been one of District Attorney Philbin's mainstays in the latter's efforts against prostitution and gambling. The previous June, Justice Jerome had stated in a newspaper interview: " People are simply ignorant of conditions on the East Side. If these conditions existed in some other communities, there would be a Vigilance Committee speedily organized, and somebody would get lynched." [2]

This vigorous statement was but a pale reflection of Jerome's campaign speeches. When the contest was at its height, he would speak half a dozen times every evening, careering through the streets in a racing automobile, to get from one hall to another on schedule.

Jerome had the knack of dramatizing the sordid tragedy of the girl victims of commercialized vice, in such a way as to leave his audience raging against the politicians who protected and fostered such woe. Even foreign-born audiences on the East Side, who could scarcely understand English, sensed his meaning and burned with indignation. Bearded Jews and swart Italians, fathers of growing daughters, sobbed and wailed as they listened to Jerome; recalled what they themselves had seen, or even suffered; and went home vowing that, come what might, Fusion should have their votes.

Jerome's tireless energy contrasted strangely with his

delicate appearance. He looked so frail that, early in the campaign, Big Tim Sullivan remarked condescendingly: " Why, that feller couldn't strike a blow that would knock a hole through a pound of butter! " But after the fiery Justice had made his first whirlwind tour of the East Side, " Big Tim " hastily revised his observations.

The Fusionists based their strategy on three main lines of attack: Protected Vice, Devery — and Croker. From the first, the Boss was under heavy fire. When Seth Low accepted the Fusion nomination, he stated: " The main issue of the campaign is the wresting of the city from those who permit one man to dominate the organization of his party in the interest ' of his own pocket all the time '; and, as if to add insult to injury, to do this from abroad, as though the proud city of New York had been reduced once more to the condition of a crown colony."

The Boss was certainly in the limelight. Each day, the Fusion newspapers carried cartoons lampooning " The Squire of Wantage," together with his race-horses, his prize bulldogs, and even his pigs. Campaign posters and campaign ditties continued the story, and held up the Boss to mingled obloquy and ridicule.

To all this, the Democrats replied in kind, and New York was deluged with the voluminous output of rival propagandas. Both sides had staffs of cartoonists, jokesmiths, and song-writers, who worked overtime and scored many a telling hit.

Perhaps the cleverest posters were those which played upon a commercial advertising theme. A leading soap concern chanced to be running a series of attractive advertisements in the form of pictures coupled with doggerel verse proclaiming the immaculateness of a place called *Spotless*

Town. A Tammany cartoonist seized upon the idea and drew a poster depicting *Spotter Town,* wherein Mr. Low figured as a long-nosed Puritan, snooping into everybody's affairs, and prohibiting such venial sins as a game of penny-ante, a stolen kiss, or a Sunday glass of beer.

But this poster had barely been distributed before a Fusion poster appeared, showing *Spotted Town* and its ruler, a most unflattering caricature of Richard Croker; while below was this bit of verse:

> *This is the Ruler of Spotted Town*
> *And known as such the world around;*
> *He doesn't care for such repute,*
> *For all he's after is the loot.*
> *But will he get the needed dough?*
> *Well, hardly, for we'll win with Low!*

Sallies like these injected a humorous touch into what was otherwise a fierce and feverish campaign. Croker, however, was in no mood to see the humor of the situation. As the great struggle neared its climax, the Boss's intuition, which never failed in local politics, warned him that the tide was setting the Fusion way. And, in his heart of hearts, Croker must have known that Democratic defeat would mean also the end of his political career.

Day by day, the Boss grew glummer and more morose. Unable to sleep, he would rise before dawn and stand silently at the windows of the Democratic Club, gazing out at street sweepers and passing milk wagons; or, again, with bowed head, he would pace the empty halls and club-rooms. Seemingly, he made no effort to conceal the strain under which he labored.

And the strain was terrific; for the Boss was putting the

last ounce of himself into the battle, grimly determined, either to win or to go down fighting. From early morning until far into the night, the Boss was at work, pouring men and money into crucial districts; driving his lieutenants to their uttermost; tapping every channel of influence and power.

The close of the campaign was enlivened by a startlingly humorous episode: Big Bill Devery blew up! Smarting under a particularly keen thrust of Jerome's, Devery vented his long-suppressed wrath to the reporters. Pulling at his huge mustaches, and interlarding his remarks with resounding oaths, the mammoth " Deputy " Police Commissioner thundered: " That man Jerome oughter be locked up on Ward's Island! He ain't sound mentally. There's somethin' the matter with him. He's like the rhinoceros up in the Park. Every time he goes down under water he comes up with a gulp and blows it all over everybody. He's goin' around insultin' everything. . . It wouldn't take me ten minutes to go an' take him by the back of the neck an' lock him up. But that wouldn't do just now. . . Will they put me out — Low and those fellers? G'wan! Never! Devery stays right here! " [3]

" Big Bill's " glaring indiscretion got him into trouble with his own crowd. Shepard indignantly repudiated the assertion that Democratic victory would mean Devery secure in his job. Also, it was currently believed that " Big Bill " was promptly summoned to the Democratic Club by the irate Boss, who realized the damage that Devery had done.

Election day came; and before the tardy November sunrise, the battle of the ballots had begun. By noon, it was evident that both sides were polling a tremendous vote. As

THE WRECK OF THE PIRATE SHIP
NOVEMBER 1901

afternoon waned, the great city gave itself up to one of those stupendous "election nights" for which it had long been famed.

By sundown, streets and avenues resounded to the tramp of crowds. Along the principal crosstown thoroughfares, from 14th to 125th Streets, rivers of excited humanity, pouring steadily from the East and West Side, converged upon Broadway. In the nipping November air, urchins were wildly crying "Extra!" And when darkness had fallen, election bulletins began flashing on the big canvas screens in front of the newspaper offices.

Soon Broadway was so jammed that the police could hardly clear passage for the street-cars. Herald Square was quite impassable. Even spacious Madison Square was filled with an immense multitude, eagerly watching election returns or gazing upward at the searchlight on the tower of the Garden, which, by the angle of its flickering beam, would announce the outcome.

On this night, however, the crowds were not kept long in suspense. The first returns from Brooklyn showed that, even in his home territory, Shepard was running badly. When figures from the East Side tenement districts began to come in, veteran observers gasped in amazement; for they disclosed a popular defection from Tammany such as no one then present had ever seen. Men looked at one another and murmured the word, "Landslide!"

A landslide it was — for Fusion. And as each successive bulletin emphasized the victory, with Brooklyn lost to Shepard, and Manhattan won by Low, the crowds were seized with a wild delirium. Horns, rattles, sirens, and cheering, roaring voices, blended in one vast diapason of sound. Impromptu Fusion parades sprang up like magic, the close-linked ranks swinging along in an ecstasy of joy, brandishing brooms and banners to the sky.

At ten o'clock, Shepard conceded defeat. Seth Low received the tidings of victory in the library of his home, surrounded by his family and intimate friends. Cheering crowds soon gathered outside his door, swelled by delegations headed by brass bands, come to congratulate him on his success. What a contrast to the scenes of another November night, four years before!

But down at Tammany Hall, all was bitterness and gloom. Shortly after the polls closed, the Tammany generals gathered around the long table in the Executive Committee Room to get the news from the front. The Boss had the seat of honor, directly opposite the whirring ticker that brought the returns. To right and left stretched a line of anxious faces, somewhat blurred by the haze of tobacco smoke which increasingly filled the room. Outside the Wigwam, 14th Street was blocked by a dense, jostling throng. When the doors were opened, the crowd surged in, and the thunder of feet trooping upstairs to the big auditorium made a hollow, booming sound.

Inscrutable, the Boss sat in his big armchair, a long black cigar tightly gripped between his teeth. Not a muscle of his mask-like face moved as the first ominous returns came in. Only when the dread tidings from Brooklyn and Manhattan's East Side arrived, did Croker begin to show signs of suppressed emotion. First, he shifted his cigar to the other side of his mouth; then he began figuring with pencil and paper; finally, he perched himself on the arm of his chair. Thus far, he had not spoken a word.

But some of the Boss's lieutenants were not cast in his iron mould. Men gnawed their lips; bit their finger-nails; hung their heads and muttered together in low tones. Van Wyck, in particular, was ghastly pale and seemed on the verge of collapse.

Only one man in this disconsolate gathering appeared exempt from the pall which was settling on his fellows. That man was Big Tim Sullivan. A sardonic smile lurking in the corners of his mouth, and a hard gleam in his eyes, " The Big Feller " strolled nonchalantly over to Croker.

" Well, Boss," he remarked casually, "you see *my* district came through o.k." Croker gave him a curt nod. Still, not a word.

When one of his trusted friends appealed to him for his verdict, Croker broke silence: " I don't give it up yet. We always finish well."

But ere long, semi-final returns quenched the last hope. Then the Boss slowly rose and said: " It would appear that Shepard is beaten. A change is a good thing sometimes; but Tammany Hall will be here when we are all gone."

Then, still slowly, seemingly deep in thought, Croker left the Committee Room, walked out of Tammany Hall, and left for the Democratic Club, through the streets of that city whereof he was no longer master.

EPILOGUE

" THE TAMMANY DERBY " — AND TWILIGHT

I⟶ is Derby Day — the climax of England's racing season. Epsom Downs is thronged with a vast multitude. Hundreds of thousands are there assembled. His Majesty the King and 'Arry the Coster; lords, ladies, and gentlemen; bank clerks and navvies, have foregathered in the wondrous fraternity of British sport.

The horses appear. They are magnificent animals; the finest the British Isles can breed. Among them is a splendid three-year-old stallion. His name is *Orby*, and his owner is Mr. Richard Croker, who reared the colt at his stud-farm, *Glencairn*, near Dublin, Ireland.

Orby is not the Derby favorite; he is entered at odds of 100 to 9. But he is the pride of a stud carefully bred over many years, and those who best know him believe in his racing powers. His master, assuredly, appraises him with a confident smile.

Richard Croker has not changed much since he resigned his Tammany chieftainship nearly six years ago, shortly after his last great campaign. His beard is grayer, and his hair is almost white. Yet his face is ruddy and his eyes have the clear light of health. Obviously, a quiet, open-air life agrees with him. From under the brim of his silken beaver, the Ex-boss watches *Orby*. Not a muscle moves; just that intent, silent gaze.

They are off! Down the course streams a blurr of horses and jockeys. *Orby* and his rider, clad in light blue silk, are lost in the straining ruck. The air vibrates with a vast murmur as the crowds, wrought to the highest pitch, follow the race with their eyes; their hearts; their very souls.

The first quarter is passed; the second; the third — and round Tattenham Corner a mass of rushing horses, topped with the brilliant colors of silk-clad jockeys, thunders into the home-stretch.

A close finish! The enormous multitude vibrates with passion. The diffused murmur deepens into a dull roar; muffled at first through straining throats, but rising rapidly towards a mighty crescendo. Ah, the hopes, the yearnings, the millions of pounds sterling that hang upon a stride taken in a pulse-beat!

Then — " *Orby* wins! " " The American horse wins! " " *Orby!* " " *Orby!* " " *Orby!* "

Epsom Downs is a mad riot. Laborers, touts, Peers of the Realm, the King himself, are swept into a common welter of wild delirium. What matter that the winner was not the favorite; that he is an American horse, ridden by an American jockey? He has won handsomely, in a splendid spurt which bore him on to victory by two full lengths! So even the biggest losers shout, yell, cheer; wave hats, veils, handkerchiefs; acclaim *Orby* the hero of " The Tammany Derby." For such is the nickname by which the great race of the year 1907 goes down in Britain's sporting annals.

Over the green turf of Epsom Downs the frantic multitudes are streaming. Amid the tumult, the stocky, white-bearded sportsman leads *Orby* past the grandstand, where Edward VII and his Court stand at attention to acclaim the victor. Mr. Croker raises his silk hat in silent acknowledgment, and the King returns the salute.

So RICHARD CROKER attained the dearest ambition of his life — the blue ribbon of the world's turf. None but a turfman can understand what this means. To British sportsmen, the Derby is the highest goal. English gentlemen of wealth and ancient lineage have vainly pursued the silken token all their lives. English families of high degree have sought and dreamed of it for generations. Ancestral forests have been cut down and castles mortgaged to the hilt, that blighted turf ambitions might be repaired. Lord Roseberry remarked in the flush of his brilliant youth that the two objectives of his career were to be Prime Minister and to win the Derby. When both were his, Britain acclaimed him Fortune's favorite. Yet a grim Tammany brave had, if anything, outmatched him in astounding success.

From the moment that Richard Croker laid down the burden of his Tammany chieftainship in the spring of 1902, he concentrated relentlessly upon his sporting goal. When the Ex-boss sailed for England, amid the plaudits of numberless friends and henchmen, he had said: " I am out of politics, and now I am going to win the Derby." And, five years later, he made good his word. To thronging friends and admirers on that memorable Derby Day, Croker exclaimed: " I have had some exciting experiences in my time. I have had my share of victories. But this is the greatest of all! "

Croker's triumph was due to no chance fluke. For many years he had planned and prepared against the supreme hour. Dollars mounting into the hundred thousands had been lavishly spent in perfecting his stud. Famous stallions and brood-mares had been purchased at fancy prices; the ablest

THE EX-KING ON THE TURF

trainers and keenest jockeys had been in his pay. Every important race-track in America, England, and Ireland had seen his Yale-blue colors ride to victory. On the turf, as in politics, Croker's dogged will and tireless patience had achieved commensurate results.

RICHARD CROKER outlived his hour of supreme triumph by nearly fifteen years. Yet this slow twilight of a long life merits scant notice and is tinged with a sadness almost sordid. Year after year, the Ex-boss followed the same general routine. Most of his time was passed on his estate at Glen-cairn, Ireland; though during the winter months he usually sojourned at West Palm Beach, Florida.

These annual migrations were made *via* New York, and Croker liked to stop a week or two in the metropolis, to greet old friends and revive old memories. But each year the friends grew fewer, and the grizzled veteran became more and more a legendary figure, almost unknown to a city which was swiftly changing out of recognition from the New York of his day.

Croker's declining years were soured by family troubles. Shortly after the death of his first wife, from whom he had been long estranged, he married again. His bride was nearly half a century his junior, and was of Indian descent.

This second marriage involved the old man in acrimonious disputes with his children, which presently culminated in bitter litigation. A snarl of law-suits began, both in America and Ireland; and those legal tangles, persisting after his death, are even yet not wholly unravelled. When a friend once asked Croker his views on the outcome, the aged man answered with a flash of his dry humor: "The lawyers'll get all the money!"

Legal difficulties were undoubtedly the proximate cause of Croker's end. Unexpectedly kept in America by court proceedings throughout the entire summer of 1921, Croker was determined to return to his home in Ireland, and finally sailed in mid-October.

The voyage was unusually stormy, and Croker contracted a heavy cold. When the liner arrived off Queenstown, disturbed conditions in Ireland (then in the final throes of the rebellion) made it impossible for passengers to land; so Croker and his wife had to go on to Liverpool, and thence to Holyhead for the Dublin packet. Reaching Dublin late at night, the Crokers, like the other passengers, had to wait on a draughty pier while their luggage was examined. This renewed exposure aggravated Croker's condition, and he arrived at Glencairn a very sick man.

The Ex-boss made a good fight for life. At times he seemed better, and on fine days of the soft Irish spring he would be wheeled out of doors, to get a bit of sun and breathe the mild air. A month before his death he was greatly cheered by the news that his favorite mare, *Orlinda*, had borne a very promising foal, sired by the Derby winner, *Sunstar*. So heartened was Croker by these glad tidings that he glimpsed fresh victories on the turf, and laughingly told a visiting friend that he hoped to attend the Dublin races that season.

However, this rally proved to be the last flicker of a waning vitality. In mid-April, Croker grew worse, and his physicians confidentially told his wife that the end was near. Nevertheless, the old man longed for sun and air, and on a fine morning only four days before his death he was wheeled out of doors to view his mausoleum, recently erected on the grounds of his estate. Silently he viewed it, built among rocks beside a shaded pool, a stone's throw from the grave of *Orby*. Then, apparently sensing his approaching end, he murmured: " I am ready for it."

On the afternoon of the last day of April, Richard Croker suddenly and painlessly passed away, in his eightieth year.

NOTES

CHAPTER I

[1] According to the census of 1790, Philadelphia was the largest city of the Union, with 42,000 population. New York ranked second with 33,000 and Boston third with 18,000.

[2] For this early period, see especially: Agram C. Dayton, *The Last Days of Knickerbocker Life in New York* (New York 1872); Carlos Martyn, *William E. Dodge: The Christian Merchant* (New York 1890); Frank Moss, *The American Metropolis*, 3 vols. (New York 1897).

[3] Charles Dickens, *American Notes* (London 1842).

[4] The major portion of this survey will be found conveniently quoted in: Denis Tilden Lynch, *Boss Tweed*, pp. 127–128 (New York 1927).

[5] "An English Workman," *London versus New York* (London 1859). This small volume is little known and is today very rare.

[6] *Ibid.* p. 3.

[7] *Ibid.* p. 36.

[8] *Ibid.* p. 37.

[9] *Ibid.* p. 37.

[10] *Ibid.* see pp. 28–29.

[11] See especially: G. W. Edwards, "New York City Politics before the Revolution"; *Political Science Quarterly:* December 1921.

CHAPTER II

[1] Boarding-house runners were of various nationalities, but they usually specialized on their respective countrymen. Since the *Henry Clay* had an almost solidly Irish steerage, Irish runners came down to meet her. Had she come from an English port, English runners would have handled the job.

The incidents of the landing of the Croker family have been reconstructed from fragmentary evidence, and therefore may not have occurred precisely as narrated. The evidence, however, does show that something very like this *did* happen to them; in other words, that they had about the average landing-experiences encountered by friendless immigrants of the period. I have, therefore, here taken some slight factual liberties, in order to portray their first experiences in New York with a vividness and local color otherwise impossible.

² These details regarding immigrant boarding-houses are taken from a book published in New York in 1849, entitled, *New York in Slices*, by a writer anonymously signing himself "An Experienced Carver"; pp. 84–85. For further details concerning hardships of newly arrived immigrants, see the book by "An English Workman" quoted in the previous chapter; also: Joseph I. C. Clarke, *My Life and Memories*, pp. 71–72 (New York 1925); Alfred Henry Lewis, *Richard Croker* (New York 1901).

³ Anonymous, "Squatter Life in New York"; *Harper's Magazine*: September 1880. For further data regarding squatters, see: James D. McCabe, *New York by Gaslight*, p. 443 (New York 1882); Junius H. Browne, *The Great Metropolis*, pp. 1–2 (Hartford 1869); Lyman Abbott, *Reminiscences*, p. 25 (New York 1915).

⁴ An excellent historical survey of the New York tenement problem is to be found in: Jacob A. Riis, *How the Other Half Lives*, pp. 1–20 (New York 1890). For further data, see: Frank Moss, *The American Metropolis*, Vol. II, pp. 357–367; Edward Crapsey, *The Nether Side of New York*, pp. 111–137 (New York 1872); Charles Stelzle, *A Son of the Bowery* (New York 1926); Frederic C. Howe, *The Modern City and Its Problems* (New York 1914). Also, Charles Dickens' celebrated description of the Five Points in his *American Notes*.

⁵ Riis, *op. cit.* p. 20.

⁶ Alfred Henry Lewis, *Richard Croker*, p. 16.

CHAPTER III

¹ See: Charles Stelzle, *A Son of the Bowery*, pp. 16–17. This well-known preacher and social worker frankly relates his boyhood gang experiences, and is not at all ashamed of them. They were simply inevitable.

² Herbert Asbury, *The Gangs of New York*, p. 246 (New York 1928). This interesting volume is full of piquant details concerning the gang life of old New York. See also: Frank Moss, *The American Metropolis*.

³ Lyman Abbott in his *Reminiscences*, pp. 34–35, gives a vivid account of a great gang battle which he himself witnessed at close quarters.

⁴ Cited by Moss, Vol. III, p. 51.

⁵ Browne, *The Great Metropolis*, p. 131.

⁶ For these and other incidents of Croker's youth, besides Alfred Henry Lewis' biography of Croker, previously cited, see: Louis Seibold, "Richard Croker"; *Munsey's Magazine*: August 1901; E. J. Edwards, "Richard Croker"; *McClure's Magazine*: November 1895; William Allen White, "Richard Croker"; *Munsey's Magazine*: August 1901: biographical sketch in *The New York Times* of April 30, 1922.

⁷ Dr. Thomas Addis Emmet in his autobiography (*Incidents of My Life*, New York 1911) bitterly assails the Republican authorities for what he considers their tyrannical and provocative attitude during the Civil War period. Dr. Emmet himself, as an anti-war Democrat, suffered official espionage and social ostracism. His charges, whether well founded or not, reveal a point of view seldom appreciated.

CHAPTER IV

1 James Bryce, *The American Commonwealth*, Vol. II, p. 637 (New York 1888). For other comment on early political practices, see: Dorman B. Eaton, *The Government of Municipalities*, p. 11 (New York 1899); Samuel P. Orth, *The Boss and the Machine*, p. 27 (New Haven 1919).

2 Orth, *op. cit.* p. 54.

3 Bryce, *Modern Democracies*, Vol. II, pp. 109–110 (New York and London 1924).

4 Denis Tilden Lynch, *Boss Tweed* (New York 1927).

5 *Ibid.* pp. 37–39.

6 *Ibid.* pp. 42–43.

7 *Ibid.* pp. 49–50.

8 *Plunkitt of Tammany Hall:* A series of very plain talks on very practical politics, delivered by Ex-senator George Washington Plunkitt, the Tammany Philosopher, from his rostrum — the New York County Court-House Bootblack-Stand — and recorded by William L. Riordan (New York 1905).

9 *Ibid.*

10 Quoted in William T. Stead, *Despairing Democracy*, p. 42 (London 1897).

11 William Allen White, "Croker"; *McClure's Magazine:* February 1901; William L. Chenery, "So This is Tammany Hall!"; *Atlantic Monthly:* September 1924.

12 Quoted in Stead, *Despairing Democracy*, p. 50.

13 The detailed evidence cited in M. R. Werner, *Tammany Hall*, p. 305 (New York 1928).

14 Cited by John D. Townsend, *New York in Bondage*, p. 158 (New York 1901).

15 Werner, *op. cit.* p. 307.

16 *Ibid.*

17 Cited by Matthew P. Breen, *Thirty Years in New York Politics*, p. 664 (New York 1899).

18 *Ibid.*

CHAPTER V

1 Werner, *Tammany Hall*, pp. 180–181.

2 In those days, each party printed its own ballots and handed them to the voters. The possibilities for fraud and intimidation are obvious.

3 This was not the precise line-up in 1872; the factions were even more shifting and complicated. But since we are not primarily concerned in this book with the political details of those years, we have sketched a foreshortening which gives the general situation for the period as a whole.

4 His standard biography is: J. F. McLaughlin, *The Life and Times of John Kelly* (New York 1885). This work is frankly favorable to Kelly. Matthew P. Breen's *Thirty Years of New York Politics* paints a less roseate picture.

CHAPTER VI

[1] The dialogue and details of this episode are taken from the record of the trial. The best summary of the whole affair easily available is found in Werner, *Tammany Hall*, pp. 308–311.

[2] Werner, *op. cit.* p. 310

[3] The article here cited was written in the summer of 1901, at the height of Croker's power.

[4] Louis Seibold, "Richard Croker"; *Munsey's Magazine:* August 1901.

[5] *Ibid.*

CHAPTER VII

[1] Alfred Henry Lewis, *The Boss: And How He Came to Rule New York* (New York 1904).

[2] *Ibid.* pp. 207–210.

CHAPTER VIII

[1] H. W. Walker, "The Trail of the Tammany Tiger"; a series of articles in *The Saturday Evening Post:* March–April 1914.

[2] The literature on the American Boss is extensive. Even foreign writers like Bryce and Ostrogorski have treated him at length. The best general works on the subject are: Samuel P. Orth, *The Boss and the Machine* (New Haven 1919); William Bennett Munro, *Personality and Politics* (New York 1924); Lincoln Steffens, *The Shame of the Cities* (New York 1904); Frederic C. Howe, *The City: The Hope of Democracy* (New York 1905).

[3] Alfred Henry Lewis, *Richard Croker*, p. 93 (New York 1901).

[4] Louis Seibold, "Richard Croker"; *Munsey's Magazine:* August 1901.

[5] Lewis, *Richard Croker*, p. 74.

[6] Lewis, *The Boss*, pp. 354–355.

[7] The conversations from which the above excerpts have been taken were published by Stead in his magazine, the London *Review of Reviews*, in October 1897.

[8] Walker, *op. cit.*

CHAPTER IX

[1] A good survey of radical tendencies in our national life may be found in Charles A. and Mary R. Beard, *The Rise of American Civilization*, 2 vols. (New York 1927).

[2] See the analysis of both Tammany and anti-Tammany psychology in Thompson, *Politics in a Democracy*, Chapters IX to XI.

[3] Beard, *op. cit.* Vol. II, pp. 396–397.

[4] William Allen White, "Croker"; *McClure's Magazine*, February 1901.

[5] Notably the so-called "Workingmen's" and "Equal Rights" move-

ments of the early Eighteen-thirties. A good survey of both these movements in New York politics is found in Myers' *History of Tammany Hall*, Chapters X and XII. For the broader aspects, see Beard, *op. cit.*

CHAPTER X

[1] *The New York Herald:* November 9, 1887.
[2] H. W. Walker, *The Trail of the Tammany Tiger.*
[3] *The New York Herald:* September 22, 1888.
[4] See account in *The New York Herald* of October 6, 1888.
[5] *The New York Herald:* November 7, 1888.
[6] Both matters will be discussed in later chapters.

CHAPTER XI

[1] H. F. Gosnell, *Boss Platt and His New York Machine*, p. 14 (Chicago 1924). This scholarly biography, based on intensive research, is the best single source for a consideration of Platt, the man and his political career.
[2] Thomas Collier Platt, *Autobiography* (Compiled and Edited by Louis J. Lang) p. xxi (New York 1910).
[3] Gosnell, *op. cit.* p. 15.
[4] Federal patronage as an important source of power to the Republican Party everywhere must not be forgotten. During the entire period from 1861 until Cleveland's first inauguration in 1883, the Republicans were in power at Washington, and thus disposed of practically all Federal offices throughout the Union. The first Federal Civil Service Act was not passed until 1883.
[5] Theodore Roosevelt, *Autobiography*, p. 274 (New York 1913).
[6] Gosnell, p. 328.
[7] Roosevelt, *Autobiography*, pp. 62–63.
[8] *Ibid.* pp. 63–64.
[9] As the city of Washington, D. C., is ruled by a Commission appointed by Congress.
[10] The forerunners of our modern primaries.
[11] Quoted from Gosnell, p. 85.

CHAPTER XII

[1] *The New York Herald:* February 5, 1890.
[2] *Ibid.* February 6, 1890.
[3] *Ibid.* March 29, 1890.
[4] *Ibid.* April 30, 1890.
[5] *Ibid.* June 24, 1890.
[6] See metropolitan press accounts under date of June 28, 1890.

NOTES

CHAPTER XIII

1 *Mazet Investigation:* Vol. I, p. 352 (State of New York, Official Publication; 5 vols. Albany 1900).
2 *Plunkitt of Tammany Hall*, pp. 3–10.
3 Job E. Hedges (quoted from Werner, *Tammany Hall*, p. xv).
4 Theodore Roosevelt, *Autobiography*, p. 168.
5 Townsend, *New York in Bondage*, p. 165.
6 *Mazet Investigation:* Vol. I, pp. 352–353.
7 *Ibid.* Vol. I, p. 442.
8 Walker, *The Trail of the Tammany Tiger.*

CHAPTER XIV

1 Asbury, *The Gangs of New York*, p. 175.
2 Junius H. Browne, *The Great Metropolis*, pp. 25–26.
3 Alexander Gardiner, *Canfield: Host to the Nineties*, p. 150. (New York 1930).
4 New York, 1894.
5 *Mazet Investigation:* Vol. II, pp. 2351–2354.
6 *Lexow Investigation:* Vol. II, pp. 1538–1539.

CHAPTER XV

1 The first edition of James Bryce's *American Commonwealth* appeared in 1888, and Theodore Roosevelt's *Essays on Practical Politics* were published that same year. To cite a few other outstanding examples of this new political literature, we may mention: Frank J. Goodnow, *Municipal Problems* (New York 1897); Dorman B. Eaton, *The Government of Municipalities* (New York 1899); two interesting series of articles on municipal affairs in: *Annals of the American Academy of Political and Social Science*, May 1893 and May 1895.
2 *Mazet Investigation:* Vol. I, p. 345.
3 *Ibid.* p. 554.
4 William Bennett Munro, *Personality in Politics*, pp. 8–9 (New York 1924). His essay on *The Reformer in Politics*, from which the above is quoted, is an excellent short survey of the subject.
5 *Ibid.* p. 5.
6 Werner, *Tammany Hall*, pp. 348–349.
7 *Ibid.* p. 330.

CHAPTER XVI

¹ Quoted from Werner, *Tammany Hall*, p. 443.
² Sydney Brooks, " Tammany Again "; *The Fortnightly Review* (London) : December 1903.
³ *Ibid.*
⁴ Finley Peter Dunne, Essay entitled " Lexow "; subsequently re-published in the volume of collected essays entitled: *Mr. Dooley in the Hearts of His Countrymen* (Boston 1899).
⁵ Alfred Hodder, *A Fight for the City*, pp. 79–81.
⁶ Brooks, *op. cit.*
⁷ Denis Tilden Lynch, *Boss Tweed*, p. 131
⁸ Werner, *op. cit.* p. 445.
⁹ *The New York Tribune:* December 17, 1893.

CHAPTER XVII

¹ See illustrated article entitled, " Mr. Richard Croker in His English Home," published in *Black and White* (London) : November 10, 1900.
² On this subject, see special article by Martin W. Littleton, entitled, " The Kings County Democracy," in: James K. McGuire, *The Democratic Party in the State of New York:* Vol. II (New York 1905).
³ Walker, *The Trail of the Tammany Tiger.*
⁴ *The New York Tribune:* September 8, 1897.
⁵ Louis Seibold, " Richard Croker "; *Munsey's Magazine:* August 1901. For other accounts of this episode, see files of the metropolitan press for early October, 1897; especially, a good article in *The New York Tribune* of October 6, 1897.

CHAPTER XVIII

¹ Gosnell, *Boss Platt*, p. 233.
² *Ibid.*
³ Leading editorial in *The American Review of Reviews:* November 1897 (Dr. Albert Shaw, editor).
⁴ Quoted from Werner, *Tammany Hall*, p. 456.
⁵ See *The New York Tribune:* October 23, 1897.
⁶ Blake, *History of the Tammany Society*, p. 177.

CHAPTER XIX

¹ Walker, *The Trail of the Tammany Tiger.*
² *The New York Tribune:* January 1, 1898.
³ *The American Review of Reviews:* February 1898.
⁴ Walker, *op. cit.*

NOTES

⁵ William Allen White, *Croker.*
⁶ Carl Schurz, "Our New Monarchy"; *Harper's Weekly:* January 29, 1898.

CHAPTER XX

¹ *The New York Tribune:* July 30, 1898.
² From an interview in *The New York Herald* of May 1, 1922.
³ *The New York Herald:* September 28, 1898.
⁴ Theodore Roosevelt, *Autobiography,* p. 296.
⁵ *The New York Tribune:* November 10, 1898.

CHAPTER XXI

¹ An amusing account of Devery in action will be found in: Arthur Ruhl, "The Caliph and His Court"; *McClure's Magazine:* August 1901.
² Josiah Flint, "York: A Dishonest City"; *McClure's Magazine:* April 1901.
³ See Chapter XIII.
⁴ *Mazet Investigation:* Vol. I, p. 7.
⁵ *Ibid.* Vol. I, pp. 38 and 55.

CHAPTER XXII

¹ Walker, *The Trail of the Tammany Tiger.*
² Quoted from Werner, *Tammany Hall,* p. 441.
³ Walker, *op. cit.*
⁴ *The Independent* of August 1900.
⁵ *The New York Tribune:* September 5, 1900.
⁶ For two symposia of anti-Croker Democratic press comment throughout the Union, see: *Public Opinion:* July 19 and September 20, 1900.
⁷ *The New York Tribune:* October 4, 1900.
⁸ See files of the metropolitan press for October 30, 1900.

CHAPTER XXIII

¹ William Allen White, *Croker.*
² See a striking description of one of these celebrations in *The Outlook* of October 12, 1901.
³ For a good survey of this subject, see: George Kibbe Turner, "Tammany's Control of New York City by Professional Criminals"; *McClure's*

Magazine: June 1909. The career of Monk Eastman is fully treated in Asbury's *The Gangs of New York.*

[4] See special article in *The New York Tribune* of February 21, 1901.
[5] *Ibid.* February 17, 1901.
[6] *Ibid.* February 24, 1901.

CHAPTER XXIV

[1] All the New York papers "featured" the Foley-Divver contest, and gave lively accounts of it under dates of September 18 and 19, 1901. For a good general description, see Turner, *op. cit.*
[2] *The New York Times:* June 27, 1901.
[3] This version is taken from *The New York Tribune* of October 29, 1901.

BIBLIOGRAPHY

Abbott, Lyman. *Reminiscences* (New York 1915)

An English Workman. *London versus New York* (London 1859)

An Experienced Carver. *New York in Slices* (New York 1849)

Anonymous. " New York City and Its Park "; *Atlantic Monthly*, April 1861

Anonymous. " Squatter Life in New York "; *Harper's Magazine*, September 1880

Anonymous. " The Dangerous Classes of New York "; *Appleton's Journal*, February 19, 1870

Anonymous. " The Tammany Hall of Today "; *Harper's Weekly*, July 13, 1889

Anonymous. " Through Broadway "; *Atlantic Monthly*, December 1866

Barnes, David M. *The Draft Riots in New York* (New York 1863)

Bayles, J. C. " Crime and Vice in Cities "; *Independent*, May 25, 1911

Beard, Charles A. and Mary R. *The Rise of American Civilization* (2 vols. New York 1927)

Bearing of the Hill-Croker Feud, The; Public Opinion, July 19, 1900

Blake, Euphemia Vale. *History of the Tammany Society* (New York 1901)

Bosses: Take Warning! Public Opinion, November 18, 1897

Brace, Charles Loring. *The Dangerous Classes of New York* (New York 1872)

Bradford, Gamaliel. " Our Failure in Municipal Government "; *Annals of the American Academy*, May 1893

Breen, Matthew P. *Thirty Years of New York Politics* (New York 1899)

Brooks, Sydney. " Tammany Again "; *Fortnightly Review* (London), December 1903

Brooks, Sydney. " The Problem of the New York Police "; *Nineteenth Century and After* (London), October 1912

Browne, Junius H. *The Great Metropolis; A Mirror of New York* (Hartford 1869)

Bryce, James. *The American Commonwealth* (3 vols. London 1888)

Bryce, James. *Modern Democracies* (2 vols. New York 1924)

Buel, C. C. " Blackmail as a Heritage; or New York's Legacy from Colonial Days "; *The Century*, March 1895

Cary, Edward. " Tammany, Past and Present "; *The Forum*, October 1898

Chimmie Fadden on Graft and the Police; Public Opinion, October 31, 1901

Clarke, Joseph I. C. *My Life and Memories* (New York 1925)

Coler, Bird S. " Commercialism in Politics "; *The Independent*, October 31, 1901

Commons, John R. " State Supervision for Cities "; *Annals of the American Academy*, May 1895

Costello, A. E. *Our Police Protectors: A History of the New York Police* (New York 1885)

Crapsey, Edward. *The Nether Side of New York* (New York 1872)

Croker, Richard. " Tammany Hall and the Democracy "; *North American Review*, February 1892

Croker, Bryan, and National Politics; Review of Reviews, February 1898

Croker System, The; The Nation, April 20, 1899

Croker's Greatest Victory — The Derby; The Literary Digest, June 15, 1907

Croker's Testimony; The Outlook, April 29, 1899

Curran, M. P. " Tammany Hall and the Catholic Church "; *Donahoe's Magazine*, November 1901

Davenport, Frederick M. " Al Smith and the Human Side of Tammany "; *The Outlook*, July 31, 1918

Davis, Hartley. " Tammany Hall "; *Munsey's Magazine*, October 1900

Dayton, Agram C. *The Last Days of Knickerbocker Life in New York* (New York 1872)

Denison, Lindsay. " Scenes from a Great Campaign "; *The World's Work*, December 1901

Desperate Plight of New York City, The; The Century, October 1901

Dickens, Charles. *American Notes* (London 1842)

Doom of the Boss, The; Gunton's Magazine, April 1901

Duer, William A. *Reminiscences of an Old New Yorker* (New York 1867)

Dunne, Finley Peter. *Mr. Dooley in the Hearts of His Countrymen* (Essay entitled: " Lexow." Boston 1899)

Eaton, Dorman B. *The Government of Municipalities* (New York 1899)

Edwards, E. J. " Tammany "; *McClure's Magazine*, December 1894

Edwards, E. J. " Richard Croker as Boss of Tammany Hall "; *McClure's Magazine*, November 1895

BIBLIOGRAPHY 273

Edwards, G. W. "New York City Politics Before the Revolution "; *Political Science Quarterly*, December 1921
Emmet, Dr. Thomas Addis. *Incidents of My Life* (New York 1911)
Fassett Investigation. *Testimony Taken before the Senate Committee on Cities, Pursuant to Resolution Adopted January* 20, 1890. (5 vols. Albany 1891)
Fawcett, Edgar. "Plutocracy and Snobbery in New York "; *The Arena,* July 1891
Flint, Josiah. "'York,' A Dishonest City" ; *McClure's Magazine,* April 1901
Foord, John. *The Life and Public Services of Andrew Haswell Green* (New York 1913)
Ford, James L. "New York of the Seventies "; *Scribner's Magazine,* June 1923
Fosdick, Raymond B. "The Police Scandal and the Good Old Days "; *The Outlook,* October 19, 1912
Foster, G. G. *New York by Gaslight* (New York 1850)
Gardiner, Alexander. *Canfield, Host to the Nineties. The True Story of the Greatest Gambler* (New York 1930)
Godkin, Edwin Lawrence. *Problems of Modern Democracy* (New York 1897)
Goodnow, Frank J. *Municipal Problems* (New York 1897)
Goodnow, Frank J. *Municipal Government* (New York 1909)
Gratacap, L. P. *The Political Mission of Tammany Hall* (New York 1894)
Gratacap, L. P. *The Political Mission of Reform* (New York 1895)
Hapgood and Moskovitz. *Up from the City Streets: Alfred E. Smith* (New York 1927)
Hawley, Walter L. "The Strength and Weakness of Tammany Hall "; *North American Review,* October 1901
Headley, J. T. *The Great Riots of New York* (New York 1873)
Hendrick, Burton J. "The Twilight of Tammany Hall "; *The World's Work,* February 1914
Hickey, John J. *Our Police Guardians, History of the Police Department of the City of New York, Compiled and Written by Officer " 787," John J. Hickey, Retired* (New York 1925)
Hodder, Alfred. *A Fight for the City* (New York 1903)
Hone, The Diary of Philip. Edited and published in 1889
Howe, Frederic C. *The City: The Hope of Democracy* (New York 1905)
Howe, Frederic C. *The Modern City and Its Problems* (New York 1914)
Howe, Frederic C. *The Confessions of a Reformer* (New York 1925)

Hudson, William C. *Random Recollections of an Old Political Reporter* (New York 1911)

Ingersoll, Ernest. *A Week in New York* (New York 1892)

Ivins, William M. *Machine Politics and Money in Elections in New York City* (New York 1887)

"Juvenal." *An Englishman in New York* (New York 1901)

Lexow Investigation. *Report and Proceedings of the Senate Committee Appointed to Investigate the Police Department of the City of New York* (5 vols. Albany 1895)

Lewis, Alfred Henry. *Richard Croker* (New York 1901)

Lewis, Alfred Henry. *The Boss, and How He Came to Rule New York* (New York 1903)

Low, A. Maurice. "Tammany Hall: Its Boss, Its Methods, and Its Meaning"; *The World's Work* (London), September 1903

Martyn, Carlos. *William E. Dodge, The Christian Merchant* (New York 1890)

Matthews, Franklin. "'Wide-Open' New York"; *Harper's Weekly*, October 22, 1898

Mayoralty Campaign of 1897, The; Review of Reviews (Dr. Albert Shaw, *Editor*) (November, December 1897)

Mayoralty Campaign of 1901, The; Review of Reviews (Dr. Albert Shaw, *Editor*) (November, December 1901)

Mazet Investigation. *Report of the Special Committee of the Assembly Appointed to Investigate the Public Offices and Departments of the City of New York and of the Counties therein Included* (5 vols. Albany 1900)

McCabe, James D. *New York by Gaslight* (New York 1882)

McGuire, James K. *The Democratic Party of the State of New York* (3 vols. New York 1905)

McLaughlin, J. F. *The Life and Times of John Kelly* (New York 1885)

Merriam, Charles Edward. *The American Party System* (New York 1922)

Merriam, Charles Edward. *American Political Ideals* (New York 1920)

Merwin, H. C. "Tammany Hall"; *Atlantic Monthly*, February 1894

Merwin, H. C. "Tammany Points the Way"; *Atlantic Monthly*, November 1894

Morrissey, John. *John Morrissey; His Life, Battles, and Wrangles* (New York 1881)

Moss, Frank. *The American Metropolis: New York City Life in All Its Phases* (3 vols. New York 1897)

Mumford, John K. "Election Night in New York"; *Harper's Weekly*, November 16, 1901

Munro, William Bennett. *Personality in Politics: Reformers, Bosses, and Leaders. What They Do and How They Do It* (New York 1924)

Myers, Gustavus. *History of Tammany Hall* (New York 1901; revised edition 1917)

Myers, Gustavus. "The Secrets of Tammany's Success"; *The Forum*, June 1901

Myers, Gustavus. "The New Tammany"; *The Century*, August 1926

"*New*" *Tammany, The: Biographical Sketches of Its Leaders* (New York 1890)

New Tammany, The; *Public Opinion*, January 23, 1902

Oberholzer, E. P. "Home Rule for Our American Cities"; *Annals of the American Academy*; May 1893

Orth, Samuel P. *The Boss and the Machine* (New Haven 1919)

Ostrogorski, M. *Democracy and the Organization of Political Parties* (2 vols. New York 1902)

Parkhurst, Rev. Charles H. *Our Fight with Tammany* (New York 1895)

Parkhurst, Rev. Charles H. *My Forty Years in New York* (New York 1923)

Platt, Thomas Collier. *The Autobiography of Thomas Collier Platt*; compiled and edited by Louis J. Lang (New York 1913)

Plunkitt of Tammany Hall. *A Series of Very Plain Talks on Very Practical Politics, Delivered by ex-Senator George Washington Plunkitt, the Tammany Philosopher, from His Rostrum — the New York County Court-House Bootblack-Stand — and Recorded by William L. Riordan* (New York 1905)

Political Bosses a Necessary Evil; *The Banker's Magazine*, June 1896

Political Mission of Tammany Hall, The: A Tract for the Times (New York 1892)

Riis, Jacob A. *How the Other Half Lives* (New York 1890)

Roosevelt, Theodore. *Essays on Practical Politics* (New York 1888)

Roosevelt, Theodore. *American Ideals* (New York 1897)

Roosevelt, Theodore. *Autobiography* (New York 1913)

Ruhl, Arthur. "The Caliph and His Court"; *McClure's Magazine*, August 1901

Schurz, Carl. "Our New Monarchy"; *Harper's Weekly*, January 29, 1898

Seibold, Louis. "Richard Croker"; *Munsey's Magazine*, August 1901

Sherman, P. Tecumseh. *Inside the Machine: Two Years on the Board of Aldermen, 1898–1899* (New York 1901)

Smith, Alfred E. *Up to Now: An Autobiography* (New York 1929)

Some Things Richard Croker Has Said and Done. Published by the City Club of New York, July 1901

"Spectator." "'The Big Feller' Celebrates"; *The Outlook*, October 12, 1901

Steffens, Lincoln. *The Shame of the Cities* (New York 1904)

Steffens, Lincoln. *The Struggle for Self-Government* (New York 1906)

Stead, William T. *Despairing Democracy* (London 1897)
Stead, William T. " Richard Croker "; *Review of Reviews* (London), October 1897
Stelzle, Charles. *A Son of the Bowery* (New York 1926)
Tammany a National Menace; Review of Reviews, November 1900
Tammany Apologists; The Nation, January 26, 1893
Tammany Banquet, The; Public Opinion, April 20, 1899
Ten Months of Tammany. A Pamphlet Published by the City Club of New York (New York 1901)
Thompson, Daniel Greenleaf. *Politics in a Democracy* (New York 1893)
Tilden, Samuel J. *The New York City Ring: Its Origin, Maturity, and Fall* (New York 1873)
Tilden, Samuel J. *Letters and Literary Memorials of Samuel J. Tilden.* Edited by John Bigelow (2 vols. New York 1908)
Townsend, John D. *New York in Bondage* (New York 1901)
Triumph of Reform, The: A History of the Great Political Revolution, November 6, 1894 (New York 1895)
Turner, George Kibbe. "Tammany's Control of New York by Professional Criminals "; *McClure's Magazine*, June 1909
Tweed Ring Investigation. *Report of the Special Committee of the Board of Aldermen Appointed to Investigate the " Ring " Frauds; Together with the Testimony Elicited during the Investigation.* Board of Aldermen, January 4, 1878, Document No. 8, New York 1878
" Volunteer Special." *The Volcano Under the City* (New York 1887)
Walker, Harry Wilson. " The Trail of the Tammany Tiger "; *Saturday Evening Post*, March–April 1914
Walling, George W. *Recollections of a New York Chief of Police* (New York 1887)
White, Frank M. " When Clubs Were Trumps "; *The Outlook*, April 7, 1915
White, William Allen. " Croker "; *McClure's Magazine*, February 1901
White, William Allen. *Masks in a Pageant* (essay on Platt) — (New York 1928)
Wilson, Charles G. " New York City in 1848 "; *The Independent*, December 10, 1908

NEWSPAPERS

Files of the New York press; especially of the *Evening Post, Herald, Times, Tribune*, and *World*.
The File of *The Tammany Times*, while inacessible as a whole, yields much information.

INDEX

B

Baldwin, "Lucky," 133, 140
Bowery (The), 27, 28, 30, 131, 177, 184, 231–236, 243
Breen, Matthew S., 240
Broadway, 6–7, 9, 21, 27, 58, 132, 184, 253
Bryan, William Jennings, 172, 216–222, 225–227, 236

C

Canfield, Richard, 133–134
Carroll, John F., 201
Choate, Joseph, 118
Civil War (The American), 32, 34, 37, 99, 100, 133, 171
Clay, Henry, 37
Cleveland, Grover, 65, 66, 72, 87, 89–93, 95–96
Cockran, Bourke, 71, 73, 74, 92, 203
Coler, Bird S., 223–224, 240
Croker, Eyre Coote (father of Richard), 2–3, 15–20

D

Daly, Joseph F. (Judge), 201–204
Depew, Chauncey M., 200
Devery, William S. ("Big Bill"), 139, 206–209, 226, 237–239, 244, 246, 248, 250, 252
Dewey, George (Amiral), 222
Dickens, Charles, 9
Divver, "Paddy," 242–246
Draft Riots, 31–34

E

Eastman, "Monk," 234
Erie Canal, 5–7

F

Fassett Investigation, 96, 99, 112, 114, 118, 135, 148
Fifth Avenue, 7, 22
Fire Department, 6, 10–11, 26, 30
Fiske, "Jim," 38
Five Points (The), 8, 19, 27, 89, 131, 231
Flint, Josiah, 208–209
Flower, Roswell P., 147, 191
Foley, "Big Tom," 231, 242, 244–246
Fourth Avenue Tunnel Gang, 30, 44–45
Fourth Ward, 22, 241, 243
Frémont, John C., 100
"Fusion," 95–96, 150–156, 247–253

G

Gangster, 25–27, 59
Gardiner, Asa Bird, 178, 182, 185, 208, 236
Gardner, Charles W., 136–137
Gas House District, 20, 40, 45, 48–49
Gates, John W., 133–134
George, Henry, 84–86, 179–182
Gettysburg (Battle of), 33
Gilroy, Thomas F., 71, 96, 113, 148
Grace, William R., 64, 67, 70, 91
Grady, Thomas F., 184
Grant, Hugh J., 71–74, 92–96, 111, 118, 132, 128, 147, 152, 172
Gunmen, 233–234, 243–246

277